Mary & Paul

Jolene's ski
friends — enjoy
the read!

Paul

THE PRIESTESS
AND
THE POPE

PAUL DIONNE

THE PRIESTESS AND THE POPE

Dedicated to Angeline, Rachel, Diane, Melodie, and Michelle

Special thanks to Steve, Peg, David, and Luc

Prologue

Northern Egypt, 1945

The blazing yellow sun lay heavy atop the large man's broad shoulders, driving thick beads of sweat down his back. A mattock hung loosely in his hand. His brothers stood behind him, ignoring the camels that tugged restlessly against their harnesses. These men had meant to take a measure of the soft, rich earth before them back to their farms as fertilizer. Several empty baskets swung from their saddles. Such endeavors were forgotten now.

The broad-shouldered man, the strongest and oldest of the brothers, had struck something in the dirt as he dug. He had come from a long line of farmers, and had been scouring this desert for rich soil long enough to know that this object, neither stone, sand, or boulder, didn't belong here among the endless dunes. No natural force had placed it there.

A camel whined and reared up behind him. One of the brothers yanked the rope that bound it, yelling in rapid Arabic. The man's heart was racing. Carefully, getting to his knees, he pushed his powerful, leathery hands into the black earth and began to scoop away the soft clumps of soil.

As he tore away at the loose earth, the lip of a large jar began to emerge, then the etchings at its top and sides. His excitement grew as he plunged deeper into the soil. He was now bent over, buried halfway up to his shoulders, his arms like pistons driving out piles of the dark sand. He called out to his brothers, who timidly unslung their shovels and began to dig around him.

Sweat pooled on their backs, but they ignored the tightening of their overworked muscles, driven on by their relentless brother. He now stood in the hole they had dug, dirt caked along his fingers and nails. He held his hand up and called for silence. Before him, parallel in height with his chest, stood an immense earthenware jar.

It seemed to glow, ensconced in the sunlight and dust. He could tell that it was the work of another age, and it was obvious that it had been carefully buried—a secret meant to remain hidden for a long time. A secret that he would soon possess.

His brothers stood back with the camels, anxious and afraid. They thought of the curses that were often put on objects like this, of the spirits and *jinn* that often made these objects their home. There was no way of telling what could be released if the jar was opened.

As the eldest wiped the last bits of dust from the jar, tracing its ancient markings, the youngest of the brothers shouted down to him, pleading with him to leave it alone. The others shuffled their feet, mumbling their agreement, not as bold as their youthful brother. They wanted to rebury the jar and go home. No good could come from disturbing something that had been hidden away so long ago.

But the eldest, a wild light in his eyes, only smiled. This jar had been buried in the middle of a desert for a reason, and after years of toiling in these barren sands, whatever it contained was to be his reward. He reached for his mattock, and raised it slowly over his head. Behind him, his brothers gasped and began to pray softly. They gazed, helpless, as the mattock hung in the air, glistening, and the hot sun coursed down around them. Their brother's forearm, thick from years of labor, bulged above his tattered sleeve. With tremendous force, the mattock came crashing down on the ancient jar in a violent collision of clay, iron and earth.

The brothers, who had looked away in fear, now turned to stare at the rubble. The eldest kicked aside the red shards. No *jinn* arose from the pile. No gold or gems glittered in a heap before them. No beam of light struck down from the heavens above. Sitting in a cloud of dust before them, a dozen leather-bound books of papyrus lay, their pages rustling in a breeze that had not touched them for a thousand years.

Chapter 1

⌇

Rome 495 A.D.

Gelasius, the Bishop of Rome, had hands like a skeleton. His fingers were narrow, white, and thick at the bony knuckles, austere in contrast with the numerous rings that adorned them. Flavius, the Pope's longest-tenured aide, watched as the pale fingers and gem-studded rings shimmered through the long hair of a Persian cat that sat perched by the Pope's wine glass. *When did this man become such a costumed skeleton?* Flavius thought.

The cat hissed, swishing its tail. Gelasius murmured and brushed the remains of his dinner off his plate towards the hungry animal. A log popped in the nearby fire, and with it, a conscious spark returned to his eyes. He turned his gaze to where Flavius stood, waiting at the other end of the table.

"I didn't hear you come in. Come where I can see you my Flavius."

Flavius stepped forward into the firelight.

"You've eaten I presume?"

"I have, Your Holiness."

Flavius avoided looking at the animal hunched over the scraps of food.

"Good, because I've been waiting for a while," Gelasius said irritably. Flavius blushed, embarrassed. "The last of the messengers arrived several hours ago, did they not?"

"Yes, Your Holiness, they did."

4

"And why is it only now that you find the time to visit me?"

"My apologies, Your Holiness," Flavius sputtered. "I had assumed when we spoke that you meant the midday meal. I was closeted with the messengers since their return and felt I needed time to consider their reports before passing them on to you. I offer my deepest apologies if I have inconvenienced you."

Flavius heard a servant come through the door behind him. He waited for the man, who appeared before the Pope with a decanter of wine. Gelasius brushed him away, and, thinking better of it, waved him back.

He waited until his glass was filled just below the brim, and nodded curtly to the servant, eying Flavius intently.

"Your apology is accepted."

Flavius avoided the Pope's gaze, looking instead at the large cross of beaten gold that hung on the wall above his chair. Flanking it on either side were twelve tapestries depicting the apostles, hung evenly around the room, their fine threads glinting in the firelight.

Gelasius is strong, but the truth flees before him, thought Flavius. *His concentration is on this world, not the next.* He looked again at the cross. Despite the orange flames that played on its surface, it seemed to Flavius to be glowing from within. *Lord, give me the strength to see past his fault, and to see how they glorify you and your heavenly kingdom.*

"I hope, Flavius, that my fervor has not been an affront to you."

Flavius' eyes fell back on Gelasius. "Not at all, Your Holiness."

"The issue at hand is of the deepest importance to me."

"As it is to me, Your Holiness."

Gelasius took a long sip of wine and set his glass down gently on the table, still eyeing Flavius closely.

"What did the messengers tell you?"

"The churches in the south are thriving, in both the cities and the countryside."

"And?"

Flavius stared down at his feet. He had spent all afternoon preparing, but was still apprehensive.

"Don't be coy, Flavius. It's not flattering." Gelasius lifted an eyebrow and stared at him without blinking. "Are the rumors true?"

Flavius' heart began to beat faster. Why was he so nervous? It was not as if he himself were flouting the dictates of the Bishop of Rome. And yet his palms were sweating. The apostles on the tapestries seemed to swirl around him, and he imagined their fabric lips mouthing out words of advice. It was an unbearable din that clouded his mind.

"Yes, Your Holiness. They are true." He cleared his throat and wiped his hands on his tunic.

The lines on the Pope's gaunt face seemed somehow to get deeper.

"How many are there?"

"It is hard to say. They are quite dispersed." Flavius felt himself choking on his words. "Several dozen in total, perhaps. Perhaps more."

Gelasius stared up towards the gilt ceiling through his clouded brown eyes, and his nostrils flared as he took a single, deep breath. The angles of his face became harsher with each passing year, and in fits of anger, his bony jaw looked sharp enough to cut parchment. That jaw was thrust forward now, his eyes recessed in their cavernous sockets.

"How dare they disobey the directives of this office—of the head of their church?" he stated harshly. "Such blatant hypocrisy. They dare defy the canons of the Council of Orange? The Council of Nimes? Laodicea? How can they possibly hope to defend themselves when they contradict the laws of nature and the Church?"

He took up his goblet and gently swirled the wine with a fine, controlled motion.

"According to what we've been told, Your Holiness," Flavius paused, looking at Gelasius' eyes, trying to gauge his emotion, "they believe their argument is a historical one."

"History?"

Gelasius guffawed and his hand became still. "We both know, Flavius, that history is what we interpret it to be."

Here is where we are sundered by religious differences, Flavius thought. He felt the same dread that had kept him in his quarters for hours, as he prayed and put off this inevitable meeting.

For a moment, he almost made known his true thoughts to Gelasius: that history exists as it is and should not be bastardized. But he held his tongue. It was not time and the Pope would not listen. They might disagree on the history, but they both agreed that this heretical practice had to come to an end. The fire flickered, dying a slow death. He stood in silence, waiting for Gelasius to speak.

"Flavius, we must purge this aberration from the Church…and its history!" Gelasius shifted in his seat and held up his hand. "Take dictation for me."

Flavius smiled, unable to stifle his bitter reaction. When they were younger, he and his brother had heard that Gelasius demanded his aides write his letters for him because he could not spell.

"Is there something amusing, Flavius?" the Pope growled.

"Not at all, Your Holiness. I am just glad we see eye to eye on this matter."

Gelasius gazed at him evenly. "Do not think that our relationship can excuse your impertinence. And do not think

I am foolish enough to mistake the fact that you disagree with me deeply on more than one issue."

Flavius stiffened, and noticed again the cold sweat resting atop his skin.

"And never forget your position. Never." Gelasius spoke clearly and sternly. "You are a scholar, Flavius, and a wise and educated man in your own right. Your books have taught you well, but you serve at my pleasure, and at any time I can dismiss you to the service of an outlying parish away from your beloved books!"

Flavius raised his eyes.

"I am the Bishop of Rome, the successor to the apostle Peter, and the representative of Christ on earth. Rome is the bedrock of Christianity, and I am its leader and its single connection to the Lord our God!"

"Yes, Your Holiness."

"So never forget your place, Flavius!"

Flavius felt his cheeks burning, and he broke the Bishop's gaze, turning to collect papyrus and ink from a nearby shelf.

"We will write a letter...no, we will issue an epistle," said the Pope, "an official church decree banning the further ordination of women priests."

Flavius nodded, the tension having suddenly vanished from his face. He had once again entered a realm of comfort.

"Take your writing materials, Flavius, and draft an epistle for my review," he said dismissively.

.   .   .

Within a few days, Flavius returned.

"Read to me the pertinent language," Gelasius ordered impatiently.

"*Nihilominus impatrienter audivimus, tantum divinarum rerum subasse despectum, ut feminae sacris alteribus ministrace firmentur, cunctaque non nisi virorum famulatui deputata sexum, cui non competent, exhibere."*

"Well said, Flavius. Let me read it. 'Nevertheless we have heard to our annoyance that divine affairs have come to such a low state that women are encouraged to officiate at the sacred altars, and to take part in all matters imputed to the male sex, to which they do not belong.'"

"The epistle goes on to condemn the action of the bishops who ordain women to the priesthood," Flavius added.

"Let us not only condemn the actions of the bishops who commit such abuses but also those bishops who appear to be favoring them by not denouncing them publicly."

"Of course, Your Holiness. There is no excuse for those who disobey the canons, either directly or indirectly."

"Out of curiosity, Flavius, is there support in Scripture for our position?"

"Not in Scripture, Your Holiness, but it finds support in the ecclesiastical canons."

"Yes, yes, that will suffice. Put the finishing touches to the epistle and bring it to me so that I might append the papal seal and sign it as the Vicar of Christ! We must work together to erase this stain forever from the records of our Church. Our written history must support our position—only then will this apostasy cease."

Flavius bowed his head. "What would you have me do, Your Holiness?"

The Pope's eyes widened. "As long as these...these heretics..." he spat out the word, "believe that history is on their side, they will continue to ignore me."

"Are you asking that we destroy the documents that support their position?"

Gelasius stood and turned to the golden cross on the wall. "These documents are heretical and must be destroyed. I will decide what is true and what is heresy, not some country church that claims history is on its side."

He paused for a moment, the furrows in his brow sinking deeper. "For their salvation, the heretics must either be converted or banished, and their history eradicated."

Gelasius sipped his wine and carefully placed the glass back on the table. "Whom do you trust to carry out this important mission?" he asked.

"Samuel," Flavius said without pausing. He had seen this coming. "Samuel can do what you ask."

"Samuel is young."

"Yes—but his devotion is deep. He will do what we ask and is devout enough to do it well."

"You're sure?"

"I am."

Gelasius nodded. "Very well. He will deliver our divine message."

With that, the Pope turned away and walked out of the room.

Flavius had been dreading this moment since the rumors had begun to trickle in from the corners of the Roman Empire. As soon as he heard the rumors, he knew they would be true, and on a moment's reflection he knew that it would be impossible to dissuade these people from their beliefs. It would require a display of force to change minds.

He stood at the window of the small austere room and looked out onto the courtyard below. Once a magnificent palace of emperors, the building had fallen into long, slow decline since given to the Bishop of Rome by Constantine. Ornamental marble had cracked, silver and gold facings had been removed and never replaced, roof tiles had fallen and their pieces kicked into rubbish piles in the corners. The city beyond the walls had suffered the same fate.

Flavius ground his teeth. The empire was teetering at the edge of ruin, and the Church was the only institution that could save it, but the heretics to the south threatened to rend its unity. Even though he despised Gelasius, he appreciated his strength in times of crisis. Gelasius was a strong advocate of papal supremacy, and he was willing to extend his authority to the temporal realm.

Flavius raised his eyes past the wall of the courtyard to the endless squalor of the city: closely packed buildings, rooftops slanting at odd angles, neighborhoods crowded and filthy. He imagined what Rome must have been like when the Caesars still ruled, and when the *Pax Romana* meant that a citizen could travel safely for a thousand miles in any direction.

It had been a dangerous time to be a Christian then. In those days it had meant risking one's life. *Were those times better than these?* Flavius thought to himself.

For the first three centuries after Christ's death, Christianity had been illegal, and Rome had been replete with political repression, religious persecution, and massacres in the Coliseum for the entertainment of the Roman crowds.

Perhaps each generation has its share of burdens, he mused. *We should thank God that we live in a time of enlightenment, when the matters of state are influenced by the men of God.* Gelasius often claimed that he wielded two swords, referring to the authority of the Pope in both the spiritual and temporal sphere.

A knock sounded on his door, and he answered without hesitation. "Please come in, Samuel."

He turned to see Samuel entering with alacrity and the deep self-confidence of youth that Flavius remembered well.

"Are you well, Father?" he asked. He was a young man who kept his dark hair shorn very short, the childlike roundness of his face not yet affected by the austerity of his lifestyle.

11

"I am, Samuel. I am. And you?"

"Very well."

Flavius gestured to Samuel, beckoning him to sit. He took up a chair across from the young scholar. A large compendium of notes and faint etchings on an ornate desk stood between them. "You've spoken to Gelasius, Samuel?"

"Yes I have...how did you know?"

"That is just his mode of operation. I take it he asked you several questions about your piety and your devotion, to a point where it seemed as if your faith was being measured."

"You are truly clairvoyant, Father."

Flavius glanced down and ran his hand lightly along the thin leather cover of a book he was holding. "I've known him for a long time, Samuel. I would expect no less from him."

"Why do you say that?"

"Because he has assigned a very important mission to you," Flavius replied, looking up. "Did he tell you what it is?"

"Only briefly. He said that you would fill in the details."

Flavius stood up and turned to the window again. Outside, the sun was setting, and birds were floating on a faint breeze in the distance. The sky past the eaves of the palace was so blue it seemed to be lit by a sapphire sun.

He closed his eyes for a moment. A young woman's face appeared, buried deep in the library of his mind. Her eyes glistened, strong and blue, and she smiled as if keeping a secret only she knew.

"There are times, Samuel," he said, "when we must act purposefully, filling our hearts with the will of the Lord while ignoring our own worldly longings. Such longings can only lead us astray from God's plan for us."

Flavius gazed out the window for a moment longer and then turned solemnly towards Samuel. "As the Roman

Empire continues to buckle under the constant invasions of the barbarians, the Pope is assuming more of the temporal powers vacated by Rome. Similarly, as the Church defends itself from the onslaught of heretics, the world must put its trust in the Vicar of Christ, as the Pope now refers to himself!" Flavius said unconvincingly.

Chapter 2

⌒

T he road south from Rome led parallel to the seashore, and the road never strayed far enough away that Samuel could not smell the salty sea air. The views were breathtaking, and a vast expanse of land and sea opened up before him. He trekked on a road that led from village to village, wide enough for two ox carts to pass each other comfortably. As he walked, he felt a newfound freedom, and at times a wanderlust that took his thoughts away from the priesthood to a world he had never experienced. But he realized this journey was for God and that even the slightest deviation could be fatal. Such travel captivated him, but he vowed not to be deterred from his papal mission.

He walked briskly in the mornings and evenings and rested in whatever shade he could find in the afternoons when the sun was at its height. Often there were small towns with churches, where the signet ring he carried was good for lodging, a meal, and fellowship. On other days, he slept at a farm or isolated houses in the countryside, and he paid for the night with the church coffers he had been given for his journey. He was generous to those he met and those who helped him, knowing that his purse was full with papal coins.

For the first days of the journey, he walked tirelessly, driven by a feeling of purpose and excitement. He spent the early hours of the morning watching the way the light of the sun turned the hills purple, then red, then pink, and the way it caught the dusty white clouds kicked up by peasants' carts that rumbled along. He spoke prayers of joy aloud as he walked, and even sang loudly when the passersby were few and far between. At times, he found that he had travelled a long way oblivious to his surroundings, his feet having guided themselves past every loose stone.

As the villages grew farther apart, he began to seek shelter beneath the stars. One night, he slept in a grove of olive trees where the ground was hard and stony. Part of him savored the pain this caused, the discomfort, because these things confirmed that the strength of the Holy Spirit was with him. This was a pilgrimage, a trip in service of the Pope, and thus in service of the Lord. The hardships he met, to him, would only serve as purifications.

But as the land became less settled, a subtle shift began to occur. Samuel's steps slowed, and he lingered longer in the brief spots of shade he found, resting more often after the air had begun to cool during his midday nap. The letter he carried in the pocket of his tunic, and the authority it bore, seemed to weigh heavily against his chest. He no longer blessed the hillsides or the sea, but prayed now for strength, annoyed at his own timidity.

It was not the letter itself or his mission that he felt was wearing him down—he believed without reservation in his assigned mission. Not only was there no place for women in the hierarchy of the Church, but any hint of deviation from orthodoxy could destroy the Church he loved so dearly. He understood all the arguments, but was fearful that the southern church he was being sent to would not accept them. He reviewed them in his mind and found them compelling. The philosopher Epiphaneus argued that men and women were different and that women possessed an inferior nature. If women had an inferior nature, then it was their fate to be ruled rather than to rule. Christian writers argued that it was inappropriate for women to hold positions of authority in the public sphere, and Roman law held women by nature to be the weaker sex and mentally frivolous. According to the leading theologian, Tertullian, women were not to teach or baptize, nor were they to engage in any kind of public discourse, either debating a theological question or asking questions for their own instruction.

There were also the Letters of Paul and the writings of Augustine from two of the most scholarly men in the history of Christianity who both believed that women possessed an inferior nature, *a further affirmation of the Pope's position on the issue*, mused Samuel as his confidence heightened.

But it was not the merits of the issue, but the character of the Pope that concerned him. Gelasius seemed more absorbed with earthly matters then spiritual ones. *This is important,* he thought, *and his character is the source of my anxiety.* If all popes were enlightened like Leo, who claimed supreme and universal authority for the papacy on the grounds that the Pope is the heir of Peter; or as courageous as Leo, who confronted Attila the Hun and persuaded him not to sack Rome; then he would feel less anxiety about his papal mission. Indeed, Leo corrected abuses, resolved disputes, and enforced pastoral practices but did so for spiritual reasons. Gelasius appeared to have the same objectives as Leo, but was acting to satisfy earthly inclination. *If Gelasius were more like Leo, I would have more confidence in my mission*, Samuel thought.

Samuel sat down by a stream at midday. He drank the cold water and ate the meat and the apple he had bought at the last village he passed through. Samuel remembered himself at an earlier age, a happy time that he spent with his parents before being placed in the convent. Then a figure stepped out of the undergrowth just ahead of him. What happened next was so quick that Samuel could hardly believe it. The man who had so suddenly appeared raised a club over his head. A horrified shout came from Samuel's throat, but before he could react, the man swung the club at him, striking him on the side of the head with a sickening sound. He slumped to the ground. The marauder then bent down and searched the pockets in Samuel's tunic. He took the bag of coins and the backpack but overlooked the signet ring. As he pushed Samuel into the shallow stream, red blood spilled into the clear water.

Samuel awakened hours later with pain running through his head. As he brought his hands up to rub his eyes, he spotted a shadow and ducked instinctively to avoid another blow. To his surprise, there was a woman standing beside the stream. "Do not be afraid," she said.

Samuel looked at her curiously. She was young, perhaps only a few years older than he. She had a wholesome face with dark brown hair that dropped to her shoulders.

"Let me help you to the tree, so that you can sit up and rest." It was all that he could do to stand, his head was so heavy with pain.

"When I came to the stream to fetch water, I found you face up in the water with blood draining from your temple. I tore strips of cloth from my tunic to bandage your wound. It was a severe blow that you must have suffered...but I believe you will heal well. When you are feeling better, I will walk to my farm where you can rest before you resume your journey."

"My coins...my backpack, they are gone!"

"I didn't see them. There are many nomads that roam this road in search of travelers to rob. You are fortunate that you were not killed."

"God protected me..."

"Maybe God. Maybe good fortune. In any case, let's not stay for them to return. They might take your gold ring this time."

Samuel looked down at his left hand and felt relieved that the signet ring was still on his finger. "It is a ring given to me by the Pope to assure my safe passage."

"The bandit must not have seen it then," she responded with a coy look on her face. "Come. We must go," she said.

When they arrived at the small house, she put Samuel to bed to rest and recover from his wound. A few hours later he awakened to the aroma of warm soup and the young woman staring curiously at him. "And what is your name?"

"Samuel."

"It's time for supper."

"And what is your name?" Samuel asked.

"Rachel is my name."

"And where is your husband?"

"He died a few years ago."

Samuel was surprised. "You live here alone?" he said incredulously. It was dangerous enough for a man to live in the country. A woman alone could hardly hope to survive.

"I manage..."

They ate their meal and engaged in good conversation until Samuel got quite tired and returned to the hay pile that had served as his bed. He left in the morning, and told Rachel that he would send payment for his food and lodging by messenger. He hugged his host before he departed and thanked her for saving his life. "God be with you," Samuel said as he departed.

"I hate to disappoint you, Samuel, but I am a pagan and I do not believe in God."

"On my return to Rome, I will return to convert you to my religion."

"You may return, Samuel, but only for companionship and not for your God!"

When he had walked along the road for a few minutes, he looked back. Rachel was still watching him. *A strong and interesting woman*, he thought.

As he continued his journey, he thought of other strong people who had been part of his life. He thought of the conversion of his grandfather, who was a Hun by birth. A soldier, he joined the Roman garrison south of his town and had been the only barbarian to inform the Romans of a coming mutiny. In the battle that ensued, he fought alongside the Romans and against some of the men he had known since he was a child. The Roman forces were victorious, and for his loyalty he was promoted, the beginning of a series of advancements that eventually put him in command of a northern legion and enabled him to retire to Rome a wealthy man.

His conversion occurred while he was in the Roman army. He had seen a Christian priest exorcise three siblings, two men and a woman, all three possessed by demons. The priest had them kneel down in front of his small church and walked from one to the other, touching his hand to their heads. Samuel's grandfather said that he saw the demons pass through the siblings' bodies and out of their mouths and a great wind rose up to sweep away each demon as it emerged. Afterwards, he said, the three pagans were full of peace for the first time in many years. His grandfather had known then that this Christ was the greatest of the gods. He learned all he could of his new faith, and was baptized when he retired to Rome. All of his children and their children after them were baptized as Christians.

His thoughts returned to Rachel and how brave she was to live in the wilderness with little protection except for her wiles. He had not been out of Rome for years, having hardly been outside the grounds of the Vatican since beginning his studies, and he realized that the idea of being alone in the world, away from the comfort of the routines and strict discipline of the Church, frightened him. The world was a fractious place, with pagans and Jews and heretics, all struggling to assert themselves. *It is these souls I am sent to save*, Samuel said to himself. The world outside of Rome was a series of candles in the darkness, bright spots of devotion in what had once been an empire of light. *So I must find the strength to rekindle the true flame of Christ.*

Gradually, over the next few days, his confidence grew and his fear subsided. The courage Rachel had shown gave him both strength and comfort.

In the late afternoon, he crested a rise and found the road falling gently before him in a long curve. Across the windswept valley rising on the opposite side, he saw the hill town of Velagio. Its details were veiled by the oncoming darkness, but Samuel could make out the profiles of several buildings. His spirits lifted at the sight of his destination. The road was bordered on both sides by sloping fields that were covered with straight rows of dry olive trees and grape trellises, and beyond the trees a broad slope of yellowed pastureland that fed a flock of sheep. Whitewashed houses were arrayed neatly along the periphery of the hills, surrounded by closely tended vegetable gardens. It was apparent from the dried stalks, though, that a drought hung over the land.

As he approached the town, the church and its grounds were nowhere in sight. Not wanting to waste time, he got the attention of a woman before she disappeared into her house. As he spoke, he noticed a small bronze idol, scowling on a small shelf outside her doorway.

She smiled and pointed him in the direction of the sea. "The Christians do many good works. My husband even talks about conversion." Her face tightened slightly. "Without them...our family..." She hesitated and smiled dismissively. "Well, either way, the church is just over..."

"What were you going to say?" Samuel interrupted.

The woman's smile softened. "My husband broke his hand in an accident at work. He's a mason and could not work for months. They helped feed our family of five for months and asked nothing in return."

"I am sorry to hear about your husband," Samuel said, looking off towards the sea. "But where is the church?"

The woman looked confused. "You didn't see it?" she asked.

"There was nothing to see."

She paused for a moment and then clapped a hand to her forehead. "Of course. The earth shook beneath us a few weeks ago and toppled part of the church and its tower. Our gods have taken much from us lately," she said, looking at the browned stems of a nearby garden. "That church was our only landmark before it was destroyed. Go straight down this road, and you will walk right into the rubble. Good day."

He nodded at her and glanced again at the small bronze idol. Turning towards the sea, he walked past a few residences that had also crumbled from the earthquake.

As he neared the edge of the town, what was left of the church came into view. It was built from a stone of darker grey than the rest of the city and sat at the edge of the bluff overlooking the sea. There were several large buildings set among a number of small but neatly manicured gardens and orchards. As he drew closer, he saw that the bluff behind the church did not fall straight down to the sea. Below there was a broad crescent of beach that held docks and a wholly separate section of the city.

His eyes returned to the destruction that lay before him. The largest building on the grounds, the church, was indeed roofless. The building was covered with a web of scaffolding, and it looked as if workmen had already cleared most of the broken pieces of stone and smoothed the old blocks straight. A single tall wooden cross, several men high, standing straight and proud, was lashed securely where the tower must once have stood. The building's new profile kept it hidden from those approaching the town from the north.

The scaffolding was empty, but as he neared the building, men began to climb onto it, laughing and joking. At the base of the scaffolding, a tall bearded man was barking out orders. Two young women stood by a large barrel, offering ladlefuls of water to the workmen as they arrived. Their heads turned towards Samuel as he approached, curious, but welcoming. They offered him a drink of water, and he declined, bringing himself up to his full height.

"Are you the pastor of this church?" Samuel inquired of the bearded man.

"I am the pastor and one of many priests," he responded. He held out his hand to Samuel and said, "My name is Joshua and I would be remiss not to mention the wound on your forehead...can we treat it in any way?"

"My name is Samuel. I am the official representative of the Bishop of Rome." Samuel offered forth his hand, the signet ring on it gleaming. "I was robbed on my way to your village but was treated very kindly by a pagan woman named Rachel, maybe a day's walk from here. I did lose all of my coins and will need to borrow money from your parish to carry out my duties."

Joshua smiled broadly. "As you know, one-tenth of our earnings are taxed by Rome annually, which is considerable. We will deduct any amount you wish from this year's payment," he said, shielding his eyes from the setting sun, "but I'm not sure your Bishop has shown much interest in our small parish in the past, except when we have been late in making our payment to Rome!" This provoked subtle laughter from the two women.

He seemed sincere, but there was a little sarcasm in his voice and Samuel was uncertain as to what to make of it.

"The Bishop of Rome has sent me to discuss certain matters with the priests of this parish."

"Of course," replied Joshua. "The Bishop of Rome...the one many call 'Papa' or 'Pope.'"

Samuel was growing frustrated but did not let his feelings show. If this was to be his first test, then he was determined to pass it.

"Yes, the leader of the Church, the successor to Peter, and the Vicar of Christ."

The bearded man appeared, on the surface, more amused than anything else, but his eyes betrayed the emotions that lurked beneath. Before he could respond, the older of the two women stepped between them.

"We have been through many struggles lately, and we are all feeling the effects of the strain. I am Anna," she said, bowing her head slightly before Samuel, "and we are honored to have a representative of the Roman Bishop visit our parish. Please allow me to welcome you. We can offer you lodging and simple meals, and the opportunity to worship in our church hall, such as it is, for as long as your obligations require."

She smiled as she spoke and her voice was sincere, but Samuel couldn't help but feel that she too was appraising him every bit as starkly as Joshua had. Even in her words, there were traces of subtle rebellion. *Flavius was right. Their intransigence runs deep*, he thought.

As much as Samuel wanted to believe, despite the forebodings of Gelasius and Flavius, that this dispute could be resolved peacefully, already he felt that hope fading. However, for the moment, he would exercise diplomacy as best he could.

"Thank you," Samuel responded while forcing a smile. "I will take that ladle of water now," he said, gesturing to the nearby water vessel.

23

The younger woman, taller and darker but with the same strong presence, stepped forward with a ladle of water. As he raised his head to drink, Samuel saw the cross towering over him, the orange glow of the sunset behind it.

The younger woman eyed Joshua inquisitively. His face was passive and still, but the fire in his eyes seemed to cool at her beckoning.

Samuel turned to face Joshua. "I neither received you as a Christian nor offered you the hospitality you are due as a brother. I ask your forgiveness."

Perhaps there is hope after all, Samuel thought.

"Of course."

Joshua nodded and his eyes met Samuel's briefly. They were much harder than his words. "Anna will make you feel at home. I'm needed here to help with the construction." Joshua looked at the young woman once more and then turned and walked into the gathering shadows around the building.

"He's been...irritable lately," said Anna, "but I believe the hard labor of rebuilding the church helps him to cope."

"I understand," said Samuel, looking to change the subject. "Was anyone injured when the building collapsed?"

"No. We were all under God's hand at that moment."

The workmen on the scaffolding had begun to light candles to ward off the dusk. The lights flickered like stars along the broken top of the building. The men talked and laughed as they swung their hammers.

"Why do they work at night?" Samuel asked.

"It's the only time they have. They have families to feed, and the men spend their days harvesting what they can from these dry lands. Their evenings they give to the church.

"The drought has been very burdensome on this town. People are suffering, and we're doing all we can, but—it isn't enough. It just compounds the tragedy we experienced just before the drought."

Samuel gave her a look, coaxing her to go on.

"A cherished member of our priesthood died, just as winter ended." The young woman's voice filled with emotion as she spoke.

"I'm truly sorry," said Samuel. "What was his name?"

Both of the women turned to face him followed by a long moment of silence. "Her name was Lucia," Anna said. "She was Joshua's wife."

Chapter 3

⌁

F lavius rose from his knees and straightened his robes. He had been trying to pray all afternoon, but at the thought of Samuel, his mind had fled to other concerns, leaving him unable to stay committed to his prayers. He stepped to the window of his small room, his hands clasped behind him and his lips pursed. Below, the cracked tiles of the courtyard were splashed with sunlight, and the weary rooftops visible over the high wall shone brightly in their red-orange tones. The haze of cooking fires had begun to rise over the city. A young acolyte passed in the courtyard below, swinging his arms and whistling, unaware that he was being watched. Flavius pictured Samuel making his way south along the coast, past Naples, past sites neither of them had seen before.

He had known Samuel since he had turned up as a precocious fourteen-year-old acolyte, voracious for knowledge. Flavius had seen this hunger in the boy and understood that if well directed, it could be turned into a powerful instrument. He took the boy under his wing and tutored Samuel intensively on the history, philosophy, and theology of the Church. He taught him Latin and Greek so that he could read the classics in their original language. The boy's mind was like a huge sponge, absorbing everything that Flavius threw its way. Within a short time he had read all of the works of the prominent theologians, Greek philosophers, and revered thinkers. Following his ordination to the priesthood, he pursued his quest for learning while mingling with the scholars of Rome. He was particularly enamored with the works of Socrates, Plato, and Aristotle.

Despite all this, Flavius realized that he still thought of him as a boy. Indeed, for all his education, Samuel was still naïve and unworldly. *Perhaps I have sheltered him too much,* Flavius thought. Perhaps he should not have been sent to the rebellious church on his own. Samuel could recite the writings of heretics, and write rebuttals as to why they should be condemned—but he had never actually met a heretic. He did not realize how persuasive, charming, and threatening they could be.

Flavius shifted position slightly. On the flat roof of a building just visible to him, a woman had appeared and was hanging a wash to dry. Among the other linens already hanging, she appeared simply as a silhouette outlined by a setting sun. He watched her as she shook out the tunics and bedding and hung them one by one on the line, reviving a memory of one he had known intimately in the past.

Samuel was facing one of the Church's most difficult problems. Official Church doctrine was clear on the matter. At the Council of Nimes, a decree had gone forth that women were not to serve as priests, which had been reinforced at the Council of Orange. But still, there were recalcitrant bishops who ignored these mandates.

Again, the face of the woman he had known as a youth filled his mind. His eyes again focused on the rooftop where the woman had finished hanging her laundry to dry. He smiled derisively at the workings of his own memory, reminding himself of the lifelong sacrifices one must make for the love of God. Their relationship had been beautiful but agonizing for him, and eventually it pitted his soul against his body. It had, of course, ended badly. He had chosen the Church, and she had fled to the city, but it had been a good lesson about the guile of women.

The church philosophers understood the weakness of

women, which required the safeguard of men. 'For Adam was formed first, then Eve; and Adam was not deceived but the woman was deceived and became the transgressor." And protection implied subordination. Thus women should be subordinate to men, a philosophy that is a true reflection of nature and God, he mused.

He had taught Samuel to view women with compassion. He defined proper roles for men and women according to household functions and public functions. This provided for a great deal of power for women in the household but enjoined them from public political life. It worried him when women spoke publicly, especially from the pulpit, because it defied women's natural subordination to men. At this critical point in the Church's history, there was no room for ambiguity.

Yet he wondered, as he had for several weeks now, about the claims advanced by the churches in the south of Italia. They were claims based on a warped sense of history, and Samuel knew this as well as anyone. But still, Flavius worried about Samuel's encounter with these women. He knew they would be full of false knowledge, confident, and strong in their conviction. For all Flavius knew, Samuel had never even kissed a woman. He would not understand the powerful influence possessed by women, let alone how they could lure a man away from his destiny—the life of the mind and the redemption of the soul. Flavius had warned him many times, and Samuel was well versed in the sinfulness of sexuality. *But that was in books...how would he do in the real world?* he wondered.

Flavius found himself looking at the olive trees in the garden off the courtyard, just visible around the corner of the building. Their squat, twisted trunks supported thin, feathery silver leaves. The trees looked half dead but still produced barrels of olives. *Am I like those trees,* he wondered idly, *coming to my sweetest knowledge late in life?*

For a moment he felt jealous of Samuel and his great adventure, his youth, his innocence, his belief in a black-and-white world where right and wrong were easy to distinguish. Maybe it was no coincidence at all that this drama would be played out by this young man, in the very region where that woman from long ago had fled to. *Put your faith in the Lord, Samuel!* he said to himself.

He left his room and walked through the long silent halls, down the quiet staircase that led him out into the courtyard. The pattern of the stones looked different up close, the web of cracks so much larger and intricate than they appeared from his window. He strolled with his hands behind his back, turning his steps towards the olive grove.

"Flavius!"

Flavius closed his eyes and tried to bury his annoyance. He took a deep breath and turned around to face Gelasius.

"Your Holiness. What a pleasant surprise!"

Gelasius regarded him for a moment. "Our young messenger should have arrived by now."

"Indeed, Your Holiness. He is very conscientious."

Gelasius eyed him carefully. "I'm certain that he is, and I hope he will not be easily distracted. Nevertheless, he is an interesting choice. I was quite intrigued by him in our meeting."

They rounded the corner and made their way onto the soft turf planted in rows among the olive trees. A gardener was in the lowest branches of one of the trees, applying a poultice to a branch he had just sawed off, and bowed his head as they passed. Gelasius raised one hand to acknowledge the gardener.

"I've been thinking on our choice, and I have a concern, Flavius."

Flavius was quiet, watching the dusty green leaves quiver

in the breeze.

"I wonder why we chose an intellectual for this mission rather than a zealot."

Flavius made a sound of protest and the Pope chuckled.

"I understand as well as you do that a scholar is sometimes preferable to a zealot...but I wonder if that holds true in this case."

Flavius swallowed hard as Gelasius continued. "Samuel is an intellectual. He lives too much in his mind. It occurs to me that you may have selected him not because he's suited to the task at hand but because you favor him—and because you are alike."

Flavius chose his words carefully. "You are very perceptive, Your Holiness, and indeed, Samuel is my most highly regarded protégé, but I would never jeopardize your mission based on emotions. He is young, competent, and adaptable, and I believe he will soon prove his worth as a peacemaker who will unite the Church into a powerful entity led by the Bishop of Rome."

Gelasius responded quietly, but there was iron in his voice. "Will he do what I've asked?"

Flavius did not hesitate. "Without doubt he will. Samuel's greatest devotion is to the Church. He'll do what you asked of him."

Gelasius paused a long time before he spoke. "Be candid with me, Flavius. Can Samuel bring about a change in this heretical group?"

"I fear..." responded Flavius, looking away through the rows of trees, "I fear that this issue may be more complicated than you believe it to be."

He awaited the Pope's reaction, but Gelasius remained placid and unreadable. "In your view, issues of orthodoxy and heresy are to be settled by a decree, or by the convening of a council, or ultimately by force."

Gelasius nodded, encouraging Flavius to go on.

"Your Holiness, this is a matter of putting history in proper perspective. We should not dispute the fact that women served as bishops or presbyters but rather, state that this is a deviance from the canons."

Gelasius perked up and listened intently. "So let us admit that in the early years of Christianity in small gatherings, women administered the sacraments of Baptism, the Eucharist, and even Penance, but that was because the clergy was not available. But we make it clear that women can not administer the sacraments when the clergy is present. In our present realm, male priests are always nearby. Therefore, women would now be usurping rights that belong to men."

Flavius added, "We both understand the extent to which there have been disputes over doctrine, especially in the early history of Christianity."

"But there has always been only one truth—and Jesus did say 'You are Peter, and on this rock I will build my church...'" Gelasius interrupted.

"And as the heir to Peter, you can never allow that authority to be undermined. But my worry is that if we attempt to stamp out this heresy by force, we'll set a precedent for tyranny in the Church."

As the word tyranny rolled off his lips, Gelasius's patience gave way. "You dare equate my divine rule with tyranny? My will is God's will on earth. My words are His words. And you ask that I reason with heretics? That, Flavius, would be a capitulation of God's will!"

Flavius softened under Gelasius's retort. "Yes, their blatant disregard for the decrees of Rome must cease immediately."

"Then why do you hesitate to enforce my decree?"

"I am simply searching for the best remedy for this difficult situation, Your Holiness. Samuel will not waver—

his faith is unquestionable. My hope is...is simply that we can convert the dissenters through reason rather than force."

Gelasius's eyes narrowed to slits. "Samuel is my representative, and he is my representative because of you. His successes and failings I will regard as yours. I do not believe, as you seem to, that this is a matter to be treated lightly. You complicate things—I strive to simplify them. So let me put this simply: If he fails or swerves from his course, your punishment will be severe."

Gelasius turned on his heels and walked back the way they had come.

Flavius watched him go, the dark wisps of doubt gathering in his mind like an approaching storm. *When long-held beliefs are challenged, we must justify each step taken along the way so as to be clear about why we have taken them...we must reflect Jesus as he lived, not how someone says he lived.*

Chapter 4

⌒

"Our Father and Mother who art in Heaven, hallowed be thy name..." rang out the communal voice of the assembly.

Samuel snapped out of his reverie. *Father and Mother who art in Heaven? God wasn't a woman...He was a man.* This was fundamental—even children knew this. *Such blasphemy can not be tolerated*, he thought while fuming inside.

He looked about at the men and women he sat amongst at this meeting of church elders. No one had flinched. No one seemed upset or surprised by what Anna had just said. They remained silent, their eyes closed in prayer.

Samuel felt panic start to well up in his chest and throat. Should he interrupt the prayer? Should he stand up and walk out? He couldn't just sit there and do nothing. He began to tap his foot nervously, waiting for some sort of reaction, some timely moment to interject.

An elderly man sat to his left. He was tall and thin, with only wisps of hair on his head, and thick white eyebrows. Samuel bumped the man's knee as he fidgeted. Tenderly, the man opened his bleary brown eyes and looked at him. He smiled kindly and put his hand on Samuel's knee.

"Peace be with you," he murmured.

"And with you also," Samuel responded out of instinct, a bit too loudly.

The old man chuckled and closed his eyes again. Samuel realized that the man was not offering the traditional greeting to him, but was trying to tell him gently to stop moving and disrupting everyone's prayer.

Samuel realized that he needed to correct these people, even if it meant disrupting their ceremony. Yet even as he built the courage to stand and speak, Joshua, who now stood before the congregation of elders, turned to him and offered him their greetings. He asked Samuel to address the group and deliver the news from Rome.

As he stood to address the group, his legs felt like noodles ready to collapse beneath him. He cleared his throat and glanced around. Through the open windows of the small room, he saw a sward of brownish-green grass that reached out to the edge of the bluff and seemed to meet with the azure sea. The breeze that flowed through the window was cool and smelled of salt water. He looked about at the curious faces, smiling bucolically, waiting patiently for him to speak.

Suppressing his anger and fear, he pulled himself up to his full height and spoke cautiously while putting the full force of the authority he represented into his voice. "My name is Samuel, and I come on behalf of Gelasius, the Bishop of Rome and Pope of the Holy Catholic Church. He has asked me to visit with you and report to him the state of this congregation."

This was a key moment, and he knew it. He was here to eradicate heresy and re-establish the orthodoxy of the Church. And yet he was hesitant to look at the women in the circle as he spoke, and so he fixed his gaze on the old man who had spoken to him.

"Word has come to Rome that a few of the churches in the area are ordaining women to the priesthood. I have been sent by the Pope to deal with these transgressions if they exist in your parish. If that is the case, the Pope will extend the opportunity to recant your heretical beliefs. If you embrace the truth of his word, you will be welcomed with open arms into the fold of the Church. But if you persist—the Pope will not look lightly upon your transgressions."

When Samuel finished, the only sound he heard was the raspy breathing coming from the chest of the elderly man. No one seemed surprised by Samuel's words. Samuel stood alone before them, trying to project both confidence and compassion—yet their stillness was unsettling.

He waited for someone to protest or to argue with him, but they all sat in silence. *Were they angered, embarrassed, or confused?* he wondered. He took a deep breath. There was nothing he could do but continue.

"To begin with, you can not open the Lord's prayer with the word 'mother'..."

"Why not?" a sharp voice perked up.

"Because it's not what the Church teaches us..."

"But it is what Jesus taught us," Anna interrupted.

"What?" Samuel squinted and pursed his lips. "How dare you make such..."

"It's what Jesus teaches in the Gospels of Matthew and Luke. He said God is like the mother hen who protects her chicks. I trust, speaking with her authority, that you are familiar with the sayings of Our Lord?"

Samuel felt the familiarity of debate wash through him. This was an arena in which he was comfortable. "Yes, but as you know, Our Lord spoke in parables. He was speaking of 'the mother hen' as a metaphor. But when the congregation refers to God as 'mother' in the Lord's prayer, that is blasphemy, because it gives the impression that God is a woman."

"Then God is a man?" Anna asked.

"God is neither man nor woman. God is..." Samuel felt the words trail off, and his mind began to flounder. How could this be happening to him, a representative of the Pope, trained by the greatest minds in Rome? He remembered

Tertullian's teachings and sputtered out, "Women were without gravity, without authority, and without discipline."

"I am grave, I have authority, and I have discipline, Samuel," responded Anna. "And I ask you, if you represent God to be 'Father' in the Lord's Prayer, are you not conveying the impression that God is a man? Is that what you mean when you say God the Father? That God has male genitals?"

He was angered by her crass reply. His eyes glowered at the woman who stood proudly before him. The corners of her lips had turned up slightly, though she remained calm and composed. She was an attractive woman who knew how to use her body to bolster her defiance. *How many men must have fallen for her wiles?* he wondered.

"Do not take my youth as an incitement," he managed. "I come as a representative of Gelasius."

"I would say the same to him," she said candidly.

"Now, Mother Anna, let us not shock our visitor into leaving before he's even settled in," Joshua added tactfully.

The old man who had been sitting beside him stifled a laugh with a clenched fist, as if he were coughing.

What's wrong with these people? Samuel thought, his disdain obvious.

"Please, Samuel, do not be offended," said Joshua. "We understand your position, but we are not in Rome here."

Samuel's teeth were clenched. "You misunderstand. This is not a point of argument," he replied. "You are outside the bounds of the acceptable. This is a matter of obedience."

At this, Anna retreated slightly. The situation needed to be defused, or it was bound to explode in front of them.

"Samuel—we aim, as you do, to act out of obedience and deference to the Lord. We respect the authority you represent, and these conversations must continue. But for now, let's go back to the house. Maria has cooked dinner, and I think we all could use something to eat and perhaps even a glass of wine."

. . .

At dinner, Samuel braced himself for their sarcastic insults and crude arguments. But when he saw that no one was going to address Anna's blasphemy, he remained silent, confident that his moral authority would assert itself. He quietly plotted out his rebuttals and retribution, determined not to lose his way again.

Still, as they retreated to the gardens to catch the last light of day, no one had come close to approaching the subject. It was as if he had never delivered the Pope's message and the afternoon's debate had been nothing more than a dream. Instead, he watched as they drank wine and told stories until the last threads of light fled into the approaching darkness.

The beauty of the sky, stretching away blue, and the sea turning gold under the sunset worked like alchemy on Samuel's heart, replacing the heat of his anger with a bright light he wanted to ignore. He tried to convince himself that the calm of this landscape was itself another form of deceit. Yet their gentle discussions, their hospitality, their provincial ease—each made it more difficult to cling to this impression and to the anger that had enflamed him earlier. Under different circumstances, he might have enjoyed himself here, he told himself. But as the glass of wine he drank went to his head, he began to suspect they were trying to lull him into forgetting why he had come here.

He studied the interactions of Anna and Joshua. There was an obvious intimacy between them, but it was coupled with an underlying tension he could not fully grasp. After all, she had been the one who told him about the death of Joshua's wife. Had there been a relationship? A love neither could speak of?

He was similarly confused by their relationship to Maria, the girl who had prepared their dinner. She had stood beside Anna, the one who offered him water when he first arrived. While she seemed to be an initiate or a pupil of Anna's, their interactions suggested they were more intimate. Were they sisters? Was Maria related to Joshua? His niece, maybe? It was not his place to ask, but his curiosity turned quickly to annoyance.

Maria did not have Anna's arrogance, but she was devilishly well spoken. She had a grace of movement he knew Flavius would attribute to sinful temptation, but she seemed as unaware of it as of the fact that her opinions, like Anna's, were wholly inappropriate for a woman to possess, much less profess openly. It was obvious that neither understood theirs should be a private role, not a public one.

According to Tertullian, women were not to teach or baptize, nor were they to engage in any kind of public discourse...that the only proper roles for women lay within the household.

"I need to see your library," Samuel blurted out during a pause in the conversation. He was mad at himself for accepting even a single glass of wine, for it had made him irritable.

"What?" Maria said in the middle of a laugh.

"While I'm here, my mentor...a man named Flavius, who is a good and brilliant man, the most scholarly I've ever met,..." Samuel paused to gather himself, "has asked me to inspect your library and see if there are any documents of historical significance."

"You think we might have documents here that you don't have in Rome?" a bemused Joshua asked.

Anna stilled her laugh.

"One never knows," Samuel responded bluntly.

Joshua nodded. "Of course. Tomorrow we will show you our modest library."

"Yes, I think we've all had a bit too much fun tonight to go and read dusty documents," Maria spoke up suddenly, catching Samuel off guard. "Tomorrow I'll take you myself."

It was an offer he was quick to accept.

"And it's flattering to think you will find something of importance in our little collection of documents," she added.

.   .   .

In the morning, Maria took Samuel to the study in the back of the church. There were shelves of texts lining the walls, all carefully ordered. She set him up with some fresh bread and cheese and a pitcher of water, as Samuel paced around the room, pulling nervously at his lip.

"Is there anything else I can get for you?" Maria asked.

"No, nothing. I just need some time alone with these texts."

She looked unconvinced. "Are you all right, Samuel?"

"I'm fine," he said, looking around at the shelves, avoiding her eyes.

"All right," she said, looking at him askance. "Well, I won't be around this afternoon. I'm going to visit the sick in our town. It's part of my duties as a deacon."

"I was just ordained three months ago," Maria said with pride. Samuel fought the urge to wince. "But Anna will be home working on her homily for the Eucharist celebration on Sunday, so she can get you anything you might need."

"She preaches?"

"Yes, of course she does. Don't priests preach in Rome?"

"But she is not a priest!"

Maria did not answer. Their eyes locked. He shook his head and turned away.

"You said last night that you were interested in seeing works you might not have come across in Rome," Maria said as she looked at Samuel entreatingly. "I spoke to Anna this morning, and she suggested you might not have seen these." She stepped to a shelf and indicated a short line of texts.

"What are they?" he asked.

"A kind of history we've assembled. Some of them are very old, and some are our transcriptions of old documents. You might start with this. It's particularly relevant to this place."

She took a scroll down carefully and handed it to him. With a glance at the first few lines, he knew no one in Rome had seen this document before. He forgot her, holding it carefully in his hands and looking fixedly at the faded lines impressed upon the papyrus.

"I'll leave you to your reading," she said, as she walked out of the room.

Chapter 5

S amuel held the scroll gently in his hands. The title read, "The History of the Church of Saints Priscilla and Aquila During the Reign of Emperor Diocletian (305 A.D.)." He started to read.

. . .

Alexandra looked down at the delicate child whose head was nestled in her lap. She ran a cool cloth along his forehead and held his hand tightly.

Her husband, James, entered, smiling weakly.

"He's coming around slowly," Alexandra said.

"Where did this one come from?" James asked.

Her blue eyes glistened as she turned towards the window. "I found him on the road to the east. He lay beneath a tree, asleep, holding tightly onto this."

She handed James a small wooden cross, dangling from the worn threads of a necklace. A storm brewed in his eyes as he looked at it, and he balled his fist around the cross, squeezing tightly.

"I will see what we have left in our grain bin. He must eat."

"James." He stopped in his tracks, and looked at his wife through a cloud of tears. "This can't go on," Alexandra wailed. "We can only care for so many, and our food is running out. Soon the floodgates will break and the persecuted will wash over this land. Our church alone can

41

not provide a home to all the sick, the old, and downtrodden who will arrive at our doorstep."

He raised his hands. "What would you have me do?" he responded. "We can not abandon these people. God will give us the grain and fish we need. We must have faith."

The baby shuddered and began to cough. Alexandra held him closely and whispered quietly in his ear, soothing him back to sleep. She took a deep breath.

"There is only so much food, James. But faith...faith is endless. Faith is what we must give these people." She dipped her cloth in the bowl again.

"What are you suggesting?"

She smiled, and the calm of her voice and features pervaded the room. "God has given us a gift, James. We must bring it to the people. We must bring them faith."

James stood in the doorway, leaning up against the wall. He looked at his wife: her dark chestnut hair outlining the soft, round face that hung above the child in her arms; her work-worn hands. He could not disappoint her.

"We will discuss this later. The child needs food."

With that, he was gone.

. . .

Later that night, Alexandra and James convened the parishioners and refugees who were strong enough to discuss the fate of their church. Those who had survived the persecution of the Emperor Diocletian confirmed what had been their worst fears. Christians in the surrounding towns and cities were being seized, bishops and priests persecuted, churches razed, and sacred objects desecrated. Holy scriptures were burned and altars smashed. Men, women, even children were being tortured. Their tongues were torn out and their limbs sawed off, even burned at the stake or nailed to the cross to suit the whims of unbelievers.

The Church of Saints Priscilla and Aquila had been protected for a long time because of an agreement Alexandra and James had struck with the territorial governor, Titus, whose brother-in-law was Christian. Each year, Alexandra and James paid him money in exchange for protection of their church. Poorer congregations, however, even those within the territory governed by Titus, had seen their churches destroyed and their members scattered or killed. Alexandra and James knew it was only a matter of time before their agreement broke under the weight of Diocletian's decree against Christianity.

"You can not fight against the armies of Diocletian," spoke one young man whose cheekbones protruded grossly from months of hunger and despair. "To fight is to submit ourselves to further persecution. We must, with the time we have left, recant our beliefs and submit to the will of the emperor."

There were rumblings of agreement from around the table from others. James raised his hand, calling for silence.

"My brothers and sisters, I recognize I have not faced the terrors you've faced, nor borne the burdens you have had to bear, but we dishonor ourselves and our Savior when we speak of such things."

"Jesus would have argued on behalf of reason," the young man went on. "He would have understood that we can not all sacrifice ourselves as he did."

The boldness of this proclamation brought a heavy silence upon the room. Even James could not find the words to speak. Many at the table bowed their heads, while others looked anxiously at the large cross at the back of the room. The young man shifted back into his seat and persisted. "If we are to survive, we must give in to Diocletian."

"Are we not His disciples?" came a voice from the back

of the room.

All turned to see the one whose voice had broken into the fray. Alexandra rose from her seat by the door.

"Are we not the disciples of Christ?" she said. "Are we not here to do His will on earth?"

"Yes, but who will be left to do His work when we are all burned at the stake?" another protested.

"All those who hear his message and accept him into their hearts," she replied. She walked among those gathered at the table, casting her powerful eyes on each as she spoke.

"Diocletian may try to kill every one of us and destroy everything that we stand for, but he can not put an end to our faith. No matter how powerful his army, how fleet of foot his executioners, how many circuses he holds, he will never match the infinite flame of Christ's love. We must spread His word throughout the empire until our legions of followers are greater than Diocletian's army."

Those whose families had been murdered, whose homes had been burned, and whose children were taken were still not convinced. James moved towards his wife, taking her hand in his. "But how will we accomplish this grandiose task?" he asked.

"God has spoken to me, James, and I know now what we must do," she said to him gently. "Will you come with me James...will any of you come with me...to preach the word of the Lord?"

No one responded, except for James. "I will preach with you, Alexandra!"

He turned to the group. "And who among you will take care of our church while we are gone?"

No one responded.

.   .   .

They began preaching quietly in the oldest manner, in houses and in poor, rundown buildings, on ships in port cities—anyplace where a humble few could gather without attracting the attention of Roman sentinels.

The people in these battered towns were starved for the Word. As James and Alexandra gave the sacraments, cared for the sick and poor, and spread the Gospel, their furtive congregation grew larger and larger. Alexandra preached with a heartfelt fire that lifted up both Christians and pagans alike, giving hope to the downtrodden and beating back their terror of the emperor with her message of love and salvation. She often quoted the words of John: "So, if the Son set you free, you will indeed be free...you shall be free from hatred, fear, despair, oppression and the sinful ways of life."

After many months of preaching clandestinely, Alexandra found herself one day in the small home of a family who lived in a decrepit section of the city. Their church had been destroyed and its stones and timber thrown to the bottom of a water-filled quarry. She began preaching within the four small walls of their tiny room, but soon, so many had gathered to hear Christ's message that she moved to preach from the stairs that wound up the side of the building. Still others crowded the staircase around her, and more filled the staircase across the alley. Those seeking the word of God gathered in the windows, on the rooftops, and in the alleys below. Most were Christians, but unbelievers as well flocked to the place, anxious to hear of this God who inspired such courage and hope.

Alexandra felt the Spirit upon her, and offered a vision of salvation to the starved people gathered before her. Her voice came forth like a hammer ringing from an anvil, pure and true. The afternoon had passed and night had fallen as she spoke. For several hours, the air was filled with her sonorous voice, made great by the Lord.

As her inspired sermon ended, and as she blessed those who wished to accept Christ into their hearts, she worried for James, who had been preaching in another part of the city. She longed to tell him the story of her preaching from the rooftops and of the victory it represented. She thought also of her daughters, asleep in their beds, dreaming the undaunted dreams of children.

In the alley, an old man who had been standing at the back of the crowd beckoned to her. She could hardly see his face beneath the cloak and hood that he wore, and he was hunched over, keeping his face hidden from her. Exhausted as she was, she approached him, having made a promise to herself to help all in need.

"Are you Alexandra?" he asked as she came near. His voice was rough and gravelly, as if he had not had water to drink in days.

"Yes, that is my name. How can I help you, my brother?"

The old man snickered beneath the thick folds of his cloak. An instinct deep inside Alexandra flared up in that moment, and the exhaustion she had felt turned quickly into the heightened state of fear. By the time her conscious mind could process what was going on, the old man had lifted his fingers to his lips and whistled loudly. Two Roman soldiers came from around a corner, seized her, and pushed her against the wall of the alley, and holding a torch above her head examined her features.

"Do you profess yourself to be a leader among the Christians?" one of them barked.

Alexandra's head was spinning from the blow against the wall. "I profess only that I have cared for the sick, have given food to the hungry, shelter to the homeless while spreading the good news of Jesus."

At this, the old man standing before her lifted his cloak. The scars on his face appeared fresh in the living light of the

46

torch, and he now rose to his full height, a full foot above Alexandra. He was much younger than she had taken him for, and his vicious smile bore into her heart like a hot needle.

"To spread the word of your pathetic religion is an act of high treason against Rome. If you were to renounce your God now, I might find it in my heart to grant you mercy and only have you flogged for your crime." His words were seething with disdain.

"I suspect that you will do what you want, regardless of what I say," she said, glowering back at him.

With a sudden movement, he leapt forward and seized her jaw in his iron-like hand.

"I seek to grant you mercy, and you repay me with such bile?" He released her jaw and slapped her in a single motion. The back of her head slammed into the wall once more.

"Admit that your God is worthless before me—admit to your treason, and I may spare your life," he snarled at her.

She closed her eyes and spat out the blood that had begun to pool in her mouth. Breathing deeply, she tried to find some measure of the peace and calmness in the Lord. "I admit only to trying to help these people find the road to salvation," she said.

Her lack of deference, so unbecoming of her gender, enraged him. Pressing himself against her, his breath hot upon her face, he dug his fingers into her cheeks, lowering his voice to sinister whisper.

"Then you have chosen death."

He pressed his lips harshly against hers, and then looked at the two soldiers who held her pinned against the wall. The last thing she saw was his savage grin, flickering in the torchlight, before he smashed her face with his fist.

Chapter 6

⌒

F or two days she sat in a prison cell with only bread to eat and a cup of water to drink. She prayed that James would find her, but not even a ray of light found its way into the prison where she was kept.

On the third day the soldiers dragged her out of the cell to the street outside, where a large cart pulled by several oxen carried six people bound in a wooden cage.

"Your regional governor, Titus, has received word of your activities here and considers your incitements a betrayal. Your church is being torn down by its own believers on pain of death, and you are to be taken to Rome for punishment."

Emperor Diocletian was determined to restore peace to his vast empire, and the citizens of Rome had grown restless and wrathful. They longed for the circuses of the past, and Diocletian began to gather Christians to satisfy the bloodlust of the land.

Alexandra fell forward into the cart filled with filthy, moaning bodies. Behind her, she heard the voice of James, who had fought through the crowd to get closer to his wife. The soldiers began bludgeoning him with the butt of their spears. Alexandra reached out through the wooden bars of her cage as the cart pulled her away from her family. Her eldest daughter, Sarah, wailed, while the youngest, Ruth, stood with her father. Seeing the agony in their faces, Alexandra's spirit broke and she wept. She was taken out of the city to join a long procession of soldiers, prisoners, animals, and wagons along the Appian Way.

At the sight of the barren, unknown land around her, she

grew afraid and begged the driver to set her free. She tried to pray, but her faith remained behind with her daughters and her husband.

Her days imprisoned in the cramped and foul-smelling cart passed as if in a dream. More prisoners were added as the company of soldiers travelled from village to village, until their numbers grew to a thousand and more. Alexandra spoke to no one, thinking only of her husband, of her children, and of the life that had been taken from her.

Alexandra hardened her heart against God, longing only to return home to her family. God had placed in her the love of a mother, and that love had now overwhelmed her love of Him....

It came to pass then that on a day filled with rain and cold, the caravan approached the city of Rome. The many roads that led there were congested with merchants and farmers, travelers, fortune hunters, street urchins, peddlers, and caravans from the East. Alexandra rose to her feet for the first time in days to see the city. Its buildings and walls were bigger than any she had seen, many of them adorned with marble and gold. Soldiers filled the streets, watching the crowds, drinking wine in stalls, and harassing the merchants. The crowds they passed jeered or turned away in disgust at the sight of the derelict prisoners.

The guards shoved the manacled prisoners into a long column, whipping those who were slow to move and beating them with the heavy handles of their whips. They marched the column through the city to a large encampment where many others sat awaiting their fate.

Alexandra shuffled along with the others, her eyes on the dreary scene around her, on the muddy ground, on the large and hastily erected prisoner huts that were more like cages than huts, on the wretched prisoners everywhere, of which she was one. The clouds had fallen so low they hung like fog above the mud and the prisoners' huts and cages. Alexandra saw through all of this tumult a small ramshackle cross made of two slats of wood lashed together and stuck in the mud next to one of the huts. The humble cross beamed with the light of the Holy Spirit, and filled her again with a warmth she had forgotten. She kept her eyes fixed on it as long as she could, even as she was herded into a large wooden cage, and as the rain poured down from above. Once inside, Alexandra worked her way around the perimeter of the cage until she found a place where she could see the frail cross standing in the mud.

"You're a Christian," said a voice from behind her. She turned to face a small man with a pleasant open face and light-colored hair slicked down by the rain.

"Yes, I am," she said.

"You were looking at the cross. Someone in that cell over there always puts one up. It usually lasts a day or two before a soldier notices and kicks it over. But he always puts another up."

"Are you a Christian also?"

"Most of us are."

"Speak for yourself," said a figure sitting against the bars at their feet. "I don't have anything to do with your madness. But it didn't stop them from throwing me in here, did it? And it won't stop them from doing whatever it is that they're going to do to you."

The figure stood and Alexandra saw a woman, as large as a powerful man, with a shock of red hair turned a purple brown in this rainy light.

"Why do you call us mad?" asked the blond-haired man.

"To believe that your God was killed and then came back to life is madness," the woman told them.

"If you're not a Christian, why were you arrested?" asked Alexandra.

The woman shrugged. "For a belief of my own, which may have been as mad as yours," she said bitterly.

"What was that?"

"I believed a member of the emperor's court when he said that he loved me, and I believed that there would be no punishment for consorting with him when he was married."

"You're here because of adultery?"

"I'm here because when his wife found out, he denounced me as a prostitute in front of her and I brained him with a calabash. I did not know that he would fall as he did and never get up." She shrugged again. "Such are the whims of life."

"You don't have to feel abandoned to the whims of life. Our faith is always open," the blond man said gently. "My name is John."

"Junia," she said curtly.

"And I'm Alexandra." She turned her back to the bars and slumped down next to the woman.

"At least the rain is letting up," John said after a while. "That's good news, isn't it? A sign that God is still with us." He smiled.

"Are you serious?" Junia asked. "Don't you understand what's going to happen to us?"

"I understand. But there is no better sacrifice than to die for my faith in the Lord. He is a kind and merciful God, and He gives me all the strength I need and washes me free from fear. If He calls on me to be a martyr, I will do His will gladly."

"Washed him free from his sanity," Junia muttered to Alexandra.

Alexandra chuckled, smiling for what seemed like the first time in an eternity. John smiled also.

"No, Junia," said Alexandra. "John is right. The Lord Jesus has the power to even destroy the sting of death."

51

"If He is so powerful, why don't you share John's cheerfulness?"

Alexandra thought of her daughters and of her realization in the back of the cart that she was torn between her family and her faith. "I am not as strong as he is," she said. "Everyone struggles at times to trust in the Lord."

"I don't believe that you're not as strong," Junia said slowly as she watched her. "That's not what was in your face. I think you understand what's waiting for us up there better than John does." She jerked her head up. Alexandra did not understand.

"Where?"

"The Coliseum," she said.

Alexandra gasped. What she had taken to be a dark bank of clouds pushed up against the open field was not clouds at all but a building. The rain had let up, and it was visible now, massive, shadowed, with arches that reminded her of open mouths, howling in agony. The sight was terrible, and she felt the fear run through her like cold water.

Chapter 7

E very morning guards threw loaves of bread into the cages where the prisoners were kept. People scrambled for the food, shoving it down their throats or hoarding it in their clothing. There was never enough for all the people kept in the holding cells, and hunger was rampant. But Alexandra did not shove or fight for food. She thought of her hunger as a sacrifice for Jesus Christ, and when she was able to get some sustenance, she took tiny amounts and gave the rest to the sick and weak in the cells. She spent her days praying for strength and thinking about her children.

In the afternoons, Roman soldiers took some of the prisoners outside and lined them up in the muddy square. They were counted and then marched at spear point in one long winding line into a passage at the foot of the Coliseum. Twice Alexandra saw men try to escape. They dashed madly out of line, pushing other prisoners out of their way. Their eyes had the look of rabid dogs and their limbs flailed with terrified panic as they slipped in the mud and the Roman soldiers surrounded them. Both times the men were captured before they even got past the mass of captives. The soldiers laughed as if this were a game, beating the men with scabbarded swords then dragging them, screaming, into the Coliseum along with the rest of that day's unlucky victims. After they disappeared into the building, there was a long period of silence. Then a great roar of voices flooded out from the Coliseum like a heavy surf pounding a beach. Just like the buildup of the next wave, there was a lull, followed by a low steady hum of voices, punctuated by roars of excitement and cheering.

None of the prisoners ever commented on the sounds, but after each bout of chaotic cheering, a heavy silence fell over all of them. They knew what those sounds meant.

On the fifth day of their imprisonment, Alexandra and Junia were sitting and talking quietly, Alexandra about her family and Junia about the man she believed had loved her in Rome. They were interrupted by the first roar of the crowd, and they both involuntarily glanced up.

"They're bringing the prisoners into the arena," said John. He stood next to where they sat, looking through the bars at the Coliseum. His face was fervent and intent, as if he could see through the massive blocks of stone. "The crowd always yells the loudest when they first see the people enter. They stand and shake their fists."

Junia's face grew pale beneath her dark red hair, and both women looked up at him.

"How do you know this?" Alexandra asked.

"I was not always a believer," said John. "When I was a young man, I watched captured barbarians and criminals in the arena many times." He spoke without looking at them.

"Was it awful?" asked Junia very quietly.

"Yes. And it's usually reserved for people who are not Roman citizens. You aren't, are you, Junia?"

"No. I'm originally from the North."

"Well, now the Christians join you, no matter their citizenship." He paused. "Great Rome executes her own people for believing in the truth. Knowing the truth is a crime."

Alexandra took a deep breath and allowed the enormity of what John was saying to sink in. She had known since childhood that Christianity was not a legally sanctioned religion in the Roman Empire, unlike Judaism or some of the so-called mystery religions like the cult of Isis. But that technicality had never bothered her before. In her lifetime, Christians' beliefs, activities, and religious services were, for the most part, just ignored by the authorities. In many towns there were separate church buildings that everyone knew were where Christians worshipped, but no one stopped them, let alone arrested them or executed them. Never before had Alexandra thought of herself as a criminal, awaiting the same cruel fate as them in the Roman Empire. For years, Christians lived in fragile peace with their pagan neighbors. But now the persecutions had started again, even more brutally than before. The Emperor Diocletian called on all people of the Roman Empire to make public sacrifices to the Roman gods and goddesses, knowing full well that Christians would refuse. He then used their refusal as a ploy to slaughter them as a public spectacle. He blamed Christians for the economic and political disasters of his reign instead of his own greed and foolishness. Distract the people from the real problems of the empire by drawing attention to those who are different—it was a trick as old as time, Alexandra thought, and yet the people fall for it time and time again. She felt a deep heaviness in her chest, and it took all her strength just to breathe.

"What will they do to us?" Junia asked.

But it was as if John had not heard her. His mind was somewhere else entirely, and he stared at the horizon. "Some people couldn't stay in the audience long," he said. "They didn't understand beforehand exactly how it would be. When they saw the spectacle, they couldn't stand it and had to leave." John began rocking back and forth on his feet. The pitch of his voice went up, but the volume went down. "For some people, it became more alluring each time they went. I was one of them. I couldn't get enough of it, of the killing and the blood and the terror on the victims' faces. I was..."

John checked himself and lowered his head for a moment. He breathed deeply and looked up. "I was a very different person," he said. "I was a great sinner. The Lord has brought me here for a purpose, to allow me to become a martyr in the place where I committed my greatest sins, enjoying the torture and death of my fellow men. When my time comes, I'll stand in the center of the arena and gaze up at whatever decadent officials are sitting in the boxes, and I will not raise my hand against whatever man or beast comes for me. I will let them kill me while I sing the praises of Christ. The whole world will see that I am not the same man who once sat in the stadium and cheered at the sufferings of others. Now my suffering will cleanse me."

Alexandra touched him on the leg and he looked down.

"God has already forgiven you, John," she said. "You were forgiven of all sins when you were baptized."

"I know," he said quietly, "but can my fellow men ever forgive me? Could I ever be forgiven if they knew that even after I was baptized, I sometimes still thought about gladiator fights and circuses?"

Alexandra paused for a moment and then said, "If you'd like, I can reconcile you to the people of the Church through the laying on of hands now."

He looked surprised and frowned. He nodded stiffly and then walked away.

"That man frightens me a little bit," said Junia.

"He seems gentle and sorrowful to me."

"But he's so eager to die. He's even cheerful about it sometimes. He always seems to be thinking about what will happen and looking forward to it."

"It doesn't work the same way for everyone," said Alexandra, "but the power of the Lord can make wonderful things happen for people. John is a troubled man, I believe, but his faith gives him strength."

"But that look he gave you before he walked off?"

"I think John is grieving his past life and feeling such shame over his sins. But I think that look has to do with the fact that I'm a woman and a priest. Most people aren't used to women speaking freely, equally with men. Even many Christians aren't used to us being leaders in the churches. I surprised him when I offered him the sacrament of penance."

"Why was he surprised?"

"Well, because now he knows I am a priest, and even though women have been priests since the beginning of Christianity, some people still have a hard time accepting a woman serving as their minister. Even though they are Christians, they are also still Romans, and as Romans, they expect women to be subservient, to keep quiet."

"Are there a lot of disagreements, then, in your religion about the proper role of women?"

"Oh, Junia, there have been a lot of disagreements in my religion about everything, almost from the very beginning. If you take ten Christians from different churches, you might end up with ten completely different pictures of the real meaning of Jesus' teachings, who Jesus really was, what God is like, and how we humans should act in the world."

Alexandra sighed. She didn't want to get into details. There were not just deep disagreements among different groups of Christians; there was terrible infighting as well. Some churches were always trying to tell others how things must be done, and some teachers and theologians denounced other teachers as "heretics" and said that they weren't true Christians. Some Christians claimed to have "secret knowledge" that others were not allowed to know. The Bishop of Rome was constantly trying to consolidate his political power and drive out those people he saw as a challenge to his primacy.

Jesus' message was simple, Alexandra thought: Heal the

sick and preach that the Kingdom of God is at hand. Trying to figure out how to do those things in the midst of the Roman Empire seemed to be too hard for mere human beings. Alexandra just didn't have the energy to start to explain all that. It was all she could do to focus on getting through the day.

But Junia wanted to know more. "Is it difficult in your religion for women?" Junia pressed her.

"Well, not in the church I belong to. We believe that men and women share equally in the benefits and tasks assigned by the Lord. I share all of the priestly duties with my husband, James,...."

His name caught in the back of her throat. It was the first time Alexandra had spoken his name out loud since she had been arrested. She let out a gasp at the pain it caused her. She realized that a large part of her had been trying to avoid thinking about him and about Sarah and Ruth.

"Oh, Junia," she cried, "I can't imagine never seeing them again, my family. I keep thinking that something will happen and we'll be let free before they come to take us to the Coliseum. But it won't happen, will it?"

"We will not escape. You know that. We will die terribly in the arena. Your God has taken your family from you."

"No. God is with me through all of this." But even as Alexandra spoke, she felt her faith waiver. She put her head down on her knees and wept.

"Alexandra, please don't. You've been so strong this whole time. I don't think I can take it if you break down now."

"I can't help it."

"Tell me about your Jesus. Please."

"He feels so far away. I don't know what good it will do anyone."

"What else are you going to do, sit and cry? You can

educate me a little. It will give us something to do."

Alexandra looked up and rubbed her sleeve across her cheeks.

"I'm not going to convert to Christianity," said Junia. "You don't have to worry about that. I'm too set in my ways. But it might be nice to think about something else for a while."

Chapter 8

❧

As the days stretched on, Alexandra told Junia about Christianity and the Christians she knew. They were such good people, Alexandra explained, people who would give their last morsel of food to a stranger and then thank God for the chance to do so. The things of this world—money, luxury, fame, power—were meaningless to them.

She told Junia stories about Jesus' life and explained that Christians followed not just His teachings but His actions as well. Alexandra told Junia her favorite story of Jesus, that of the unnamed prostitute who washed His feet with tears and dried them with her hair. When the men around Him asked Jesus how He could let such a despicable person—and a woman at that!—touch Him, He said that she had shown more love for God than any of them had by following their rules and laws.

Jesus had a way of turning things upside down, Alexandra explained, of making you realize that what you *expected* God would be is not necessarily how God actually *is*. He was a radical, a revolutionary of love and acceptance. Alexandra told Junia the beatitudes, the teachings from His Sermon on the Mount. Junia asked Alexandra to say the beatitudes over and over again, as they sat in the mud and cold rain, till she herself had them memorized.

She told Junia about Jesus' death by crucifixion at the hands of the Romans, the most painful execution ever thought up by human beings, and how Jesus never lashed out at anyone who treated Him so cruelly. Alexandra shared with her about Mary of Magdala, one of Jesus' closest friends and greatest supporters. When all His other followers had abandoned Him at the end, only Mary, His mother, and Mary of Magdala remained with Him as He dropped His head and died of suffocation. It was Mary who went to Jesus' tomb to grieve and instead saw an angel, who told her that Jesus was not there—that Jesus had defeated death. She told Junia that since then, Mary of Magdala has been known as "the apostle to the apostles," the first to proclaim the good news of the resurrection to all of humanity.

Junia interrupted her. "If Mary of Magdala was the first person to preach this message, why then would John be bothered by you preaching now?"

"Well, I guess people don't always think through their assumptions about what Jesus would want or do. People have their own agendas—they only remember the things they want to remember. Mary may have been the first priest, but that doesn't make it any easier for female priests today. The men who rule the churches are afraid of the truth. They are afraid of women, so they can and will do everything in their power to stamp out the priesthood of women. We Christians must struggle not just against the Romans but against these powerful, misguided men in the churches."

"Being a Christian has been hard," Junia said, more than she asked.

"None of us were ever promised that life following Christ would be easy," Alexandra murmured, "but He is with me, here, now, always, and there is so much joy in that."

"Are you like John, so eager to go to your death?"

"No, I'm not." Alexandra paused. She surprised herself as soon as she spoke, but she knew her answer was an honest one. "I had always thought I would be honored to be a martyr," she continued. "As a girl growing up, I imagined myself spitting in the eye of the Emperor and staring down legions of Roman centurions. I even secretly imagined becoming a saint. But I would do anything to live."

Junia was quiet for a moment, but she moved restlessly and rubbed her face. Then she took a big breath. "I know a way if you are desperate," Junia gazed steadily into Alexandra's eyes, "but it would mean becoming like that prostitute."

Alexandra gasped. "What...what do you mean? Somehow I don't think you mean washing someone's feet."

"I only wish...It would mean selling your body for the chance at life. The centurions will pass over our group or will transfer us into a different cell when it comes time to choose who will go to the Coliseum. As long as you continue to have sex with them, you will be safe."

"But what about when all the cages are empty and we are the only ones left? Will they let us go free?"

"I don't know what will happen. All I can promise is that it will give us time."

"Perhaps enough time for James to find me," Alexandra murmured. "I just want to see him again."

"Are you willing?"

Alexandra swallowed hard. "I am. Whom do I need to talk to? But first, tell me everything that will happen. I have to get my mind ready for this. I need to know."

That evening, when the guards came to their cage to count prisoners, Junia and Alexandra approached one. The guard knew Junia and raised his eyebrows and smirked as they neared him.

"Well hello, Junia. Is this another whore who just can't stay away from me?" The centurion grabbed his crotch and snorted at his own base, crass humor. He was a tall man, and he stared down his long straight nose at the two women.

Alexandra fought the urge to slap him. Junia squeezed her hand. She had explained to Alexandra that they should just remain silent and let the centurions do all the talking. They liked to hear themselves, she explained.

"You're not bad-looking." He lifted a lock of her hair with his meaty fist and stroked her ear lobe with his dirty fingernail.

Alexandra thought she would throw up and choked down the feeling with all the strength she had. The centurion's face was distorted by the light of the torch he held in the descending evening's light. He looked like a monster, and he smelled of sweat and dirt and sex. "But you're a bit padded, aren't you." He pinched her hip. "Had a couple of children, haven't you?"

The thought of her girls steeled Alexandra. She would do anything to survive, she realized, even if it meant debasing her own body.

"But I think you'll do," he continued. He turned to Junia. "Well, we'll have some fun tonight, won't we? You know the routine. One of us will come and get you. And for the love of Mars and Venus, clean yourselves beforehand." He threw a bucket at them.

That night, Junia and Alexandra waited by the gate at the front of their prison. In the distance they could hear the guards singing and shouting. They were getting drunker as the night wore on. This was actually a good thing, Junia explained. It meant that the orgy would not last too long before the centurions passed out in pools of their own vomit and semen.

Junia had encouraged Alexandra to try to get some sleep in the early hours of the night because she would not be sleeping much for the next few days, but it was impossible. She was terrified of what was going to happen and torn over whether she had made the right decision. Should she go willingly to her death, singing, as the great martyrs before her had done? Was she turning her back on all she believed as a Christian by defiling her body? She had to be true to her faith.

But she also had to be true to her daughters and husband. She had a responsibility to those children and had to do everything in her power to have the chance to raise them to adulthood. *Don't I have to do all in my power to escape and return to my family?* she questioned.

She prayed incessantly to God for guidance. *What is God's will,* she wondered, and she begged for guidance. But the answer was not forthcoming.

Then around midnight, her praying was interrupted. Another guard, this one much younger than the first, arrived at the gate where Alexandra and Junia stood waiting. He smirked and grunted at them, threw open the gate, and roughly grabbed their wrists.

Alexandra prayed, over and over, "Lord, give me strength."

Suddenly the young man stopped and snapped his head around. "Shut up!"

She had not realized she was praying aloud.

They arrived at the soldiers' quarters, entering the brightly lit tent through a flap in the canvas. As Alexandra's eyes adjusted to the light, she could not understand what she was seeing. Then she realized she was looking at bodies, a dozen naked bodies rolling around on hay-stuffed sacks.

"Hello, my pretties." A heavy hand clapped Alexandra on the back. "Let's have some fun. Off with your clothes. Hurry up! The men want a show."

The senior guard whom Alexandra first saw that afternoon staggered towards them through the bodies. "Wait, wait!" he yelled. He was drunk and grinning. "She's a Christian," he slurred as he pointed his finger at Alexandra.

The other guard let out a whoop. "Now this will be fun! Isn't it true that you Christians think you are cannibals, eating the body of your God? I've never fucked a cannibal before."

The centurions started laughing. Junia squeezed her hand, and a spirit and anger she had never known flowed through Alexandra. It made her strong.

"Well, before we let any Christians join our little party here, we make you swear an oath to Eros, the god of love. We find it makes for a better time."

Alexandra knew what she had to do. "No."

Junia turned towards her, a look of panic in her eyes. The guards seemed not to have heard her and had begun to look around for an idol for her to pray to.

"I said 'no,'" she repeated.

"What are you doing?" Junia asked.

This time, it was Alexandra who squeezed Junia's hand.

"No? No, little missy? Then what exactly are you here for?" the guard breathed hotly into her face.

"To tell you that the true God of love is Jesus Christ—the only God."

The older and larger of the guards spat in her face. Alexandra calmly wiped the spittle off with the back of her sleeve.

"What's the holdup?" called one of the soldiers from the back of the tent. "Get those clothes off!"

Another made a sound of agreement, and then another.

The man who had spit on her leaned close to Alexandra. "If you break our agreement, tonight could be your last night on this earth! Are you ready for that? Just a few hours ago you would do anything to live!"

"I'm ready."

"Stop all this talking," said a younger soldier. "These are women, are they not? Let's make them do what women do."

He pushed forward and began to grope Junia, who yelled and kneed him in the groin. He gasped as he doubled over.

The older guard knocked him to the ground dismissively and then raised his hand to still the other soldiers who had stepped forward angrily.

"No one touches these women until I say they do," he growled.

"Don't try to spoil our fun," said another soldier. He was drunk and naked, and he staggered forward holding his sword.

The older guard turned and looked at him. "If you raise that weapon in my direction, I'll kill you before you take another step," he said.

The man hesitated. "Why do you care?" he said. "Step out of the way and let us have them."

"There are fifty women in camp who will give themselves to you willingly," snapped the older guard. "These two intrigue me."

He turned back to look at Alexandra. "You know, if I allow it, these men will have you whether you like it or not."

"I know," she said.

For a moment he met her gaze, and then he motioned to one of the soldiers behind him. "Go find two other women," he said to them. "Unless you want to dance for us again tonight?" he asked Junia.

She squeezed Alexandra's hand, took a deep breath, and said, "I am going to the Coliseum tomorrow as well."

"Very well," he said. "I'll let you go back to your cages and to your death tomorrow. I'll do it because it amuses me. The emperor wants his prisoners strong so they can fight, and these packs of dogs behind me would tear you apart if I let them, but that's not why I'm stopping them. I'm doing it because it amuses me to show you how pathetic your God is. He's not helping you—I am. You're dependent on my mercy at this moment, not your God's. And sometime in the next few days, as you are dying, you will finally understand that

66

all along it was my mercy you should have begged for. You were worshipping the wrong being. You should have been worshipping me. I'm more powerful than your God is, and that amuses me."

He reached forward and kissed Alexandra savagely on the mouth and then pushed her away from him, already beginning to laugh mightily. "Get them out of my sight," he said. "I have given them my blessing, more powerful than that of any gods. We'll find others who won't befoul us when we touch them. Rome is mighty and her women are plentiful."

As a younger guard took them back to their cage, Alexandra said a prayer of thanks. She had known what she must do, and she was thankful for that. But her heart sank when she thought of her girls.

Chapter 9

Each day another cage had been emptied until there were only three left. All of the prisoners had learned to gather when the guards entered the large yard and watch which cage the guards approached. The captain of the guards had, in turn, begun to make a kind of sick game of the selection, grouping his men and then walking slowly from cage to cage smiling at the inhabitants and often doubling back or changing course, knowing that they were all filled with terror at where he would stop.

The sun was already shining brightly when the captain appeared in the yard and began his stroll. The prisoners watched in horror and the guards stood in a group, watching with their own grim amusement. A woman in one of the cages had again managed to come by two sticks that she had bound together to form a cross and stuck into the dirt. The captain spotted the cross and walked over to pick it up. He examined it for a moment and then turned to survey the yard of empty cages, smacking the cross in the palm of his hand. Alexandra felt him looking at her across the expanse of dirt. He smiled and she knew which cage he would choose. He looked away at the other cages, and then he raised the cross and pointed it at her and said something that sent the guards streaming in their direction. The captain slapped the cross into his palm a final time and then broke it into several pieces. He dropped these on the ground and walked off.

The guards came into the cage with their swords and whips and drove the prisoners out into the yard. They herded the prisoners into a line and then moved them towards the tunnel that led into the Coliseum. In the bright sun it didn't look so terrible, but Alexandra had tears in her eyes as they moved out of the light and into the cool, damp darkness of the tunnel. It smelled like sweat and urine. She walked between Junia and John, who was praying softly and continuously. Junia touched her on the elbow.

"Alexandra, do you think there is time for me to be accepted into your faith? How much time does the ritual take?"

"All it takes is belief, belief in the Lord and belief in the sacrifice of Jesus that I have been telling you about."

"All around me are people going to their death and yet they are not screaming or running. They are praying, and even this death is no match for their faith. I want to have that strength, if I can...if there's time."

"You do?"

"I've been thinking about it, and it's like I've begun to feel something wonderful surrounding me when I do. Today when that man broke that cross, I felt so sad. I think that it took me this time to understand what I was feeling and what I was sad about. I thought about everything you have told me about Jesus, and I realized the emotion I felt was pity. I wanted that man who had just sent me to my death to understand that there was more in the world than hatred. I wanted him to know there was love also, the way you have told me that Jesus taught. I knew as soon as that man started marching us that everything you have been telling me has opened my eyes to this and that I want to be a Christian. But I don't know if there is time. Wouldn't I have to be baptized?"

Alexandra looked at the taller woman in the faint light of the tunnel. Junia's expression was eager and unafraid.

"In our church," said Alexandra, "we believe that baptism by water is not the only way. You can be baptized by your desire for it. Your love of Christ will baptize you into the Spirit of the Lord."

She said John's name and plucked at his tunic. He turned towards them. He was trembling uncontrollably. "Bear witness with me?" she asked him.

He nodded and she could see that in the darkness his eyes were opened very wide.

"Do you believe that Jesus Christ, begotten Son of the Father, died on the cross for your sins?" she asked Junia.

"I do."

"Do you take Him as your Savior and open yourself to Him and His commands, turning your soul over to His glory?"

"I do."

Alexandra took John's hand in hers, squeezing it to quell the violent trembling, and with her other hand she touched Junia's forehead. "Then with all of the joy that has been granted us by the Lord in our short lives, we welcome you to your life as a Christian. You are reborn."

She could see the tears flowing down Junia's strong, beautiful face. They stood for a long time, all holding hands, in the close darkness. Alexandra felt her strength returning. This is who she was, she thought, down to her very core— she was a priest for Jesus Christ, shouting to the world the mystery and joy of His sacrifice.

"Thank you," said Junia. "Now I'm ready for whatever death awaits us."

"Don't talk like that," said Alexandra. "We're strong, the three of us, and if we fight well, we have a chance to survive."

"What?"

"Ask John. If we are still alive at the end of the day, there is a chance our lives will be spared by the crowd. Our faith is gentle, but it doesn't demand that we submit easily. Now it's time to fight."

Even in the darkness she could see the glimmer in Junia's eyes. "Then I will fight like no one they have ever seen before."

The doors at the far end of the tunnel were thrown open and bright yellow light flooded down the tunnel. The guards behind them began beating them to force them to move into the Coliseum. Junia started forward, but John did not. He was crying now.

"Alexandra," he said. "I can not...I can not die. I've seen what happens. I just can't do this. It's impossible!"

The prisoners were pushing blindly past them now, yelling and weeping. There were curses from the guards behind them and someone began to scream.

"Be strong in the Lord," Alexandra cried. "He is with you. He will make us strong enough to survive."

"I can't," he said.

He turned towards the guards. There was a terrible smell in the tunnel, and the guards were approaching not with swords or whips but with lit torches dripping globs of burning pitch.

"Please," John yelled to them, "you can not kill me. I don't believe. I am no Christian! I will do anything you ask of me!"

Alexandra knew they would not stop, so she called to Junia to help her. They grasped John's arms and began to drag him down the tunnel. They burst out onto the yellow sand, and the guards slammed the wooden gate behind them. The sun was momentarily blinding; the noise of screaming people engulfed them. The floor of the Coliseum was a vast expanse of sand filled with a jumble of boulders and wooden platforms. Bodies in all states of decay were spread here and there, the carcasses of gladiators mixed in with those of prisoners. At the top of the walls, Romans sat comfortably in wooden stalls, shaded by brightly colored cloth, eating and drinking wine. Beyond them rose level after level of benches filled with a sea of drunken revelers throwing their food scraps down on the people in the sand. The largest and most opulent box was occupied by the emperor and his drunken retinue. A messenger there stood and blew a trumpet, and the crowd quieted. He shouted something that Alexandra didn't hear. She and Junia were still holding John, who had fallen to his knees and was sobbing loudly.

"John," said Alexandra, "the Lord is with you, stronger than ever." She knelt in front of him. "We can survive this. We have to fight!"

"What do you know, woman? Oh God, I've lost everything! I denounced Christ! God won't want me now!" John was weeping uncontrollably, and his body shook with his convulsive sobs. He seemed mad, like a man possessed. He started scratching his face with his fingernails and curled into a fetal position.

Junia had run to the body of a gladiator and tugged free his dagger and shield.

"Take one of these, Alexandra," she said. "It's time to fight."

"We have to help John!"

"I would leave him behind if I were you," said another voice. Alexandra looked up. A short, very stocky man stood above them, holding a pair of broken spears in one hand. "I will join with you two women if you want to fight together, but I would hurry. They're getting ready to open the gates."

"We can't leave him." Alexandra grabbed John's wrists and looked straight into his eyes. Her voice was steady and strong. "You haven't lost anything. God forgives all things. I have heard your confession and God has heard your confession. You are forgiven. Now get up and fight."

"On your feet, man, or you will be left behind," said the

stocky man. "There's no time for this!"

He reached down and began to shake John violently by the shoulders, but Alexandra stayed his hand. She took John's head gently in her hands and said a brief prayer for him.

He stopped wailing and looked at her. She saw a calmness come into his eyes. "Yes," he said, "I can do it."

The crowd roared again, and people around her began to scream. Alexandra knew something terrible had been thrust into the Coliseum with them but did not take her gaze from John's.

"Have faith, my brother," she said.

He nodded, his eyes wide, and scrambled to his feet.

"Alexandra," said Junia tightly, "we need to move."

"What is it?" she asked.

Junia pointed across the Coliseum where an enormous dust cloud obscured half the arena. Alexandra could see bodies running and falling, people looking behind themselves and screaming. Her mind could not make sense of what she was seeing: enormous creatures, the color of the sand. She had never seen anything like it before. Several large lions had been let into the Coliseum. The animals loped among the frantically fleeing people and then pounced, almost immediately beginning to eat. The crowd roared deliriously as each made its kill.

"This way!" yelled the stocky man. "There is strength in numbers."

He led the way to a place where two large boulders stood next to each other, where they would make their stand. They had among them only the dagger, the shield, and the two broken spears.

"What's your name?" Alexandra asked the stocky man.

"Marcellus," he said.

They each said their names, readying to fight. Even John

was steady on his feet now and had begun to collect stones to throw from behind the shield.

More lions were introduced into the arena one by one over the course of the afternoon, each accompanied by a roar from the crowd. They were starving beasts that immediately began to tear at each other and then to hunt, chasing down the prisoners and swatting aside any attempts at defense. Two mangy bears were let in, and the crowd roared as if it were a great joke when they fought over a wounded man and ended up tearing him to pieces. A bull came in, wounded and bleeding from wounds the guards had given it. Enraged, it tried to gore and kill anything that moved. For a long time Alexandra and the others, hiding in their rocky crevice, remained unnoticed in the fray, but finally they were discovered by several of the lions. The animals began to pace back and forth, looking for their chance to leap forward.

"I've never liked Christians," said Marcellus tightly, "but if we get through this, I'll give you the chance to convince me."

"You're not a believer?" Alexandra asked.

"I'm a Roman and a thief," he said, and at that moment the first lion sprang towards them. They went forward to meet it, flailing at it with their makeshift weapons and yelling at the top of their lungs. The other lions came forward also, and for a moment Alexandra thought they would all be torn apart. But their resistance scared off the animals, and they shied away, off to find easier prey. The group retreated again to the lee of the boulders. They were alive, but each of them had deep tears in their flesh and large bruises.

"We can not survive long," gasped Junia.

"Anything is possible!" said John. "Look at me. I didn't expect to survive even an hour and I feel as strong as a lion myself now."

"Don't get ahead of yourself, friend," said Marcellus. "We still have a long time to go."

The crowd and the music became more frenzied throughout the afternoon as the ravenous animals continued to attack the prisoners. The crowd called for more, and eventually a second batch of prisoners was thrust out onto the arena floor. The royalty in the ornate viewing box added their mockery and derision to the spectacle by sipping wine and chatting among themselves, seemingly oblivious to the carnage in front of them.

Marcellus pointed them out and cursed them.

"Not me," said Junia. "I pity them. It is forgiveness they need."

Alexandra smiled grimly. "You're a wise woman," she said.

"You've shown me how," Junia responded.

Again and again throughout the afternoon, they fended off attacks from the animals, always staying close to each other and defending their space between the two boulders. They received many wounds, and eventually John was so weak that he could not fight. The other three stepped in front to protect him.

Finally, a trumpet blew and heavily armed gladiators rushed into the arena, prodding the animals back into the tunnels with spears and torches. The dead carcasses of animals and humans were dragged to the center of the arena, stacked up like cords of wood, and set on fire. The crowd roared as the flames erupted into the evening sky. The sickening stench of burning flesh covered everything. The gladiators walked the arena, looking for the wounded, who were thrown alive onto the blaze. Eventually, one of them spotted John, lying near death behind Alexandra and the others. The gladiator yelled to his companions, and they drove forward behind a wall of shields, impervious to the frantic blows of Marcellus and Alexandra and Junia, until one of them was close enough to John to grab him by the foot and drag him away across the sand. He struggled and screamed as he was thrown into the flames.

"Have strength, John!" Alexandra shouted, crying and still throwing herself against the shields. "The Lord is with you."

She could hear Marcellus cursing and Junia sobbing next to her.

When the wounded were cleared away, the few remaining survivors were then urged by the crowd to come out of hiding. Alexandra and Marcellus and Junia walked from behind their boulders towards the center of the arena. Another dozen survivors joined them. They stood before the bloodthirsty crowd and wondered what would come next. The heat from the bonfire beat on them heavily; its stench was overpowering. A few in the crowd stood to wave white handkerchiefs shouting, "Free them! They fought bravely! Free them!" But the large majority of the drunken spectators rained their last pieces of food down on the spectators and howled "Crucify them!"

Alexandra looked at the others. "I will not be crucified."

"Nor will I," said Junia.

"Nor will I," said Marcellus. He looked at Alexandra. "I'm sorry I have had no time to acquaint myself with your God," he said. Before she could reply, he turned and rushed towards the viewing box where the emperor sat, leaping in the air and catching the edge of the wall, trying to pull himself upwards. "You have destroyed all that is good with Rome!" he yelled. But before he could get any farther, a gladiator pierced him casually with a spear and slammed him back to the earth. He shook violently, his hands clenched around the shaft of the weapon, and then went still.

The other gladiators ringed the two women and began to

advance.

"Alexandra," said Junia, turning towards her. "Thank you. I have lost my life but gained my soul. I'm not afraid."

"Nor am I," said Alexandra.

Together they rushed towards the gladiators. One of the men hit Alexandra on the head with a mace and she fell to the ground, nearly losing consciousness. She saw Junia struggling with another man, who pivoted suddenly and thrust his sword deep into her abdomen. Sighing with a quiet, tremendous agony, she collapsed around the blade.

Alexandra felt one of the gladiators grasp her by the hair and drag her across the sand towards a cross they were constructing. They stripped her naked, nailed her wrists to the cross, and drove large spikes through both ankles. As they lifted the cross upright, the crowd cheered wildly. The men kindled a fire beneath her and she felt the first touch of heat on her shattered feet. The pain was unbearable and her final thoughts were of James and her daughters, Sarah and Ruth, far away. She hoped desperately that they could live in peace.

Chapter 10

S amuel sat for a long time looking down at the scroll resting on the table before him. The wax of the candle Maria had left for him was burning down, and he watched as its light played along the underside of the papyrus.

He had never read anything like this story before. Of course he had read of martyrs in the Bible, and of the lengths to which those like Abraham and Jesus were willing to go to perform God's will. But never before had he read such an unsettling story, of a life ended so brutally in the name of an earthly power—and the life of a woman no less.

In reading about Christian martyrs, there had always been a beauty to their death, a salvation and a learning that came with their passing. Samuel could not find this in Alexandra's story. Her death came so abruptly, and at the height of her faith. No one came to her aid—no angel from Heaven or prophet in the street. There was no reassuring conclusion that affirmed she had been taken to Heaven to be with her Lord.

Where was He when she was brutalized and murdered by the Roman guards? How many more had suffered her fate, and how many of their stories remained untold?

Samuel felt the tightness growing in his throat, and moved to replace the scroll on the shelf. As he did so, he noticed a tattered piece of papyrus left behind on the table, and he realized it must have fallen out as he had been reading. He lifted it up to get a better look in the dying light of the candle.

This scroll contains all that I could uncover about my wife's disappearance and death. After scouring the city for many days, I came to hear of her sermon from the stairs. I spoke with as many of the townspeople as I could find who had gathered to hear her preach, and from the bits and pieces I gathered, I've come to understand that she had been taken by Roman soldiers on that night.

The soldiers did not kill her, but those who saw her the next day say they wished she had given in to death. She was savagely beaten and tortured, and following her battle in the Coliseum, they dragged her like a common thief to the cross, where they nailed her naked body to a crucifix. Those who were present tell me that she was declared guilty of treason and that she was burned alive as an example to all who would follow in her footsteps.

As I write these words, I know that my life has left me. I feel nothing but anger and hatred from the beginning of my being to its end. I do not know where my Lord has gone, and why He left her to suffer. She spoke only of love, and was met with the vilest offerings of this dark world.

I can not return to lead our church, and I fear the fate that lies before me. All I can do is ask that you carry on her message of love, and *make sure it remains always in the hearts of those who dwell within our church, as long as its stone walls stand tall and strong above the ground. My soul is lost, but so many remain to be saved. Let them not wander astray.*

Those who were present say she professed her love for God, even as the flames were struck beneath her. They say she cried out only of her love for him, and her family. Let her faith be a vessel of light for you, and a pillar of strength and truth for those you will care for. Keep her story safe.

As for my daughters—you will agree they are too young to understand. In time, I trust I can teach them what they need to know of their mother's death.

As Samuel's eyes fell upon these last words, the candle beside him burned out, leaving only a wisp of white smoke in the darkness.

Chapter 11

᷎

S amuel could not sleep that night. He kept pouring over the story in his mind, and he could not shake the words James had written in his heartbreak. *Who was he was writing to?* Samuel wondered. *Are they trying to deceive me?*

In the morning, he woke feeling dispirited and confused. He ate a cold breakfast in the large kitchen that was attached to the back of one of the buildings, and took his writing materials to the bluff that overlooked the sea.

It was a quiet morning, the sun hidden behind a shell of clouds. The ground was smooth beneath his feet, with pebbles visible between low dried clumps of grass. He settled himself on the ground out of sight from the church and thought for a long time. As he looked out on the rolling waves of the ocean, creeping up the beach towards the dark cliffs, he began to write a letter to Flavius. He dipped his pen in ink and moved his hand slowly, choosing his words carefully. It was late morning when he finished, and he knew that the service would be starting at the church. Anna was going to be delivering the sermon, and he was not ready to stand before her again as she so blatantly disregarded the teachings she claimed to uphold. He imagined her stepping into place behind the altar and beginning to speak, delivering communion to the unquestioning members of her congregation.

He thought of the story he had read, and of the debate that had raged in his head over the course of the previous evening. Its raw emotion had indeed reached out and touched him, but he knew that his feelings could not be allowed to blur his stance on matters of doctrine. Through the mortification and subjugation of her sinful flesh, Alexandra could attain holiness, and she deserved praise for overcoming her feminine weakness at the time of her death. But she also should have known her place. God did not abandon her as James claimed He did. Though she acted out of love, it was she who had abandoned the Word and law of God.

He thought of what theologians had written, "It is not permitted for a woman to speak in the church, nor is it permitted for her to teach, nor to baptize, nor to offer, nor to claim for herself a share in any masculine function—not to mention any priestly office." He was not shocked that Alexandra had baptized Junia, for he knew that women had been doing that from the earliest Christian times. What upset him was the implication that this was normal, that it was a natural and right thing to do.

He quoted Augustine to himself, and he ran through the arguments about the inferiority of women that Aristotle and Socrates had put forth. These were the wisest men in history, both Christian and non-Christian. This was the wisdom of generations in the Church hierarchy. These were inspired men who knew the world. How had James and Alexandra failed to see the basic hypocrisy of their relationship and their actions? How many more might have been saved if Alexandra had stayed home, and if James never had to cope with her death?

As a youth in the schools of the Roman episcopate, Samuel struggled with the inclination to question everything. It was only through discipline and rigorous study that he had been able to commit to believing, and from that point, his faith had been unerring. He had learned over time to keep himself from speaking his questions aloud, but he could never fully silence that questioning part of himself. It was this part of him that jabbed at him now.

What were the arguments of all the wise men in the world when put up against the singular truth of God? How could the ideas of Aristotle matter in light of the example set by Jesus? Aristotle posed that women were naturally inferior and flawed, but Jesus welcomed them into his ministry as equals. Why should the theories of philosophers hold more weight than the actions of Jesus? If women are so weak, why did the angel first announce the resurrection—the heart of Christianity itself—to Mary of Magdala? Why, for that matter, was it Alexandra whose example was to live on in the Church of Saints Priscilla and Aquila?

Samuel knew that since the time of Clement, it had been agreed upon that the structure of the Church was the doorway to God. The Lord had delegated His authority on earth to the bishops, and they delegated to priests and then down to deacons. The decisions of bishops were not just the decisions of wise men; they were the decisions of those who had direct access to the Lord, and the dangers of straying from the divinely ordered structure of the Church were grave. If individual church communities were to decide who could be a priest, then who knows what misunderstandings could creep into people's souls? The laity could not be trusted to make these decisions.

There was one God, and there was one Bishop of Rome —the Pope—to explain God's will to the people. In stepping outside of what Rome thought, a person was stepping away from the one God. *This is the problem with the priesthood of Alexandra and Anna.* The Pope knew best. He knew that it was against women's nature to be priests, to administer the sacraments of baptism and the Holy Eucharist. Samuel had to try to make Anna, Maria, and Joshua see that. It bothered him that they seemed to live with such joy here, ignorant of the path they were on. In Rome, Samuel always felt a quiet dread in his gut. Try as he might to resist the feeling, here beside the ocean, smelling its salt as he walked among the gardens and through the endless fields, he was overwhelmed by the peace of this place. He smiled to himself and thought, *On earth, so it shall be in Heaven.*

Doesn't Jesus know better than Gelasius? he asked himself. At that moment, it was as if another voice inside of him had spoken. It had been years since he had allowed himself to hear such questions. This had all seemed so clear in Rome, inside the thick, quiet walls of the library. Somehow the bright light of day and the peace of the countryside only brought him confusion and trouble.

Samuel again imagined Anna, standing and preaching, and he wondered what she would say in her sermon. *Stop thinking of such things!* It was as if even the thought dishonored Gelasius and Flavius. Anger and frustration surged through him, while outside, the waves continued lapping peacefully along the shore. He put aside his writing materials and knelt on a patch of soft turf, closing his eyes to pray. His mind tired as he chastised himself, and asked for strength and forgiveness. He prayed until there were no more words to send forth. In this emptiness of self, a calmness had settled over him, and he knew that he would be guided in his actions by the Lord. He looked dispassionately out at the grey sea and gathered his materials to walk back to the church.

.   .   .

Back in the kitchen, he folded his letter carefully and lit a candle, dripping wax onto the paper and imprinting it with the signet ring he had been given. He walked out of the kitchen, passing the large roofless building where the service was still in progress. The murmur of voices passed through the high windows and the demolished roof. *Let them pray as they will for the moment*, he thought. *The Lord will express His will through me soon enough.*

.   .   .

Samuel set off from the church once again, this time heading the opposite direction, down the rocky road cut into the side of the bluff that led down to the lower part of the city and the sea. As he arrived at the wharves, he asked the seafarers lounging by the docks for a ship that was headed north. The gritty sailors eyed him and his robes with amusement, and pointed to several boats that were moored further down the beach. The only one that appeared to have anyone aboard was a slender ship, composed of dark, foreign-looking wood. There were strange carved symbols all along its sides, and a pink bird stalked angrily around the deck on long legs that looked like stilts. Its wings were clipped, and it sent up a great commotion when Samuel arrived at the top of the gangplank. At its call, a man came grumbling forward from the hold, aiming a vicious kick at the bird, which squawked and danced out of the way.

"Demon bird! Don't you know I be restin'?"

His skin was darker than any man Samuel had seen, and he had a row of small scars cut into each of his cheekbones. As the man turned to eye his intruder, Samuel noticed he was missing two fingers on his right hand and the lower half of his right ear. The hair atop his head was sparse and white.

"And what do you want? Here to pick a fight I hope?" he asked with a sinister glee. His teeth, or those that were left, glowed yellow in the sunlight.

Samuel almost turned and walked down the gangplank, but knew that time was of the essence, and that this man

85

might be his only chance to deliver his letter north. He would see where this game led.

"I'm looking for someone to deliver a message to Rome," he said, ignoring the putrid stench of the man's breath.

"Aye? And what makes you t'ink we'd want anything to do with dat?" the man asked.

"The men on the docks. They said you were heading north."

The man's eyes narrowed, and his three fingers fell to his side, where Samuel saw a rusted cutlass. "What did dey tell you?"

"Nothing," said Samuel, looking him straight in the eye. "Only that you were sailing north."

"Who are you?"

"My name is Samuel. I need a message delivered, and its reply returned to me. Money is of no consequence to me in the matter."

"You don' say? It's not nothing to you...," the man looked slyly in one direction and then the other. "It's nothing...untowards, is it?"

"Of course not," Samuel blushed. "You need not concern yourself with the message—it is simply..."

The man burst out laughing. "A joke, boy. Dese days it seems dare's not much untowards a man can do. Not since the demise of the empire, at least." Samuel forced a smile as the man went on. "What kind of money are you offerin'?"

Samuel hesitated. There was no telling what this man might do with his message, and this game was not going well. "What's your business to the north?" he asked.

"You heard right, boy. We're on our way to Rome," the man said, seeing his confusion and talking in a placating way. "My brother owns this boat and I bin usin' it to carry my old bones and these barrels across de sea. Dere's a dangerous drink popular in Egypt, made of honey. Were I to tell you its secrets, bot' you and me would mos' certainly be dead." The same wild glee appeared in his eyes as he spoke. "It is difficult to make and expensive—a well-kept secret, but dere is a rich man in Rome who reaches for it like a babe for 'is mother's milk," he said chuckling. "Whenever I can get my hands on some, I know he will buy it for a, shall we say, righteous sum."

The man's eyes twinkled as he said this, and Samuel felt his shoulders and face relax.

"And this man's name is Gelasius?" Samuel asked.

The man was suddenly serious, making a gesture with his hand that Samuel did not recognize.

"How do you know dat?"

Now Samuel found himself cracking a smile. "I am here on official business on behalf of His Holiness. I've seen him drink it many times."

The man sighed in relief. "I t'ought for a moment only a demon could know such t'ings. But I see Isis favors me on dis day."

"No demon. Simply a humble servant trying to deliver a message."

"Aye? And your church doesn't have...a more righteous means of communication den?"

Samuel shifted uncomfortably. "You ask many questions for a man being offered money."

"Indeed boy—and for dis reason, I still stand before you." The man smiled and rubbed his hands together. "How much will dey be willing to pay for such secrecy in Rome?"

"I will give you this now, and a note instructing them to pay you the rest," Samuel said, holding a small sack out to the man. "And, as I say, there will likely be a return message for you to bring back."

The man opened the sack, and the light of the sun hitting its contents reflected along his leathery face. "If such money awaits me, I'll deliver it to your door."

"That won't be necessary. I will return to the docks to seek you, and you may summon me if needed from the church on the hill there."

They both looked up. The fragmented buildings stood out starkly against the cloudy sky. The man shivered. "Christians...you make an honest man like me uneasy."

"Have you never visited one of our churches?"

"Not in your life, boy."

Samuel smiled once more. "Perhaps when you return, then, I will show you there is nothing to fear from the one true God in Heaven."

"Who said anything about fear?" the old man grinned.

Samuel couldn't fathom how this man lived, but knew that he would do what he was told. "Very well—it is important that you know this letter is intended for the Pope, but when you arrive in Rome, I want you to deliver it to a man named Flavius. He also resides at the Pope's palace."

"Flavius?"

"That's right."

"If he will be the one who pays me, den to him it will go."

"He will. I'll make a note out to him now."

"You are mysterious to me, you Christians," said the man. "But as long as dere's money involved, I don' mind you at all."

The old man took the letter in his hand and stuffed it into his tunic. He cleared his throat, spat on the ground, and began to turn away. Samuel shifted uneasily from one foot to the other. As if reading his mind, the old man looked him in the eye. "Go on, boy. Your precious letter will get dere— unless my boat sinks!" He started to laugh as he disappeared into the hold.

The man slammed the door behind him, and Samuel was

left alone. The shrill squawking of the bird once again filled the air.

Chapter 12

⌒

S amuel made his way slowly back up the road towards the church behind two women carrying heavy baskets filled with fish. They carried one basket in each hand so they were balanced as they walked, slowly and patiently, their shoulders bent from many years of performing the same task. As Samuel drew closer, he heard them discussing the morning's sermon. Neither of the women was a Christian apparently, but it was clear they had both been impressed by Anna and by the message of the sermon. They spoke of Anna's conviction and inclusiveness: In difficult times like these, the Christian community offered aid and charity to anyone in need, regardless of their beliefs. Greed was a dark sin, Anna had said, and charity was its counterweight. Only with kindness would the people of this village ride through the storm of evils that assailed them in their daily lives. The women spoke with particular animation about the power of kindness to strangers, to adversaries, and to your enemies. Before they reached the top of the hill and turned off towards their neighborhood, Samuel heard them agree to try to convince a few friends to accompany them the following week.

He continued on towards the church, where he found Maria hanging the clothes she'd laundered, casting a wary eye up at the sky as she did so.

"Worried about rain?" he asked as he approached.

"Not really," she smiled at him. "These clouds don't speak of coming rains, though I would welcome it if they did. What do wet clothes matter against the end of this drought?""

"I'm certain it will come, sooner or later," he said reassuringly.

She cocked an eyebrow at him. "We thought maybe we'd run you off last night after you saw what was in those manuscripts."

"Not at all," he responded. "They were precisely what I was hoping to find."

"Interesting." She spoke with a smile that seemed to be teasing him, as if she knew exactly the depth of his discomfort. She went back to hanging the linens. "I was sad to see you missed the service this morning."

"Next week perhaps."

"Planning to stay for a bit then?"

Samuel held his hands clasped behind his back, and moved to the other side of the clothesline where she could see him. "There seem to be many works of interest in your library, and of course, I still have points of doctrine to discuss with—" he paused, "with the elders of your church."

"I'm glad," she said earnestly and smiled at him again. "It's not often I get to talk to someone with an education such as yours!" She looked down after she had spoken, as if embarrassed by her enthusiasm. There was an awkward silence, and Samuel felt the need to keep talking.

"Tell me," he said abruptly. "There was a document I found—a small note that dropped from the scroll you had given me. It was a note written by James to someone. Do you know...?"

"Of course," she interrupted. "He was one of our most notable priests. He took care of our parish, assisted James in the care of his daughters, and of all those who came to our church in their time of greatest need. He was a very charitable man."

"Oh—I just...well. I wasn't sure what to make of the

connection."

"Umm," she responded, smiling.

Her look brought a lump to his throat. There was another moment of silence, and Samuel looked to change the subject.

"Yes, well—either way, I've been wondering—what is it that bothers Joshua? He seems be both angry and sad, and yet he withdraws when approached about it. Is it the death of his wife that still pains him?"

Maria cast a furtive glance around them. In her anxious movements, Samuel saw that, despite her firm words and quick mind, she was still a girl, so much more so than Anna. She lowered her voice. "Can you keep a secret?" she asked.

He nodded, allured despite the childishness of this game.

She leaned close to him. "I think..." She paused to look around once more. "I think Joshua and Anna have fallen in love," she said. "No one here knows for sure—but I think everyone suspects it. And I don't think anyone finds it inappropriate. It's not something we control in ourselves, and they are both very blessed in the Lord. But it's difficult for Joshua. He loved Lucia very deeply, and Anna was like a daughter to her." She bit her lip, and Samuel nodded that she continue. "I wish he could get over it and just admit that he loves Anna and that the Lord has provided him a second life after taking away his first. This whole ordeal is beginning to weigh on everyone around him."

"Samuel," said a voice, and they both jumped.

It was Anna, approaching from the gardens, behind her Joshua, staring into the distance.

"I'm glad you've decided not to leave us."

"It is my intention to stay as long as is needed," Samuel said firmly.

"Good," she replied, leaving Samuel to wonder again if she had thought at all about the message he had delivered on behalf of Gelasius. "Did you find what you were looking for in the library?"

"I began to, at least, but I think there are many works there that will need my attention. And I need to have a discussion with you."

"That's fine," she replied, "but it will have to wait. We received word this morning that a little village to the west of here has been even more severely affected by the drought than us. Some of the members of the church and I are leaving this afternoon to deliver what food we can gather to them."

"I see," he said with ambivalence.

"I will be gone for a few days."

"Is Joshua going with you?" asked Maria, beaming with innocence.

"No," said Anna bluntly. "He's staying to work on the church. We found another deep crack today that we had missed, and there is a tremendous amount of work to be done if we are to save our church. When this drought breaks, I'm certain we are going to need a solid roof over our heads."

"Maybe I can help him?" suggested Samuel, surprising himself with the offer, but quickly reasoning that it would give him a good chance to talk to the man alone. "There is only so much time I can sit in the library and read."

"That would be lovely, brother," said Anna, smiling. "Go and speak to him now, if you wish, so he has time before tomorrow to decide how to use you."

Samuel glanced at Maria, and she met his eyes quickly with a subtle smile. Samuel felt the corners of his mouth twitch as well, as he set off and left the two women alone.

Joshua was still standing in the garden as he approached, staring out at the sea.

"Anna said there is more work to be done on the church."

"There is," said Joshua. He reached up distractedly to

scratch at his beard.

"I would like to help if I can."

Joshua turned his head towards Samuel, but it was a moment before he shifted to look at him directly. He nodded sharply, as if he had been expecting the offer all along. "Good man," he said, smiling a little as he said it. He kept his eyes on Samuel for a moment and then reached out to grasp both of Samuel's wrists, turning his hands over. He smiled wryly at the softness of Samuel's palms and fingers.

"These will be sore at first," he said, "but all parts of us grow strong in working for the Lord, don't they?"

"It appears there's at least one thing we can agree on," Samuel said with a nervous chuckle.

"You've never done work like this before?"

"No. It feels sometimes that I sit too much and move too little, so I'm eager to learn."

Joshua nodded. "Indeed," he said, letting go of Samuel's hands. "We will work together then, and I will teach you."

"Perhaps, brother, it will be an opportunity to learn from each other."

Joshua stared back at him intensely. His wry smile widened, and Samuel shifted uncomfortably in the silence.

"Perhaps," Joshua said with a wink.

"Now go and get some working clothes from Maria. You'll want to get a good meal in you before we begin. Something tells me you'll need it."

Chapter 13

F lavius sat in his tiny office, rolling a stylus back and
forth between his fingers. Just off the main library,
he retired here often to think when his spartan room
seemed too familiar or when he did not feel like walking the
grounds. Much to the annoyance of the head librarian, he
was also in the habit of bringing his own books and scrolls
here to study them. However, Flavius's position in the
Pope's hierarchy ensured that he had the only key to the
small office and was the only person allowed to enter it.

Flavius closed his eyes, forcing himself to focus. He had
not heard from Samuel yet, but the news from the other
heretical churches was not encouraging. All had been
extremely and even violently resistant to changing their
ways. Was there any reason to hope that the one to which
Samuel had been sent, the most intransigent, was any
different? Was the young man truly prepared for his mission,
or had Flavius sent him only out of sentimentality?

Flavius rubbed his temples. If only he had not grown so
fond of Samuel. He had come to see him almost as a son,
and someone who could accomplish all of the Lord's work
that was set before him. Given the other reports that had
begun to come in, he was growing more and more anxious.

Samuel's greatest asset and his greatest weakness were
one and the same: He believed with all his heart and mind
that his task was about Truth with a capital "T." Flavius
knew that it was not.

The Church could no longer be concerned only with
eternal and spiritual truth. Jesus' message was now the

Catholic Church, and the Catholic Church was now the bedrock of society. Christianity was no longer just the astonishing message that God became human and that Jesus rose from the dead and abolished death for all people. It had grown into schools, basilicas and chapels, shelters for the poor, and palaces for bishops. It established structure, a philosophy, political power, and social support for a crumbling empire. Christianity had become a huge institution that had to be maintained and closely controlled. If the Church fell into the same chaos as the empire, it could mean the end of Western civilization. The Church had a heavy earthly burden now, one that the early Christians could never have guessed at.

God, Flavius mused, had seen to it that when civilization became Christian, Christianity became the guardian of all things civilized. And while the truth of the Holy Spirit was mediated through the Church, it could no longer be the only concern of the men who ran this complex institution. The Church, and men like Gelasius and himself, now had to worry about the state of society as well as the state of the soul.

This was the reality that Samuel failed to grasp. Given that he had spent most of his formative years witnessing the Pope's political activity the purity and single-mindedness of Samuel's faith were astounding. And yet despite the dogmas he clung to so desperately, from years spent buried in books analyzing every passage of the Bible, there was nothing cold and calculating about Samuel. As hard as he might try to appear worldly, Samuel was an innocent.

Flavius knew this odd mix of dogmatism and innocence was the reason he had chosen Samuel to investigate the library of the Church of Saints Priscilla and Aquila, and why he believed he could succeed. When Flavius heard that the church claimed it had "history on its side" to justify its female clergy, he knew he needed to send someone as stubborn and as guileless as Samuel. It was the only way to discover exactly what that history was comprised of. A treasure trove of banned, heretical, and rare documents could be hiding in the tiny library of that rural church by the sea, and he wasn't about to let this history be lost.

Flavius eyed the large book and stack of papers that sat atop his desk, and began flipping through its contents. *There is so much that remains to be told*, he thought to himself. *And so much of it may rest in Samuel's hands.*

These documents represented what Flavius considered to be his life's work—a history of the first five centuries of the Church. While he served as a teacher and a priest, Flavius understood himself as the man who would save history from the clutches of those who feared the ragged and confusing origins of their faith. It would be a history that traced the Church's transition from the private to the public sphere and the change of the role of women during its evolution.

He pulled one of the loose papers out from the stack and looked it over. It was covered with his own notes and droplets from his pen. He traced a few of the underlined passages with his index finger before slowly bringing the tip of his finger to his mouth and breathing deeply. It was hard to believe the amount of time and ink he had invested into this secret book. He looked over the many yellowed documents and small scrolls that accompanied each page of notes, each of which Flavius had taken immaculate care of. The book that sat beneath these myriad papers and musings was to be his opus—the compendium of his thoughts and observations—sorted and redrafted, chapter after chapter of unaltered history and truth

It was the history of women in the Church. For the most part it was a history that detailed the closing off and shutting down of women's importance and activity in Christianity.

Since female priesthood, once a common and accepted practice among all Christians, had been declared heretical by the Popes, many of the documents that might support a woman's claim to the priesthood had been destroyed. Even those that suggested their importance Flavius had found altered or hidden deep within the Vatican archives. Whatever documents resided in the little parish church by the sea he knew would be integral to the completion of his work.

He was unsure as of yet what he would do with his manuscript when it was finished. It contained copies of essays, letters, Gospels, and meditations that had all been deemed heretical, and detailed ideas and beliefs that people held close in their hearts and in their souls—a history of passion and of pain.

He was certain that no Pope would ever consent to have it published, but he could not bring himself to believe that simply destroying the evidence of an idea was equal to defeating it. His hope in compiling this history was not to validate it, but to confront it, and to deal with it as a reasonable theologian. It was only in fully understanding these heretical beliefs that they could ever be fully overcome. An idea erased from the Church's history could just as easily be sowed by the devil again in a time when all arguments against it were forgotten. To record these heretical notions, and the arguments against them, was to ensure the future stability of the Church.

Flavius knew that the Church had been built to resist such affronts to its dogmas. Thus, there was another reason he had chosen Samuel to make the journey to the south. He was the only person within the Church hierarchy whom Flavius could trust to report directly to him rather than to Gelasius.

Gelasius had in mind that Samuel was to investigate the depths of the rogue church's beliefs and to convince its members of the correctness of Church doctrine by delivering his epistle. If their congregation and their priests refused to relent, Samuel was tasked with destroying whatever documents supported their position.

If the documents were destroyed, that record of history would be gone from the world forever. Gelasius was not interested in an accurate history of events and ideas; he was solely interested in maintaining control and power of the papacy. He viewed these rare documents not as a treasure, but a threat to be eradicated for the sake of orthodoxy.

Flavius knew that political maneuvering meant nothing to Samuel. He also knew that he could manipulate Samuel's innocence and naïve righteousness. What he didn't know was what he was prepared to do—or prepared to ask Samuel to do—on his behalf. Part of him hoped that the Church of Saints Priscilla and Aquila would comply and that the Pope would simply let Samuel confiscate their documents and return them to Rome.

Flavius looked at the wall above his desk. He felt compassion for the people of that parish and for the women who served as priests, and had no doubt they were good people—loving, passionate people. A passionately faithful woman he had known once felt called to be a priest by God —and who was he to question her faith? He felt a weight on his chest at the thought of her.

Flavius shook his head, taking the heavy key that hung around his neck and unlocking the box beside his desk. He lifted a fresh stack of parchments on which he had been organizing his most recent thoughts. He put his hands on it, feeling the solid weight of the leather beneath his fingers. *The Church, and the lives of Christians, had changed so much in just five hundred years,* he mused. It had begun with Jesus, an itinerant Jewish carpenter, preaching the good news of love and salvation. Following his death, a motley group of men and women followed in his footsteps, preaching to Jews that the Messiah had come, died, and been raised from the dead. At first they thought their message was only for other Jews, and remained in those first few years after Jesus' resurrection a sect of Judaism. But the apostle Paul, himself a Roman Jew, understood that Christianity was not just for one group of people. Jesus' message of radical equality and pure love was for all.

Paul preached that in Christ there was neither male nor female, Gentile nor Jew. Women were powerful allies in his work, and he mentioned many of these women by name in his letters. Since services and gatherings were held not in church buildings but in people's homes, the traditional domain of women, it made sense that many of the earliest leaders in this new religion were women. As Paul spread the Gospel of freedom all over the Roman Empire, Christianity was born. It was no longer Jewish in nature; it became Hellenized and Romanized.

And that is where my history begins, he thought. As Christianity spread throughout the Roman Empire, it was viewed as a threat to Rome, an illegal practice oftentimes observed in secret. There was no one single authority that determined what was right and what was wrong. In the shift from Judaism to Christianity—in which women were powerful leaders and prophets—misunderstandings and differences between house-churches were rife. These differences were regular topics of Paul's letters, in his attempt to bring uniformity to the religion. This shift from being a small Jewish sect to an all-pervasive religion was the first chapter of Flavius's history.

The next chapter dealt with the creation of a single canon of orthodox books that became the Christian scriptures. In the early days of the Church, it seemed that every parish wrote its own version of the life and death of Jesus. Flavius already had numerous disparate Gospels in his collection and had read about or heard of a dozen more, to say nothing of all the other writings that had circulated since the death of Christ. The diversity of these parishes, both culturally and ethnically, with different practices and rituals, was reflected in the writings that Flavius had uncovered. Some of the writings stressed Jesus' openness and acceptance of women and highlighted the crucial role they played in His ministry and in the first two centuries of the house-churches. Other writings relegated women to the private realm, based on society's beliefs about gender and the writings of still other authors. The latter was accepted by many of the bishops as they consolidated their authority over their regions during the second and third centuries. Still, even the four Gospels that were accepted by the Church, those of Matthew, Mark, Luke, and John, could not hide the fact that it was Mary of Magdala who was Jesus' most loyal and trusted disciple. After all, it was she who remained with Him as He died on the cross. It was she to whom the resurrection was first divulged. It was she who first preached the good news. And it was she who was the "apostle to the apostles."

The face of a young woman framed with luminous black hair invaded Flavius's mind along with the words she so long ago had spoken to him.

"Peter might be the rock the Church is built on, but Mary is the water that allowed it to flourish," she had said with gaiety in her voice.

Flavius let his mind's eye linger on her face. As much as he tried to convince himself otherwise, he knew he was compiling this history because of her. He wondered what she would think when she read it.

Flavius flipped to the next section of his work. This was the chapter that changed the course for Christian women—the era when a collection of persecuted and disparate churches were transformed to the powerful church of the

Roman emperor.

After half a decade of vicious battling and vying for power, Constantine became sole emperor in 312 with his defeat of Maxentius. When he did, he proclaimed that it was the Christian God who had helped him in his conquest. At this point, the melding of the empire and Christianity was inevitable, signifying a fundamental change in the nature of the Church. It had gone from simply being one religion among many to becoming the most powerful spiritual and political force in the world. Thus, being a member of the clergy soon meant holding a measure of worldly, as well as religious, power, binding the Church inextricably to earthly matters.

The impact on women could not be underestimated. Women had run the earliest churches out of their homes in the days of Paul, and women had been among the bravest and strongest of martyrs during the three great persecutions. Back then the churches were on the margins of society, and Christian women had a power and influence unlike their pagan sisters. The Christians saw themselves as radically different from Roman society and challenged it in every way, including how it viewed women. But once Christianity became the religion of the empire, Christian women were expected to act like all other Roman women—they were expected to keep quiet. The Church was no longer a challenge to the status quo, but an institution that demanded the subjugation of women.

While Flavius understood the tragedy of this history, he also believed firmly that the Church, and its views on women, had evolved as God had seen fit—for while individual women might long for the equality of the early days, it was not God's plan. Women, by their inferior nature, were vulnerable and required the protection of their fathers or husbands.

Flavius came to this understanding of women through his study of Saint Augustine, the greatest of Christian theologians. Women, as brave, strong, heroic, or intelligent as they might be, were always inferior to men. Women could never lead a local church because they could never lead a man to virtue, only to vice. Like Eve herself, women distracted men from God.

He replaced his notes in the box and drummed his fingers on it. The changes and shifts in Christianity and in its philosophy in the past five hundred years had been enormous. Women may have been involved at the beginning of Christ's Church, but that was because Christianity had to operate outside the boundaries of society. Since it was God's plan that Christianity become the religion of the empire and the guiding force of a civilization, it had to adapt to Roman society and disavow its heritage of equality.

Ahh, but shouldn't Rome change to become more like Christ rather than Christianity change to become more like Rome? he asked. It was, as always, the woman's voice, haunting him as her face flashed once more before his eyes.

The need to constantly remind himself, to justify his thoughts and the Church's stances, had begun to eat away at Flavius. It exhausted him. He wrote his history and his meditations based on the lives and thoughts of those who were declared heretics to assuage his own sense of guilt for the part he played in suppressing their voices. He wrote it to answer that woman who still spoke to him in his memories and in his dreams—the woman who long ago had fled to the South.

Chapter 14

⌒

S amuel had never worked so hard in his life. Given the extent of the new damage they had discovered, the men of the town had decided to work full time along with the clergy on the church, and for four days they had been laboring steadily to repair it. Every day, Samuel awoke before the sun rose and worked with the other men from the first glimmer of light until the noon meal. After that, they set forth again, working tirelessly as the brutal heat of the afternoon cooled towards night. It was an exhausting schedule, but he was determined to show that the strength of his hands matched that of his mind.

The crack they had discovered ran along one of the long walls of the meeting hall, sloping from a high corner that would have to support one of the roof's large wooden beams, diagonally towards the ground. It was a narrow crack, nearly imperceptible at places, sometimes cutting through the mortar, other times through the stones themselves. To Samuel's untrained eyes, it seemed almost insignificant, but he knew it could not be ignored. Joshua explained that if they simply built on top of the wall, it could slowly shift over time, and would eventually bring down any new roof they planned to build. *Like a bad habit or a small sin,* Samuel thought—*capable of dooming the entirety of the soul if not caught early on and addressed.*

They spent the first several days breaking free the stones that sat above the crack before addressing those that had been split or damaged then chipped away the old mortar and lowered the big stones to men on the ground below them with a series of ropes that ran up through the wooden scaffolding. They carefully piled the stones that were not cracked off to the side, ready to be used again when they started rebuilding. The cracked stones, although damaged, were not discarded. Three men set to work on them with hammers and chisels, shaping them into smaller triangular shapes that they could use where the front and back walls would be angled up to support the central rafter. The cracked stones, as Joshua explained, were to become the most important in the whole edifice.

As Samuel watched the three workmen, he couldn't help but think of the Holy Trinity. The stones, like sinners, were cracked and damaged, but through the work of the three, they realized their purpose, their impurities cut away. The men were relentless, and they smiled and laughed as they worked, wiping the sweat from their brows and drying their glistening hands on their rough tunics. Samuel looked down at his own hands, coated in dust and grime. As his hands grew calloused with work, and as he became accustomed to the feeling of sweat, dirt, and soreness, he realized that the connections between his body, spirit, and mind were growing stronger. Meaning wasn't something to be found solely in books, but it filled the world and the work of the men around him. He felt as if he were becoming a physical expression of God's heavenly will.

Samuel worked at the top of the scaffolding with Joshua. It was brutally tiring work, scraping away the mortar with a chisel, using a heavy hammer wrapped with several layers of canvas to knock the big rectangular stones loose, then wrestling them by sheer force of muscle into the sling attached to the system of ropes. He wore a white tunic and a white piece of cloth tied around his head to keep the sun off, and he was very quickly covered in the fine white dust that drifted around the work site, raised by the breaking of the rocks and mortar. His hands were scraped and bruised by the stones, and his muscles were exhausted long before the time they quit working for the noon meal.

Across from him, working steadily and patiently, was Joshua. The large man was quiet, only speaking to explain what they were doing and to give instructions. Despite his attempts to convince himself otherwise, Samuel felt as if he was being judged, as if the man's silence and steady working pace were meant as tests of faith and strength.

Each morning, he willed himself to rise at the first light of dawn, hoping to arrive at breakfast before Joshua did. He poured water from the calabash in his room to wash his face in the chilly grey light, his shoulders and arms aching, and his mind slowly waking to embrace the reality of the day ahead. He dressed quickly and stumbled across the small open space to the hall where they ate, glancing first towards the sea, lying dark and placid at this hour, and then at the doorway ahead of him where he could hear the sounds of Maria cooking. The thought of seeing her always brought a smile to his face.

When he reached the threshold of the dining hall though, his thoughts again returned to Joshua. Each morning he hoped would be the morning he arrived before the large man. And yet each morning when Samuel entered, Joshua was seated at one of the long tables, with a steaming mug in front of him, gazing out the window at the sea. Samuel cursed himself, and became frustrated with his own strange desire to best this man. Why not just get the rest he needed? He did not understand why this effort was so important to him.

As the days wore on, he realized that this competitive drive wasn't limited to who rose first in the morning. In everything he did, he found himself competing with the older man. He felt an irresistible need to prove that he could work harder and longer, rise earlier, and be more devout than

Joshua. As he grew more aware of these feelings, he began to feel ashamed at the pettiness. This shame only fed his frustration, forcing him to work harder and longer each day, until he soon felt on the brink of snapping.

On the seventh day, Samuel climbed onto the scaffolding after the older man, already weary before the day began. They were working on the lower half of the building, having progressed almost to the bottom of the crack. After an hour of hauling and chiseling, Samuel's hands slipped as he was handling one of the large stones, and it fell, splintering a board at their feet and hitting the dirt heavily below them.

"Are you all right?" Joshua asked calmly.

"I'm fine," said Samuel. "It's the dust—it makes my hands slippery."

"You're tired."

Samuel could feel the hair on the back of his neck bristle. "And you aren't?" he snapped. "I feel fine. It was bound to happen sooner or later."

Samuel knew he was lying through his teeth. His arms felt like frail filaments, moved more by memory than by will, and his hands felt bruised and swollen, as if they were harboring the blood from the rest of his parched, weary body.

"We'll take a break for a moment."

"There's really no need, unless it's a break you want to take," said Samuel. Even as he spoke them, the words felt needlessly combative.

"Safety is always the first need," said Joshua. He called down to one of the men and asked him to send a skin of water up on one of the ropes. When the water arrived, he took it and climbed up in the scaffolding until he was at its highest point. Samuel followed him. There was a flat spot at the top of the wall where they sat and looked down at the open roofless room below them with its simple altar, and beyond at the town and the brown hills rising up from the sea.

"You work hard," said Joshua, offering him the water. "Have you always been like this?"

Samuel drank, unsure if this was another test. "I've never worked like this with my hands, if that's what you're asking," he said after a moment. "But in my studies, always. It was impressed on me very early on that there was no other way to succeed in becoming the man that the Lord wanted me to be."

Joshua nodded. "And what do you think it is about this project that has inspired you to pick up a hammer and a chisel?"

"We're building a house of the Lord, aren't we?"

"That we are." Joshua smiled, and Samuel handed him the water again. "But I had it in mind that you were here to deliver the Pope's message and to investigate our library, not to engage in simple labor on our behalf."

Joshua looked at him steadily as he spoke, and it felt as if the man had seen into Samuel's mind all along—had known that he had been trying to beat him to the breakfast meal, and that he had been trying to outwork and outperform him in every way possible.

"It is important to me that I represent the Pope well in every endeavor."

"Even when he has not tasked you with building a church for heretics?"

"Yes. Even then."

Joshua looked away, out over the town and the hills. "Tell me," he said, "do we seem happy to you, Samuel?"

Samuel was unsure of where he was going with this, but Joshua did not return his gaze. "Excuse me?"

"Have you felt that this life out here in the countryside is a happy and pious one?"

"Well, I suppose...but..."

"Does it bother you then that although we allow women into our clergy, we are still joyful and productive, and preach the ways of our Lord Jesus Christ?" Joshua turned to look at him once more. "Is this why you are so eager to keep up with this labor?"

"No," said Samuel, "Of course not." He looked down at his feet, dangling off the scaffolding, and at the splintered board below. "It's not my place to judge you in your mistakes. The Pope and the Lord Himself will do that. I only want to do well at any task I am given."

"And if you are given a task by the Pope that runs counter to the commands of the Lord?"

"Impossible. The Pope is the direct repository on earth of the Lord's commands. There can be no division between them."

Joshua smiled faintly. "Anna will have plenty of thoughts on that subject when she returns, I'm sure," he said, taking a long swig of water.

"I don't see what any of this has to do with my work here."

"Well, Samuel, it seemed to me that maybe you felt the need to prove the worth of your theology through the sincerity of your effort," said Joshua softly.

"The only proof of my theology lies in the words of Holy Scripture, in the books of the canon."

Joshua nodded. "Ah, the canon." He was silent for a moment. "And what of the other books and letters by our earliest Christian brethren? Are they of little worth or meaning to you?"

"Well, no," Samuel started, then hesitated, unsure of what Joshua knew or suspected about Samuel's real mission. "The non-canonical works are important, surely—or at least some are. But they do not have the importance and authority of the Gospels of Mark, Matthew, Luke, and John, the letters of

Paul, Peter, and John and the Apocalypse of John."

"And the Acts of the Apostles?" Joshua responded, a smile playing on his lips.

Samuel felt the blood burning across his whole face. It was humiliating to make even a minor slip in front of this provincial pastor.

"Yes, of course, and Acts."

"And what do you make of the other Gospels? The Gospel of Philip, of Mary, of Thomas, and others? The Didache? Letters?"

Samuel's heart began to thump violently in his chest. He tried to maintain a calm exterior but could feel sweat tingle all over his body. Did Joshua have copies of these books?

"Well," he began, "most of those books have been deemed heretical by the Popes, making them unfit for the eyes and ears of a devout Christian. They should have been destroyed over a hundred years ago. They may have been written by early Christians, but the ideas are heretical and misleading."

"But Samuel," Joshua said softly, "many early church fathers argued for the inclusion of some of those books in the canon and argued against the inclusion of others. The Gospel of John, for instance—there were many who said it was too strongly Gnostic. How do you make sense of that?"

It was the gentleness in his voice that infuriated Samuel. "I don't have to make sense of it. I trust in the Lord, I trust in the Church, and I trust in the wisdom of the Pope, as should you," he fumed. "It was the misguided ideas in those writings that led to aberrations like women in the priesthood."

He had lost his temper. While he truly did believe that women in the priesthood was an aberration, he knew that he had insulted Joshua and everything his church stood for. But Joshua did not show any physical response at all to his

110

words. Instead, he responded very calmly. "Samuel, we both believe in the same God. We both believe in the word of Jesus. We both acknowledge that women served as presbyters in the early church. We merely differ on the means by which we find God. The Church at Rome takes a very narrow view and restricts the means by which we can find God, which is through the men of the Church. Our modest church, as well as many others, believes we can find God either through the men or women. And we further believe that we can even find God within ourselves. The Gospel of Thomas says: 'If you bring forth what is within you, what you bring forth will save you.' In other words, in our church, one can discover the light within, on one's own, or with the help of a priest, or with the help of a priestess. In this manner many more will find God."

"Joshua, when you say that 'one can discover the light within,' that is contrary to the teachings of John which says that we can only experience God through the divine light embodied in Jesus. John challenged Thomas's claim that this light may be present in everyone. And, of course, the Gospel of John became part of the New Testament and the Gospel of Thomas did not. And ever since, the Church has denounced the teachings of Thomas as heretical."

"No, unfortunately Constantine and the bishops at Nicaea included the Gospels of Mark, Matthew, Luke and John, and the letters of Paul but not the Gospel of Thomas."

"And should that not put an end to this debate...the bishops have spoken?" Samuel retorted.

"I believe it was as much Constantine's will as it was the will of the bishops. It was his desire to unify the Church and model it on the government of Rome."

"And do you believe, Joshua, that your secret documents will convince the Pope to change Church doctrine?"

"I would hope that you would keep an open mind in

regard to these documents, and try to understand how decisions were made due to outside forces."

"I will keep an open mind, but I will also consider that the bishops have viewed such documents as blasphemous and heretical!"

A long silence ensued as the two men stared each other down. Was this the time to pursue a theological discussion with this man? He knew Joshua would not concede to his beliefs in the time they had.

"I'm sorry we can not seem to do anything but argue," Joshua said, as if sensing Samuel's thoughts. "I hardly know you, Samuel, and before we continue fighting over that which we may never agree on—I think it would do us good to discover what brings us together."

Samuel nodded, surprised that Joshua was the first to raise the flag of truce. Though Joshua's opinions and blasphemy angered him, he could not deny that there was something refreshing about his earnestness.

"Why don't we get something to eat," Joshua suggested, and together, they walked back down to the kitchen.

.   .   .

"Tell me son—do you have a family back in Rome?" Joshua asked, breaking bread for the two of them. "Your mother, your father—what did they do?"

"Well, I suppose there's another reason I've taken to this manual work," Samuel said, accepting the bread that Joshua offered. "My father did a great deal of work with his hands"

"Did he? And what is it he did?"

"He was a laborer. He began by making bricks and building with them, and by the time he was my age, he had a number of men who worked for him and was on his way to becoming wealthy." Samuel paused, taking a moment to chew his food. "Even so it was a disgrace when my mother married him. Her family did not look kindly upon my father's occupation and the modest living it brought him. When he died several years later, the rest of my family attempted to forget him as soon as they could. But she kept him close to her heart, even when she married again."

"I'm sorry to hear that, son," Joshua said, bowing his head as he did. "May I ask what your mother is like?"

Samuel hesitated. "She was an intelligent woman," he finally said, "but her weakness revealed itself as I grew older. Her second husband was a strict, powerful man, and she could not match him in his rigor or his discipline."

"Did he ever...did he ever hurt her?" asked Joshua quietly.

"What?"

"I thought perhaps from the way you spoke..."

"No," said Samuel sharply. "He was strict, but he was godly. If they had conflicts, it was only because she refused to be subservient to him as a husband."

"I see."

Samuel could not tell what Joshua was thinking. He was always so placid and unshakably thoughtful. "Was it he who started you on your education?" Joshua continued.

"It was my mother. A year after they were married, she announced that she felt that the best thing for me would be to attend one of the schools run by the Church. I've always wondered if she believed I shared her weakness somehow— as if I could not match the rigors of her husband's faith any more than she could."

"Do you feel that was true?"

"Of course not!" snapped Samuel. He took the water in the bowl before him and raised it to his lips to cool his frustration. *How can this man ask such questions without a second thought?* Samuel sighed before continuing on.

"Either way, I never got the chance. She succumbed to a

fever years ago, and he could not escape catching it from her."

"I'm sorry," said Joshua.

"Well—they're in a better place now, are they not?"

"Indeed."

"Anyway," said Samuel, "it was all a long time ago." He set down his bread and stood up, anxious to change the subject. "When will Anna return? I need to convene the elders and speak to them."

Joshua shrugged. "I had been expecting her today, but I have no idea how long she will be away. If things are bad in the south, it could be several days."

Samuel began to pace around the table, looking at the knots of the wooden wall as if they were of great interest. "And what is there between the two of you?" he asked, turning suddenly to face the old man. *If he wants to pry into my life, I shall pry into his.*

"We love each other, as fellow Christians," he said.

Samuel chuckled softly. "I see. And I'm sure as Christians, Christ would look joyfully upon the love that you share?"

Joshua's expression did not change, but he swung his leg over the bench, clasping his hands as he sat, hunched over the floor. "Perhaps that is enough for today," he said. "We've had time to rest and to speak. I have other things that need attending to, and I'm sure you are anxious to get back to the library."

"Of course," said Samuel.

"You should speak with Maria...I believe Anna spoke to her before she left about other documents you may find edifying."

"I will."

Joshua nodded sharply, and left Samuel alone with the

unfinished bread and water, wondering about so many things.

Chapter 15

⌒

"Samuel…Samuel…are you here in the library?"
"Yes, I am. What's the matter?" Samuel asked responding to Joshua's tremulous voice.

"I'm worried, Samuel…Anna should have returned by now. She is a few days overdue and has not sent a message letting us know the reason for the delay. Will you journey with me to find her?"

"Of course, I will…but why me?"

"Because you have the signet ring and it will be helpful in our search for Anna. There are many who will not get involved unless it's for money or the papacy."

"Do you understand the irony of this situation, Joshua? I was sent here to eliminate women priests and now I might end up saving one."

"It is the Christian way, I believe!"

"When do we leave?" Samuel asked.

"As soon as you are packed."

It was early morning when the two left the village travelling with the sun to their back. Neither spoke, but Samuel had become intrigued by women who defied the rules. Anna was a priest, she ventured out on her own, she ostensibly answered to no one, she cared for those in need, and she was a leader in the church. But had Anna defied the rules to the point where harm had come to her? She was older, but she was attractive. Men would be attracted to her, and seeing that she was travelling alone might make them think that she was a person of loose morals. He looked at Joshua's face and saw a worried look. The journey took one full day, and very little conversation took place between the two until they reached the edge of town. "We will visit the church first and see if Anna is still there or whether they know her whereabouts," Joshua said thoughtfully.

The parish priest recognized Joshua from his prior visits to the town. "Father Joshua. To what do we owe this pleasure?"

"We are looking for Anna, and we thought she might be here."

"She was here, but she left almost a week ago. I was under the impression that she was returning to your town."

"Oh, my God!" Joshua uttered. "Do you have any idea where she might be?"

"No, but you must rest now. We will begin our search in the morning...We will scour the town to find any trace of her. Someone must have seen her and knows her whereabouts."

The search began in earnest the next morning. The three went to all the neighborhoods in the town, but no trace of her was found. The next day the three searched the countryside but to no avail. "Tomorrow we will search the little fishing villages that dot the seashore," said the parish priest with a glimmer of hope. But that search also proved to be futile. "Only prayer remains," said Joshua that evening. "Tomorrow we will set aside the morning for prayer and meditation!"

The three prayed and meditated in their individual ways. The parish priest presided over mass and then strolled through the streets of his parish assisting those in need. Joshua walked to the seacoast and communed with God through nature. Samuel attended mass and read passages from the Bible. Early afternoon the three met in the rectory in hopes that their prayers had been answered. Joshua was distraught. Samuel was silent. But the parish priest had an idea. "Anna was worried about the edict from the Pope. She brought it up often and was concerned about what would happen to her parish and all other parishes that had ordained women to the priesthood. She said she had an old friend in Rome that had influence with the Pope."

"Oh my God," gasped Samuel. "Flavius!"

"Flavius...your mentor...aide to the Pope?" Joshua asked, obviously baffled.

"Flavius oftentimes spoke of a woman he was close to in his youth who fled Rome because of the restrictions placed on women."

"That could very well be Anna...but the road to Rome is fraught with danger. I must go to Rome."

"She is walking. Take our horse and you will make up some time. But she is probably already in Rome!"

"Samuel. Return to the church and bring news of our plight. Oh, and let me borrow the signet ring, if that pleases you..."

Without hesitation he removed the ring from his finger and tossed it to Joshua who was already moving towards the barn.

. . .

Flavius had received a note to meet an old friend in a remote tavern in the heart of the city. He had been waiting for nearly an hour. As he prepared to leave, the door from the street side opened and a tall, attractive woman came in. It had been many years since he had seen her, but his youthful emotions returned like a bolt from the blue, leaving him breathless. She was older, a little heavier than he remembered, her hips more rounded, and her breasts fuller, but that only added to her appeal. The sight of her made him ask himself why he had not married her. All of his achievements paled in comparison to the love he had lost. "Flavius, you have not changed since I left Rome many

118

years ago."

"You have not lost your charm, Anna, and your presence brings me back to our youth."

"If only we could return to those years, Flavius. I believe we would do things differently."

"I think of you often, Anna. Do you sometimes think of me?"

"I do, Flavius. I think of you often and hope that you have found happiness. But most recently, I have been thinking of you in a different vein. Samuel arrived at our church a while ago, and even though we all like him, he carries a message of doom from the Pope. When we parted years ago, it was the prohibitions of Rome that I was running away from."

"Then it was not me that you were fleeing from?"

"I loved you too much for that, Flavius, but I could not live in these surroundings. You should have followed me to the south."

His heart sank when he heard these words. How foolish he had been not to have left Rome with her. How foolish he had been to take a vow of celibacy to serve as a papal aide. But that was in the past, and for the moment he was with the woman he most loved in the world. And as in the past, he could not express his love for her.

"Now, Flavius, the prohibitions of Rome have found us in southern Italia. I do not care to flee the long arm of Rome again, so I have returned to Rome to seek your help."

"What can I do, Anna? I am in the service of the Pope and have sworn a vow of obedience to him."

"And you have also taken a vow of celibacy. How much of your life are you going to give up for this Pope?"

"Anna, it is not for the Pope that I have taken these vows; it is for my salvation."

"And would you be willing to break these vows for me

and for the other women who serve the Church for the love of God?"

Flavius hesitated. What did she intend for him to do? The dreadful thought crossed his mind that she wanted him to conspire against the Pope. He would have to think more about that. For now, he said, "I haven't had a chance to think about it."

The smile left her face and that saddened him. He knew he should speak words of encouragement but could not find them. There was an awkward silence, but she was not yet finished.

"Flavius, it's time to speak the truth!"

"Anna, all I can do is record the truth."

"You are now as you were then, engrossed in your musty books and documents living for the generations to come and not living for yourself. I thought you might have changed, Flavius."

Chapter 16

S amuel ran his finger across the dusty leather folders containing old papyrus sheaves and touched the stiff, tightly wound scrolls that lined the library shelves. The morning sun shone in through the small window, illuminating the sheen of the leather bindings. He had been there for more than an hour, but he could not settle down to read. He worried about Anna and Joshua, and he was concerned that he might be wavering in his assignment. Admittedly, he did not feel prepared for this task, though he was not sure there was anything he could have done to change that. He sighed deeply.

"Need help getting started?" a voice asked from the doorway. Samuel's heart began to pound. It was Maria, standing amidst the sunlight with a pitcher of water in hand.

She stepped into the library. "I thought you might like something to drink. And some good news."

"Yes, thank you," Samuel stammered as he poured water into a mug. "And what is the good news?"

"Joshua and Anna returned last night. They were tired but so happy to be back. He mentioned that you had been very helpful! And he asked that I return your signet ring."

"And they are well?"

"Yes, they are well." She paused briefly. "Have you found anything else of interest?" she asked as she looked around the library.

"No—it's just that there is so much. I wasn't sure where best to move next."

Maria reached up and around him, her shoulder brushing his chest. The dark strands of her hair brushed his cheek as she pulled down one of the thicker volumes from above.

"I think this might interest you. It's about a woman named Michella."

Maria handed him a sheaf of roughly cut documents bound with an ungainly piece of twine.

"How old is this?" he asked, looking down at the stack of papyrus. It was yellowed with age and appeared to be extremely fragile.

"This is a copy. The original is over a hundred years old," she replied. "The things it tells about happened fifty years after the death of Alexandra, the woman you already read about."

Samuel carefully put the bundle down on the desk. "How old is this congregation?" he asked.

"Very old," she said. Their eyes met and he felt his stomach flutter.

"I'll leave you to read," she said. "Would you like me to have food sent over when the meal is ready?"

"Please."

"And Samuel—please be careful with the documents," she said seriously.

"Of course," he said breaking out in a smile.

"We have only one copy of these documents. The originals are almost too delicate to handle. I'm in the process of making another, but it is slow work."

"You write well enough to do that?" he asked.

"There are many things I do well," she answered returning his smile.

Her smile was devastating. As she turned towards the doorway to leave, Samuel called out to her. She turned again to face him.

"I've decided to take a day off from working tomorrow,

after I finish this reading," he said. His voice sounded stiff and formal in his ears. "I thought, well, when Anna is fully rested, I am going to be busy with her and with my correspondence with Rome—and I thought that maybe I would go on a walk in the countryside and I wondered—that is, I expect that you know this area well because you live here." He felt himself blushing.

She looked at him, waiting for him to continue.

"Would you like to go on a walk with me?" he asked timidly.

"I would like that, Samuel," she said.

Even more embarrassed at the gentle happiness in her voice than he had been at his own halting tones, he looked down, shifting his attention back to the pile of parchment.

"I'll come and find you tomorrow, then," he said.

"I'll have your dinner sent over," she replied, and then she was gone.

He listened to the sound of her footsteps receding across the stone, thinking what a fool he was. Had he not listened to Flavius when the old monk told him about the perils of women? Did he not know as well as the next man how insidiously dangerous they are? And yet what was the danger of a simple walk? *If you do not want to go, then you can beg out of it tomorrow*, he told himself. *Now concentrate on this task at hand.*

He closed his eyes and said a quick prayer for strength, and unwrapped the papers with extreme care. It was titled *The Story of Michella and Her Husband Joseph, Monastics.*

Samuel sighed and shook his head condescendingly. Even as a child in school, he had known that monasticism precluded marriage. How could anyone take a history such as this seriously? And why in the world did Maria give him this to read? The warm, joyful feeling in his chest vanished, and the nagging anxiety that had been growing since he arrived at this church replaced it. He considered putting the document aside and looking for the forbidden scrolls that Gelasius had told him to search for instead. But he knew that Maria might want to talk about it tomorrow and he did not want to disappoint her.

Chapter 17

I t was hard to believe the man's pale face had once glowed with life. Michella watched as his frail lips mouthed out the prayers she knew by heart. His eyes were closed lightly, but she could see that the movement beneath his eyelids was beginning to slow. She wondered if he could see the Lord reaching out. It was only a matter of time now.

The man began coughing harshly, and Michella held tightly to his hand. "You will be with Him soon," she said to him softly. "If you truly accept Him into your heart, then He can not but accept you into His. For as we are born on earth, so we enter His heavenly kingdom as babes born anew, adorned only in the everlasting light of His love." She lifted a small pitcher of water to his lips, and he drank slowly.

For many years, Michella had served as a midwife, caring for those as they first entered the world. It was during this time that she came close to God, and felt she understood the beauty of His own birth. She became well known for bringing hope to all those she touched, even those on the edge of death, by helping them see the eternal life that had been granted by Christ.

This man had summoned her from a neighboring province, having seen too late the error of his ways. Now the eldest in his village, he had accumulated a great deal of wealth, which he had kept to himself until God stripped his voice from him. It was only in writing that he could repent, and it was in this way he had sought out Michella.

"We are forever being born," she told him. "Continue to

pray—continue to open your heart to Jesus and He will carry away your sins that you may be washed clean and born again."

At this, the man's eyes opened wide, and his chest rose in the air. Michella stepped back, and stood by as the man's arched back shook above the bed. A strained syllable left his lips, the dull moan of a man whose life was being pressed out of him. As suddenly as he had arisen, he fell back to the bed and the tension that once had held him so tightly seemed to slowly seep away from his body. Michella listened as his soft moans became one long exhalation, and as a look of peace settled onto his face. The hand that she had been holding fell slackly by his side, and she watched as a single tear that had fallen from his eyes coursed slowly down his face before falling to the floor.

She reached up to close his eyes, and began praying softly, issuing blessings over his body and giving thanks to the Lord.

"You have done a great thing," came a voice from the door.

Michella turned and saw the man's wife standing in the doorway. She was younger than he had been, but Michella could see how time had worn itself into the skin around her eyes and mouth.

"He has done a special thing in accepting the Lord into his heart," Michella replied. "That is something only he could do."

Michella could see the tears forming in her eyes, as she looked at her feet.

"There is something I want you to have," the woman said, wiping the tears from her face. "In his life, there was nothing he treasured more. He slept with it every night beneath his pillow, afraid one day it might be taken."

She held forth a small object wrapped in a white cloth,

and moved to hand it to Michella.

"I am flattered but I'm not sure I can accept..." Michella said, but the woman had pressed the gift into her palm, wrapping Michella's fingers around it. As she stepped away, Michella began peeling back the folds of the cloth to see what it held.

"What...what is this?" In her hand she held a slender bone, gray with age.

"It is a relic of Saint Persillia—a bone from her hand. My husband obtained it on a pilgrimage he made to Rome many years back. He was convinced it was what brought him his long life and his fortune. It was only later that he...," she paused, fighting back a second flood of tears, "that he wished he had given more to the people of the village."

"Please," she went on, "use it in your work to heal others. They say Persillia was a powerful holy woman. They say that because of her connection with Jesus, this relic can heal others. Use it—and make sure that those healed by it lead lives that are truly saved, as you have saved my husband's."

Before Michella could respond, the woman had turned to the door and walked briskly away. She looked down at the relic in her hands, and back over at the man, lying with a peaceful expression on his face.

"My Lord—you work in mysterious ways."

She rose, and left to fetch the sons who would bury their father.

·   ·   ·

Mother Michella was well aware of the rising power and importance of the cult of the saints in the last hundred years. As the priest of a small congregation in northern Africa, she knew of many who had come to believe that the relics of saints—their bones and clothing or other items that had touched them during life—were portals that allowed people to draw closer to God. But she had never seen or touched one before, and she was not sure what she should do with what she had been given. She brought it back to her home at the church, and kept it on the table where she wrote her sermons.

Given her extensive work with the sick and the needy and her consistent service to the parishioners of her church, a few months prior she had been elevated by the elders of her church to be its pastor. With this position came new responsibilities and new questions, many of which she did not know yet how to answer. Her church, far from the heart of Christianity, in Alexandria and Rome, was filled with independent thinkers, none more so than she. It was in this context that she toiled over the relic, unsure of how her congregation would react to her harboring such an object. *A good night's sleep will help me to figure it out*, she thought to herself before retiring for the night.

.   .   .

"Mother Michella! Mother Michella!"

Michella wheeled out of her bed as the young girl's panic-stricken voice burst through the open window of her bedroom. She had fallen asleep hours ago, and she looked outside into the pitch-black night.

"What is it, my child?"

"Please come! Please!"

"Come inside, my dear! Are you in trouble?" Michella asked, opening the door to see a very young girl with the dried streaks of recent tears along her cheeks.

"No, Mother, you must come with me! Mama is dying! Her baby—she's stuck! We can see her head, but she's not moving, and Mama has passed out. Please!"

Michella's body responded out of instinct. Even before the little girl was finished speaking, she had dressed herself and began pulling together the utensils she had once carried as a midwife.

"Is no one there to deliver the child?"

"There are three women there, and no one can get the baby out. They can't stop the bleeding, and it has been going on for hours."

The blood drained from Michella's face. The child might not understand the severity of the situation, but Michella did. Without immediate help, this woman was going to die, and likely her child as well. Michella did not know what a fourth midwife could offer, but with her things together, she moved quickly towards the door, until she spotted the relic. Knowing she had no time to consider its value, she scooped it up in her hand and threw it in her case.

Together, they ran through the darkness to the laboring woman. Upon entering, the room was silent, and two of the midwives were busy trying to turn the baby, hoping to ease the pressure that was preventing its birth. But Michella could tell by their grim faces that there was no hope.

"Mother Michella!" the third midwife, sitting in the corner, called to her. "We have been trying to save her, but the bleeding...it has not stopped since she first went into labor. I have been praying, but..."

Her words trailed off, as the other two women continued to toil away.

"Let me speak with her," Michella said, unsure what she was doing.

"But Mother Michella—she has been unconscious for a while now."

Michella ignored the midwife's pleas and kneeled down beside the pregnant mother. The woman's face, bronzed by outdoor work, was now pallid from exertion and glistening with sweat, with strands of her dark hair laying like fault lines across her cheek and forehead. Reaching into her pocket, Michella pressed the relic against the brow of the laboring woman and began praying quietly, whispering in her ear as she spoke. The others were silent, and she began to whisper more intently. *Push*, she thought. *Push!* She thought of the old man, dying in his bed, and of the sadness in his wife's eyes. *Lord, let me save her. Please let this child be saved!* She bowed her head and squeezed the relic tightly in her hands. "Push," she said aloud. "Push!"

"Here she comes!"

Michella looked up to see the two midwives staring wide-eyed at the head of the baby girl before them. They moved quickly, and gently began to massage the woman's stomach, easing the baby out as Michella held the relic tight against her head. The third midwife, having gotten up from her seat, kneeled between the two others, her hands held out expectantly. "Push," Michella urged her again. "Push! Push!"

The shrill cries of a small child filled the room. The third midwife beamed with exultation, and Michella turned to see her holding a perfect, beautiful baby girl. The afterbirth followed, and with it, the copious life-draining bleeding ceased. "She will survive," Michella whispered to the others.

It had all happened so fast. The midwives stared at Michella, unsure what to say or think.

"Mother Michella—how is this possible? This woman and her child...you saved them."

Michella was shaking. She did not know what to make of what had just passed.

"It was not I. It was the Lord who saved them," she replied. "He heard our prayers."

"It is a miracle, Mother Michella. The Lord has worked wonders through you!" a midwife exclaimed as she began to clean the child. "You are a living saint!"

The others looked at her in awe. "I do not believe so," Michella said to them calmly. "But it may be that a saint has come to our aid."

She unwrapped the relic of Saint Persillia for all to see. The midwives' faces were filled with wonder as they moved to get a closer look.

"There will be time to explain," Michella said, "but we must now tend to this mother and child. There is still work to be done here."

With that, she directed the midwives to fetch warm water and extra clothes. As they busied themselves, cleaning the child and coaxing her mother back into consciousness, Michella stepped outside to breathe in the cool night air. *Was it a miracle, or the mother's will to live—or the hope in my heart?* she wondered.

. . .

The story of the miraculous birth spread like wildfire through the province. People spoke of the relic that had saved the mother and baby, and the story soon became mythical in proportion. Michella was now being summoned to all births within miles of the church. And at every stop, when the relic was held against the laboring woman's brow, the baby came swiftly and safely. People also came to believe that Saint Persillia could hasten a Christian's birth into Heaven just as surely, so Michella was called to bring comfort and hopefully salvation to the dying. She was rarely at home anymore, and was summoned to ever more distant places to minister to the needs of the living and the dying.

At the same time, pilgrims travelled to the site of the powerful relic of Saint Persillia. At first, dozens and then hundreds of pilgrims came from across northern Africa to both glimpse the miraculous object and implore Michella's intercession for their causes. When Michella was away with the relic, people pressed bits of fabric against the reliquary where it was held, and those who met her in the streets bowed their heads, asking humbly if they could glimpse the relic she carried. Many pilgrims donated generous sums of money, and in time, both the church and Michella became wealthy and politically powerful. As the church prospered, she worked tirelessly to recruit new members and to glorify God and the saints. Those who were most devout among her congregation were sent to evangelize and convert the people of the surrounding region. As they welcomed Christ into their lives, their idols were melted down and recast as crosses, statues, and chalices to adorn the church.

For months after the miraculous birth, the church prospered and grew, and the people of the village were elated. But the demands placed on Michella began to take its toll on her husband, Joseph, who was left at home to address the day-to-day needs of the church and its grounds. With Michella gone, he grew more and more restless and agitated. When she returned one day, she found him disconsolate, sitting and waiting for her in front of their house, his head bowed above his knees. His hands were covered in dirt, and the garden to the left of the house lay half weeded.

"Joseph—is everything all right?" she asked.

He looked up at her through swollen, red eyes. "No. No, I don't think they are," he replied.

He took her by the hand and led her to the side of the house where they had placed a small bench in the shade of a trellis covered with grapevines. They sat down together, and he held firmly on to her hand. "I need to make a confession to you," he began. "This morning, as I started to work in the garden—I found myself getting angry. It has been happening a lot lately. I was thinking of you, off on a journey, or going to save someone's life, or raising money for the poor, and despite telling myself to admire the goodness of these acts, I couldn't help but feel insignificant—weeding the little garden and repairing the house. As this anger grew, I saw another woman in my mind, a woman who would spend her time laughing with me, the way you used to, and who would listen to me as I told of the happenings of my day, the way you used to."

He squeezed her hand tightly as she looked away. "This upset me deeply," he said, moving to look her in the eye, "because this is the way in which I used to imagine you. I stopped my work, and prayed for strength. Michella..." He waited until she turned to face him. "The Lord has put it in my heart to understand, and to tell you, that I am jealous of your position and your favor in Christ. As much as these past months have been profitable for the church, I need you to know how difficult it has been for me. I am going to continue to pray for strength, and hope that you will pray with me."

The expression on Michella's face was pained. *Have I been consumed by my own aspirations?* she thought. She had feared the worst when he had mentioned another woman, but when she saw the sincerity in his eyes, she knew he had simply wanted to confess everything that had passed in her absence.

"My dearest," she said. "I'm so sorry...I love you and need you, and need for you to be happy. I'm so very sorry."

She raised his hand to her lips and kissed it.

The sensation that passed through her in that moment was overwhelming. It felt as if her body had fallen away and everything inside her was replaced with the sensation of a cool breeze. She gasped, and shook slightly, as she felt the divine breath glittering outwards from her heart, running like a soft current beneath her skin. A cave out in the desert appeared to her, clearer than any dream or vision she had experienced. It took no more time than the brief contact of their skin, and as soon as it had come, it was gone.

"Joseph!" she cried, startled and a little bit scared, "I think—I think I felt God's hand on me just now!"

Joseph nodded, his eyes wide. "What did He tell you?"

"I saw a cave in the desert and you and me in ragged clothes but with joy in our hearts."

There were tears in his eyes. "What do you think it means?"

She laughed with joy. "I don't know! But it's a sign that our lives must move to another destination."

Seeing the exultation written on the other's face, they fell together and held each other. They swayed slowly back and forth on the bench, embracing, clutching each other tightly, and promising one another to heed this vision of a better time to come.

.   .   .

They contemplated their course for a few days, and gathered together the congregation and its elders in the tightly packed halls of the small, but now ornate, church.

"My brothers and sisters, Joseph and I stand before you with difficult tidings to share," Michella said. "We have prayed, and the Lord has answered our prayers. He has put it in our hearts that we must again commit ourselves to each other and to our faith...and we have decided to heed His call."

She looked out upon the crowds that had assembled, and saw the admiration in their eyes. They were hanging on every word. "'Go, sell your possessions and give to the poor, and you will have treasures in Heaven,' Jesus tells us. And tomorrow, we are following his words and leaving to live in the desert, for that is our new calling."

The crowd gasped. It hit them like a blow to the stomach, and murmuring filled the church.

"We will take with us nothing more than we need to survive, and leave all that we have with you," she continued.

"But when will you return?" asked a young woman in the crowd.

"When we are commanded by the Lord," Joseph answered, stepping forward.

"But what of our church?" asked a man indignantly. "How can you just abandon us?"

"The Lord will not abandon you, and will provide for you as He will for us," replied Michella.

The murmurs at this point grew into a din of shouts and confusion. Joseph looked at Michella and knew, despite her placid exterior, there was a great sadness churning within her.

For several days following the announcement, the parishioners and the townspeople were in an uproar. Certain men in the congregation claimed that in spite of all she had done, this abrupt move was evidence that women were not meant to be leaders in the Church. Through it all, Michella and Joseph ignored the criticism and pushed forward with their plans, giving away most of what they owned and preparing for their journey to the desert.

Prior to their intended departure, a priest from a neighboring town who had heard of their decision journeyed to speak with them. The morning they were to leave, he arrived and found them at their home, their meager belongings in hand, looking out into the distance with a sense of adventure in their hearts.

"Michella...Joseph!" he cried.

They turned to see a short man, strands of grey interspersed among the dark, bushy bristles of his long beard. He told them of the chaos and confusion that had rippled to other parishes after their announcement. Though it was rumored that God had summoned them to the desert, he wondered if they too had been struggling with more pressing earthly concerns. He told them of his conversations with other priests from the region, and it quickly became clear to Michella that many of the clergy across the land were deeply concerned about the evolution of the Church during these difficult times. Were they to preach the Gospel of Thomas or the Gospel of John...was Jesus human or was He divine...was God found within oneself or through the clergy...adorn the churches or give to the poor...include women or exclude them?

"These are the questions that are being asked, and these are the questions you should be present to answer," the priest pleaded.

"The sheep are scattered, and the shepherd who tends them is gone," Michella said to the visitor. "At the beginning there was a purer and simpler faith where all believed in basic teachings, such as love God and love thy neighbor. With time an institution developed with a hierarchy of priests and bishops. They developed a Testament, a Creed, and Canon Law. Now the Bishop of Rome is asserting a privileged position among the bishops. And who will herd and tend the flock tomorrow? Will it be the power of the bishops...the persuasiveness of the theologians...or the example of Jesus? That is one of the reasons we are leaving for the desert, to find the true course."

Michella and Joseph nodded to the visitor then shouldered the small bags they had prepared and walked out of the town. The villagers stood next to their houses and watched them go in silence.

Chapter 18

⌒

It was morning, and the desert was dry and red around them. They walked until the sun hung high above their heads, and rested in the shade of boulders and shrubs. Neither knew where they were going, and they spoke rarely, often too tired and parched to speak during the hottest hours of the day. Yet, when the land cooled, or when a stray cloud passed before the sun, both felt peaceful in the other's company, and in the company of the Lord.

For three days they travelled like this, moving slowly and resting often, until they found themselves drawn into a narrow canyon choked with bushes. They looked at one another, and in their silence, heard the trickling of a small stream. As they wandered through the canyon, the sound grew, echoing among the high rock walls. Michella began to run, anxious to find the source of this sweet sound, leaving Joseph behind in her excitement. By the time he caught up, he found her kneeling before a beautiful crystalline pool, her hands held up to the sky in exultation. Over her shoulder, Joseph saw a large cave stretching back into the canyon wall. It was the place God had summoned them to.

With the simple tools and small portions of seed they had brought, they settled into a life of simplicity and asceticism, rejuvenating both their marriage and their faith. They fasted and prayed; they made love and took pleasure in each other's company.

Several months passed in this fashion before they came in contact with anyone from the outside world. They were both kneeling with their eyes closed, meditating, when they heard someone approach quietly. In their heightened state of awareness, both of them sensed that there was nothing to fear from this intruder, and they listened as the newcomer sat before them. Michella spoke aloud the Lord's Prayer, and they opened their eyes. The son of one of their oldest friends sat before them. He was sixteen years old, blond, and he bowed down to the ground when they looked at him.

"Thomas," said Michella, smiling, "why are you doing that?"

"I thought it might be proper," the young man said. "I hope I didn't disturb you."

"We're the same people that you've always known, and you've never bowed to us before."

He lifted his head to look at her. "Back in the village— there are some who say you've become holy—that the relic of Saint Persillia and your dedication to God have made you a living saint, Mother Michella."

Michella almost laughed aloud. "Thomas, how did you find us? And how did these rumors start?"

"There are those who have visited our village who spoke of a man and a woman living in the desert," the youth began. "I spoke with them, and they mentioned a canyon far beyond the roads normally taken by traders and pilgrims. It took some time, but in the last few weeks, I made the necessary preparations and followed their directions to this place."

"You are a brave young man, Thomas," Michella replied, "but I fear you may be disappointed if you are expecting saints. We are living as closely to the Lord as we know how, but that doesn't mean you need to bow before us. Every person has to find his own path to the Lord. This is simply the one we have chosen."

"Do you still eat food and drink water?"

"We eat enough to sustain us," responded Joseph with a chuckle.

"Some people say that you no longer need those things."

"Don't be silly. We drink from the stream and have a small plot of vegetables at its bank," he said with a smile. There was a serenity in his eyes the likes of which Thomas had never seen before. "Occasionally, the Lord provides us with a small animal that we eat with gratitude, but no more than that. We live as simply as we can, but we are still two people living our very human lives, which we dedicate to God!"

"Oh." Thomas smiled sheepishly, but looked crestfallen. "I of course am happy for you—though I suppose I was hoping that you would have some deeper secret to tell about gaining favor with God."

Michella chuckled in spite of herself. "Is that why you came all this way, Thomas?"

Thomas again looked befuddled. "I have felt lost," he said. "And in looking for answers I came to you."

Michella and Joseph exchanged glances, and she turned to address Thomas. "We are glad you've come, and we can offer you a chance to live quietly here with us for a few days, away from the distractions of the world. This may indeed allow you to come closer to God, but there is no magic to it. Simply prayer, meditation, and peacefulness."

Thomas nodded uncertainly. He stayed with them for two full cycles of the moon, sleeping under a tree on the other side of the stream, following their routine of prayer, work, and fasting. When he departed, he had been touched by the experience and felt closer to God. He returned to the village and spoke to all that would listen about the transformation he had experienced. Michella and Joseph's reputation spread quickly throughout the region. People from every walk of life travelled to the desert for sundry reasons, some to find a greater understanding of the religion, others to experience a conversion, and still others for the sake of curiosity.

"You can begin by kneeling here beside us," Joseph would say to the visitors, "and by listening."

"Listening?"

"To the sound of the stream, to the sound of your breathing—to the sound of your own heart beating," Michella joined in calmly, settling back in to her meditation. "You may hear more than you expect."

With a deep breath and the sound of water singing along the walls of the canyon, the visitors would close their eyes and sit between them.

.　.　.

Some would stay a few nights, others for longer, sleeping under the stars by the nearby stream, following closely Michella and Joseph's routine of prayer and fasting. They lit a fire as the sun went down each day, and spoke long into the night. Both Michella and Joseph were anxious to hear news from throughout the province and about the development of the church. To the extent they could, they shared the revelations they had in the desert, and the joy and peace they had felt living the monastic life.

When the visitors were ready to leave, it was as if they had been transformed. Away from the strictures of society, they could see things more clearly, and the channel to God seemed clearer and more direct.

Michella and Joseph made sure their visitors had adequate supplies for their trek back across the desert, and embraced them lovingly before sending them on their way.

Based on accounts of their visitors, it was not long before Michella and Joseph had become more famous in the region than any others before them. It was a joyous and reverent time for all who met and prayed in the desert, and Michella and Joseph found their love for one another renewed and stronger.

Chapter 19

⌒

The rainy season had settled upon the land, forcing Michella and Joseph to spend much of their time within the confines of the cave. The pool and stream grew in size, and the sound of the torrential rains pouring into the canyon reverberated loudly as they sat meditating. With her eyes closed, Michella imagined the sound was that of God exhaling, while the stray drops that cracked and plopped in their cavernous home were the pings of creatures born to life.

Visitors had grown scarce, and many of the seeds they had planted by the bank of the stream had been washed away. The two of them were now forced to survive on what they could find, as well as the few items people had brought and left. Meditation and long periods of fasting had prepared them well for this time of scarcity, and they only stirred to gather roots or to boil water for tea.

Michella, rousing herself from the deep immersion in the sound of the rain about her, opened her eyes to see that Joseph had left to forage. *He is growing strong with the desert*, she thought to herself. The two of them had an ongoing competition to see if they could move without disturbing the other's concentration, pushing one another to be one with the Lord and His earth at all times. After listening for so long, both had learned to blend with the rocks, to move beneath the sound of the stream, and to hide among the dirt and the dunes.

Michella jerked her head towards the entrance to the cave, as she heard a break in the rainfall. A blurred figure was emerging from the gray dusk, approaching the cave, stopping and sitting at its edge outside the entrance. It was easy to tell that this was not Joseph—the heavy rains seemed to break upon the frame of this silhouette rather than embracing and running down its sides. Michella studied its edges, trying to determine the nature of this visitor. She walked slowly forward, careful to move in concert with the rainfall. The figure of a man became clearer, his hair long and ragged, and his clothes as decrepit and worn as her own.

"I have heard that there is a hermit living off of this road who is unparalleled in his faith," the figure said, keeping his face from her. "Are you this man?"

His voice startled her, and she stood for a moment behind him, unsure if he was talking to himself or to her.

"I know you are there," he went on. He turned around to look at her where she stood. "My name is Cyprian—I mean you no harm."

His voice was flat, and his face gaunt, pale, and emotionless. Despite his effusive calm, his presence clashed with the peace of this place.

"Cyprian—I am Michella," she said. Neither bowed or extended a hand in greeting. "I do not know if I am the one you seek, but if you would like, you can come in out of the rain and warm yourself in my home."

Cyprian stood up and turned back away from her, towards the rain. "You are a woman," he said.

"As God made me," she replied.

"I mean no offense," he said casually. "I am not one of the many who believe that a woman must follow a man into the Lord's presence."

"Nor am I," Michella said, unsure of the man's tone.

He revealed nothing and simply nodded sharply. "If a woman knows her place, she can partake in His joys as equally as a man."

"I believe this may be a conversation best had inside, where we can sit, warm and dry. My husband will be home soon, and he may be the man you seek."

"I will wait here then," he said, gesturing broadly to the canyon. "I believe that it is only by enduring every hardship of God's world that we shall be drawn closer to Him."

The hairs raised on the back of Michella's neck as he spoke, but her curiosity compelled her on. "It takes tremendous devotion to embrace such an ethic. You must consider yourself very close to the Lord."

"I am," he said, as if he were simply stating a fact. "How long have you been in the desert?"

"Nearly three years—although neither of us knows exactly. Time moves differently out here."

Cyprian nodded stoically. "Very good. I myself hope to live as you have. You eat only what the Lord provides through the land?"

"Yes...cultivated wild roots, along with watercress from the stream, and occasionally a mouse or the locusts when they come."

"I believe that we should renounce ordinary human experiences. We should pray and work enough to provide for our subsistence."

"We have certainly tried to organize our lives around a principle of simplicity, taking joy in God's creation."

Cyprian nodded once more, and did not speak further. Michella watched as the rain fell in curtains upon him, bewildered by his stubbornness as much as she was drawn by his peculiar and stringent beliefs.

"Are you sure you won't come in out of the rain?"

"No," he said. She could not see his face clearly through the rain, but something in his voice seemed troubled. "There is a flat space across the stream where I will make my bed. I will leave you now."

"You must be careful of the stream," she said as he moved away. "When it rains like this, it can rise very quickly."

"I will submit myself to the Lord's will, as expressed through His word," he replied before he disappeared into the gathering darkness.

.   .   .

When Joseph returned with the watercress he had rescued from the rising stream and wild tubers gathered underground, all placed in the small basket they had woven, Michella told him of their new visitor and of his abrupt departure.

"Strange," he said. "I did not see him as I passed."

They both looked out into the downpour, but there was nothing but rain and rock to be seen. "Everyone must live as they see fit, Michella. I'm sure God will watch over this wandering lamb."

Michella shivered, and Joseph embraced her. At his touch, she felt as if her fears were slipping off to join the growing pools outside their home. They built a small fire and ate together before stretching out on a bed of reeds and falling to sleep, listening to the sound of the rain.

By morning, the sky had cleared, and they rose early to thank God for the blessings of the rain and the bounty it would bring forth from the earth. As they were preparing a small breakfast from the remains of yesterday's meal, Cyprian appeared once more at the entrance to their cave. He introduced himself to Joseph and proceeded to probe them intensely about their time in the desert. They learned that he had travelled across the land, seeking out its wisest people in hopes of discovering the truest path to God. He had heard of them while travelling along the northern stretches of Africa, and had spoken with Thomas, who knew of their location. While he engaged them on many topics, from the divine nature of Christ to the relationship of the Apostles, Michella had the strange feeling that he was circling around something, waiting for the right time to address what was troubling him.

As with Thomas, they spent much of their time downplaying the significance of their lives, inviting Cyprian to join them in quiet meditation, and to live and learn with them as long as he would like. Despite his unsettling presence, Michella felt safe with Joseph around, and she told herself that her heart needed to remain open to all God's children. Thus, for several days, he spent most of his time with them, studying their habits and routines and participating in their prayers and meditations. In the evenings, he retired into the darkness, but to where, Michella and Joseph did not know. Each morning, he showed up as they finished their morning prayers, gazing upon them with the same stoic eyes.

Finally, one afternoon, following an extended period of meditation, he spoke candidly.

"Tell me—does it not seem strange that you live as you do, renouncing all appetites, and yet you have not renounced your sexual relationship?"

Michella smiled before opening her eyes. *Is that what has been bothering this young man?*

"If I may speak for both of us," said Michella, glancing at her husband, who nodded, "our time in the desert has not been about renunciation for the sake of renunciation. It is our belief that sex and the relations between a man and woman are important parts of the Christian faith in a way that worldly possessions are not. To give up that essential connection would be to give up an essential part of the faith and a natural part of our being."

Cyprian's face remained stolid, but there was a new intensity in his voice. "Sexuality may be an important part of your life, but it is sexuality itself that is the cause of original sin."

Both Joseph and Michella looked at one another with concern. "Where did you get such an idea?" Joseph asked.

"This is the new understanding of the story of Adam and Eve in the Garden of Eden. This new interpretation is gaining strength and has many supporters. The fruit from the tree is simply an allegory for sexuality. It was the knowledge of this sexuality that forced Adam and Eve from paradise." Cyprian spoke smoothly and cooly. "And it was, as you know, Eve who tempted Adam with the fruit. Extending this allegory, it must be clearly understood that the apple is a symbol of women seducing men with their charms." His voice seemed to flicker lasciviously as he looked at Michella, sending a chill down her back. All the calm she had felt as they sat together ran away as his words hung in the air.

"I have never in all my years as a Christian heard such a ridiculous interpretation of the Creation story. Your understanding is flawed and dangerous," Michella replied firmly.

"The bishops at the head of the Church do not think so. It is gaining ground with all the important theologians. But then I suppose a woman will not understand the intricacies of the allegories of the Old Testament."

Joseph shot up from where he sat, and the muscles in Cyprian's body tensed.

"Joseph!"

Michella stood and put her hand gently on her husband's arm. His look was pained and furious, but she shook her head at him, turning back to face Cyprian. She was sure she could see the beginnings of a smile peeking out from the corners of his mouth.

"You claim to be devout," she said between gritted teeth, "and you have proven your resilience in the face of this world's dangers and strife. But you have learned nothing if you can speak of women with such venom." She felt Joseph relax behind her. "You disgrace your own mother in doing so."

She was acutely tuned to her own breathing as she gazed on the frail man. Cyprian sat stiffly, his hands clasped, staring back at the two of them. "I mean no offense," he said in a derogatory tone. "I am only trying to explain the thinking of the bishops of Rome and Alexandria, and of theologians like Tertullian, Irenaeus, and Origen. A brilliant young man named Augustine has clarified their arguments, and made the truth these men were reaching for clear for all to see."

Michella and Joseph were familiar with the first three, and were skeptical of their ideas. But neither was familiar with Augustine.

"Who is Augustine?" Michella asked.

"A brilliant theologian. It is he who has provided a philosophy as to the inferior nature of women and the danger of sexual relationships."

"*All* sexual relations? Even in marriage?" Joseph sputtered.

"Yes. Even though sex is permitted in marriage, the participants are still engaging in the act that brought about original sin. Sexual intercourse is only permitted for the sake of procreation."

"This reasoning is absurd!" Michella exclaimed. "Why then would Jesus have sanctioned marriage? Why would God give us such great joy in each other's bodies?"

"Augustine argues that the only allowable reason for sex is procreation, not joy. Why indulge in pleasures of the flesh, when it is our flesh that holds our soul captive from Heaven?"

Joseph stood dumbfounded, before spinning on his heel and gazing along the wall of the cave. "Is this what the world has come to in our absence?" he appealed to Michella. "Is this how far our sheep have strayed?"

"This is the enlightened Christian view of sexuality," Cyprian replied. He stood up, brushing the dust from his tunic.

"I believe I have learned all that I can here. For the sake of your own souls, I hope your time in the desert brings to light the truths of which I speak," he said. "Though, after years of living a life of such excess, if the truth has not come to you yet, I fear it may never."

There was nothing condescending in his voice. He delivered his cruel forecast as if it were an undeniable fact—one that he cared nothing about. As he began to walk away from them, Michella called out to him. He paused a moment before turning to face her.

"These views of love and the relations of man and woman—are there others who hold such views?"

For the first time, Cyprian laughed. The sound rang ominously among the boulders and rocks.

"I think you will find, should you ever return to your home, that yours is a dying breed. Those who embrace the truth of sin, and its permeation of the flesh, are those whom God has elevated into power. It is only natural that truth prevail—and that your views now return from whence they came." He glanced out beyond the stream into the desert's wavering heat and left their abode.

.   .   .

They never saw him again. But from that day on, they heard rumors from pilgrims who had trekked to the caves of other monks in the desert whose ideas were gaining currency. It was reputed that their Christianity was a new and pure Christianity, stripped of the sins of the past. Michella and Joseph knew that Cyprian had been garnering followers, preaching his dangerous philosophy to those who needed a code to live by, and infallible beliefs to guide them. Having lived amid the extremes of the desert, Michella and Joseph both recognized the difficulty of grappling with doubt. But they feared that the religion they held so dearly was being sanitized, and led down a dark path towards a singularity of convictions.

Soon after Cyprian left them, Michella and Joseph understood that their journey to the desert had ended. Without belongings to pack, they spent their final hours sitting before the stream that had sustained them their many months under the sun, pouring forth what gratitude they could to the Lord and to his earth.

Chapter 20

⌒

The trek back to their village passed as if it was a dream, and those they met upon arriving barely recognized them. They were thin, their skin deeply tanned by months of unending sun, and their clothes only vague recollections of what they had been when they left. Ahead of them, they spotted Thomas, speaking animatedly with a man in a black robe outside of the church.

"This church is the beating heart of the land!" they heard him say. "Though others may stray, we can not allow the coming storm to overtake this stronghold of truth and of love!"

They looked at one another, and quickened their pace.

"My son—your faith is strong, but misplaced," the man in black said. "We must turn our love to the truth—the truth that has been revealed to us."

"There is no truth in what you speak of! There is..."

Thomas saw them approaching out of the corner of his eye, and his eyes went wide.

"Mother Michella! Joseph!"

Thomas ran to meet them, embracing them both tightly. "Truly, the Lord has answered my prayers," he said to them excitedly. "Have you heard? The church—our church—espouses a new theology, one that is seeking to overtake us."

"This is no new theology, my son," the man in black called, stepping forward towards Michella and Joseph. "It is the religion of your Savior, washed clean of its sin and error."

He eyed Michella and Joseph, unsure of what to make of

the bedraggled couple. "My brother and sister, if you've come from the desert seeking food and water, you are welcome in the halls of our church."

Michella sensed the man was kind, but his very presence confirmed the worst of their fears. The beliefs that Cyprian had spoken of had spread, and now were taking hold in the church they had called home.

"I am Michella. I was the leader of this church, and I have returned to preach to my people."

The man's eyes flickered skeptically between her and Joseph.

"My name is Luke. I was told that this church had been abandoned," he said. "I was sent from Rome to see that its people are not left alone without a priest—without a connection to the Lord."

"Those who pray and love are always connected with God, and their priest is here to lead them as they need to be led,"

Michella spoke resolutely. The man in black opened his mouth, but did not speak. Thomas and Joseph stood by watching, as if two angels were grappling in the street before them. The man in black hung his head, biting his lip thoughtfully.

"I have been with your congregation for weeks now, and they have been hungry for the truth I have brought from Rome. Only a few cling to the scattered beliefs of the past," he said, looking at Thomas. "I am not here to displace you, and so I concede the pulpit if you claim it to be yours. But I must make sure that you do not lead these people astray."

He looked intently at Michella. "My sister, I have heard of your pilgrimage to the desert. I do not know what you found, but you have returned to a church whose beliefs have been clarified—to a people united around a common truth. A new and glorious era is beginning for the followers of Christ, and I am but a messenger, sent here in service of the one true message."

It was Michella who bowed her head now. As she listened to his words, she realized there weren't just radical zealots like Cyprian preaching this newfound "truth." This was a conscientious man, doing what he honestly believed was best before God. His faith and assurance were seductive, and in that moment, she feared for all that would unfold for her faith, and the others who held it.

Her breathing was deep and heavy. For the first time in three years, she felt tears sliding down her face, darkening the earth beneath her feet.

"Mother Michella?" Thomas's voice was filled with concern.

She wiped her face with a dusty sleeve, forcing a smile. "I'm sorry, Thomas." She took another breath and faced the man in black once more. "Luke, you may stay with us, but I fear given all you've said, you may not wish to do so. I know what I have been called by God to do. I have returned to preach and to lead the people of this village, and what I feel I must say will be said."

The finality in her voice was clear, and he stood only for a moment before nodding and folding his hands together.

"If it is to be so, then I will leave you to find your way. There are others who have never heard the Word, and who need Christ's help. I only hope that His truth will reveal itself to you in time."

With that, he turned and walked to the church, to gather his belongings, and left them.

.   .   .

From that moment on, Michella preached to her congregation the truths they had discovered in the desert:

that renouncing the importance of earthly things was indeed a key to entering the Kingdom of Heaven, but that relationships and the love that binds a man to a woman, a mother to her child, and Jesus to his people were to be glorified. Joseph was not the public speaker that she was, but with his wonderful measure of daily wisdom, helped preach practical ways of bringing worship into people's lives.

They stripped their small church of the gold and silver ornaments they had once coveted and replaced them with simple furnishings. They instructed people in the virtue of giving, and taught that love of the Lord was a rigorous and everlasting work. Their worship was joyous, lifting up their fellow believers and holding high the wonder of friendship and love and family ties that bound them. When they felt that their church had embraced these teachings and their truths, they turned church leadership over to the capable hands of Thomas and his wife, Rebecca. It was time, once again, to leave.

They walked out of their small town, as they had before, carrying few possessions. But this time the congregation of the church gathered around them, praying and laughing and wishing them well. Their next sojourn was to take them into the heart of civilization rather than into the wilds of the desert. There, they hoped that others would embrace the teachings revealed by God in the desert, and that Christ's love might blossom in hearts shrouded in darkness and confusion.

They wandered from town to town and region to region, never with more possessions than they could carry on their backs, always preaching their vision of a simple, humble Christianity. When they felt weakened by their travels, they retired to the wilderness to rejuvenate their spirits. They shared their beliefs, and where their ideas took root, they founded churches where women and men stood on equal footing, and where human relationships were glories to God. But they also encountered many Christians who disagreed fervently. Over the years, they argued and fought back against those who ascribed the philosophies of Augustine and Cyprian.

It had been clear to Michella since meeting Luke that theirs was a tenuous view of Christianity. The followers of the "new" Church were ardent and convincing people, and they had begun to wield enormous political power. But she knew that she could not deny the purpose God had set in her heart. Like Christ himself, there might be a day that the truths of the desert might arise again in the hearts of men and women.

When they became too weak and old to travel, they decided to seek out a final resting place where they could spend their remaining years and concentrate on teaching and writing. On their travels, they had heard of a church by the sea with a history and a congregation that would be amenable to their ideas, so they took a final journey to the southern part of Italia. They were welcomed at the church, where they lived ascetically, preaching when they were called to and putting their ideas into words. They died peacefully, on the same night, and were buried in the small graveyard overlooking the sea. Their writings can still be found in the library of the Church of Saints Priscilla and Aquila.

Chapter 21

S amuel finished reading the parchment for the second time. Between his readings, he searched the carefully organized shelves and found the writings of Michella and Joseph. There were both original scrolls and copies made carefully and painstakingly in Maria's fine, strong hand.

After first reading the history of the couple, he had doubted the existence of these writings' original copies. A part of him wanted to believe that they didn't exist—that this was all an elaborate ruse constructed by a band of heretics, the falseness of which would reveal itself before God. But another part of him was burning to know more. When he found the scrolls, the experience of touching the parchment and seeing Joseph's own handwriting affected him forcefully. Michella and Joseph had lived and breathed and believed fervently. They were misguided to be sure—they had to be—but their devotion had an impact on Samuel.

It was late and the night was cool. The candle flickered on the table in front of him, next to the remnants of his dinner. *No crumbs*, he thought to himself, with a short laugh. He sat for a long time, thinking of Michella and Joseph—and then of Maria. The tremors of a deep confusion had taken hold of his heart.

. . .

Samuel slept late the next morning. The work on the church had caught up with him, and when he woke, his body ached and his eyes hurt from reading late the night before. He lay in his bed looking up through the window at the rectangle of blue sky. In the distance, he could hear the sounds of the laborers atop the meeting hall, the creak of ropes and pulleys, and the crack of hammers. The air that came in through the window was warm, and the light it carried was a pure white, as if washed clean by the salt of the sea. Despite the soreness of his muscles, as the warmth of that light passed over him Samuel felt a deep peace washing over his tired body. He found himself longing to stay and hoping that he could bring change to these people, that he might remain to teach and live among them. Rome, far from the simple openness of this place, suddenly seemed a place of refuse, of tarnished gold and shadows. Just the thought of returning made him uneasy.

He knelt at the window and began his morning prayers, feeling the gentle sun and wind on his face. He crossed himself, and then rose to change from his sleeping clothes. With his bed made and his robes smoothed and presentable, he walked to the small kitchen of the church where he found a bowl of porridge, along with a wooden spoon and a small pot of honey that had been left for him.

There was something different today, but what it was, Samuel couldn't quite put his finger on it. Even the porridge he had eaten each morning prior, today seemed to announce itself with new flavor and sweetness. He ate eagerly, the peacefulness with which he had woken still with him. When he finished, he found a loaf of bread in the pantry, and soon he had eaten that as well, smearing it with the last of the honey. As he was adding the last dollop, through the window he saw a figure moving slowly away from the church grounds towards the edge of the bluff. It was Joshua.

Joshua was not aware he was being watched, and he walked slowly with his head bowed, his shoulders slumped, and his hands clasped behind him. In his heightened state of awareness, there was something in the way the older man moved that pained Samuel deeply. He watched Joshua for a long time as he stood at the edge of the bluff, looking out over the sea, ostensibly lost in deep thought.

Samuel brushed the crumbs off his shirt and walked out of the kitchen. He followed one of the gravel paths through the garden, and as he neared the bluffs, made his way slowly towards Joshua. The big man turned at his approach.

"Samuel," he said, straightening his posture, "we missed you this morning."

It was the same half-joking, half-serious tone that Samuel had gotten used to, but today, he resisted the urge to snap back. "It seems that our work along with my own study in the library got the best of me today, and my body is grateful for the day off."

"I see," said Joshua. He turned to look back at the horizon.

"I was eating breakfast this morning and I felt the peace of the Lord as I haven't felt it for some time. I saw you here through the window and I could not help but wonder..." Samuel trailed off, pondering his next words carefully. "It looked to me like you might want someone to talk to."

Joshua turned to him again. "An odd offer, coming from you, with what you have come here to do."

It was Samuel who now looked to the horizon. "Maybe you're right. I will not apologize for what I believe, but I suppose it has contributed to your problems."

"It has."

The two of them stood in silence on the precipice of the bluffs, waiting for the other to budge. Though Samuel felt sorry, he would not allow himself to say it, and he knew Joshua would not take the conversation any further. There was a reason for all of this, and it was up to him to find out what that was. "Do you think it's possible for us to have a real conversation about our beliefs? If I could just try to explain the position of the Pope and we could talk about it without becoming too emotionally attached to the discussion..."

"Is that what you have learned in Rome?" asked Joshua with a trace of bitterness in his voice. "To discuss with only your mind rationally? Never including the heart?"

"The mind must be the shepherd of the heart. The heart can be fickle, and lead men away from God."

"And what of the soul? Does that ever enter into your debates?"

Samuel paused. "The soul is my only concern, Joshua."

Joshua chuckled and shrugged slightly, raising up his hands. "Well, Samuel, you have mistaken me," he said more gently. "I am no thinker. What I believe, I believe with my heart, not with my mind. I leave that up to Anna and the other thinkers around me."

"It doesn't bother you not to use the greatest gift the Lord has given you?"

"He doesn't speak to me through syllogisms and fancy arguments, but through my heart and soul. What I feel there, I know He has given me."

Samuel knew that for all the arguments he could muster, all the points he could prove, and evidence he could provide —none of it could change how this man felt. He had met others like Joshua in the seminary: those who argued passionately, and whose words seemed to pour forth from the forges of a deep love and connection with the Lord. But all those men in time had their passion tempered by the logical reasoning of the Church. Joshua had no such guidance, and his heart, as pure as it might be, was lost unless the Church could open his mind to the truth.

"I appreciate your coming to speak with me, Samuel, but

I have come here to consider what sermon I might deliver tomorrow," Joshua continued. "I have never been—felt strong—before the pulpit. The words I wish to speak elude me."

"Perhaps I could help you," said Samuel eagerly. "If you tell me what you hope to say, I may be able to help you find those words." He felt this was an opportunity he could not miss, and he spoke excitedly. "It will be as it has been with our repairs—my pen, like my hammer, will go where you bid it go."

Joshua looked at him and then chuckled. "You are truly persistent, aren't you?"

"I have studied theology for most of my life and have prepared countless sermons and epistles. Minor epistles perhaps, but I have helped prepare them all the same."

"Samuel, the sermon I am composing deals with the strength we must have in the inevitable battle that is facing us against the Bishop of Rome."

Samuel fell silent. The peacefulness and joy he had felt were gone, sucked away as quickly as if they had fallen off the cliff onto the rocks below. He felt conflicted and confused, bitter about his own Church and about the Pope, and equally frustrated that his presence here had seemed to influence no one. He was a man of words and books and ideas. His life was not supposed to be like this, so connected to people and their fickle passions.

Samuel felt as if the wall between them that had been slowly coming down had been erected again. "My teacher, Flavius, has instructed me broadly, and I've learned since I was young that knowledge is to be shared, not hoarded."

"Flavius?" Once more, Joshua seemed to retreat to a distant place within his mind.

"Yes. Flavius is my mentor in Rome."

Joshua laughed, and the bitterness in his voice returned.

"The Lord is forever mysterious to me. Maybe he has chosen Flavius to destroy us, or maybe..." his voice trailed off.

"Do you know Flavius?" asked Samuel, confused.

"I believe I do. And if he indeed is the same man I know, I may even know things about him that you do not."

"What things? What did you mean by saying he would destroy you?" Samuel was bewildered, unsure what Joshua's words might mean.

Joshua sighed deeply, and brought his hands together above his stomach, rubbing his left palm gingerly with the thumb of his right hand

"Joshua, what do you know of Flavius?" Samuel implored him.

The older man's hands fell to his side, and he cleared his throat.

"When Anna was a young woman, she lived in Rome. She knew a man named Flavius there with whom she was," he hesitated, "close."

Samuel looked at Joshua, waiting for him to continue.

"They were very close and about to be betrothed. However, she had very strong views about her right to participate in the Eucharistic ministry. But many of the men around Flavius denounced women in the ministry because their active leadership roles in public assemblies went against society's view of women. Flavius chose to support the prevailing view. Anna left Rome at the time...but returned recently to seek his assistance. He had not changed and would not help her."

"What happened then?"

Samuel could see this was not something the old man discussed often. He hoped he was not pushing too far, but Joshua's reply confirmed his worry.

"You will not breathe a word of this to anyone. It was

said to you in confidence...and we do not wish to alarm the parishioners. Do you understand?"

Samuel hesitated, and the old man reached out to put a hand on his shoulder, imploring him. "It must be so, and I must have your word," he said.

"If that is the way it must be, I will not speak a word to anyone, not even Anna," Samuel replied, although as he spoke, he pictured Flavius and the sadness he often carried. He had rarely spoken of his own youth, and Samuel realized that, for all the time they had spent together, he hardly knew Flavius at all.

At this, Joshua smiled. "Perhaps, though, there is something you can help me with," he said. "At this point, there is no point in keeping secrets between us, and you heard through Maria, I'm sure, about the situation between myself and Anna."

Samuel nodded, still distracted.

"You are well read—certainly more so than me. Surely, you must have some knowledge of what wiser men than I have said about love and marriage—marrying again, whether it is appropriate, and after what time."

Samuel felt a deep and terrible sadness open within him. All of this, about Flavius and Joshua and Anna, was too much to take in. In his studies he had read little about love and the relationship between men and women, but he sensed that Anna and Flavius at one point must have had a deep love for each other and now Anna and Joshua seemed to have a deep love for each other. Was that the way with love, that something always seemed to get in the way? Was that what was happening between Maria and himself? If he returned to Rome, he would never be permitted to marry Maria. However, if he led a normal life here in the village, he could marry, listen to the sounds of babies, enjoy the camaraderie of his friends.

"I must go, Joshua!" and before Joshua could respond, Samuel had turned and was running back towards the church.

What is happening to me? Why can't I control myself? Once back in his room he shut the door, closed the shutters, and knelt to pray. But he could not concentrate. Thoughts and emotions rushed through him, bringing in both hope and resignation.

At the knock on his door, he nearly jumped out of his skin.

"Yes? Who is it?" he asked.

"Maria."

He froze.

"Samuel?" she said. "I saw that you had returned to your room and I thought we might go on that walk before I had to begin to prepare the evening meal."

He had completely forgotten. He opened his mouth to tell her he wasn't feeling well, but choked on the words. He moved instinctively towards the door and opened it. She stood in a simple brown dress, her hair pulled back; she was smiling at him, a charming smile that melted his heart. In that instant, all the voices in his head ceased, and there was only her, there before him.

Chapter 22

S amuel followed Maria out through the gardens along a path he had never been on before. It led across the road and up into the brown hills that surrounded the town, and then turned through an olive grove to run along high above the water. The leaves of the trees rattled dryly in the breeze, and the ground was parched and hard, even in the shade. After a short distance, the grove ended, and they found themselves at the top of a bare hillside. To their right was the sea, and to their left were the rolling yellow hills of the coast. Beyond the hills, a range of low mountains stood, covered with dusty green trees. They walked slowly now, following the dirt trail as it rose and fell along the crest of the bluffs overlooking the sea.

"You know, Samuel, I hardly know anything about you," Maria said, breaking the silence.

"What is it you want to know," Samuel asked shyly.

"Anything. Tell me about yourself, about Rome, about where you come from."

"Well, I am a student, I suppose, and a priest. I'm an aide to the Pope and have lived my life in Rome. I know very little of the world outside."

To his surprise, she laughed.

"What is it?" he replied, "Did I say something?"

"We are both very young, Samuel. Has it not occurred to you that we are not supposed to know everything in the world yet?"

"Really? That never occurred to me," Samuel said with a serious expression.

She looked at him skeptically, until she realized he might be serious. He held his straight face for as long as he could, until he broke down smiling. She laughed again, pushing his arm, and he laughed with her.

"In Rome I have been taught that what there is to know in the world can be learned through reading and discussion and prayer," he said. "I've done a tremendous amount of all three."

"And what is it that we outside of Rome have taught you?"

"I have found that people are more complicated than I thought."

"And your beliefs? We haven't corrupted you entirely, have we?"

She smiled, expecting him to laugh once again, but this time his expression was solemn.

"Despite there being much to learn of people and of the world, I know what I believe."

Samuel spoke more sharply than he intended and he glanced at her quickly to see if she had been offended. But she walked with her eyes straight ahead, and he could not read her expression. Still, he felt an intimacy developing between them, and he was beginning to enjoy it. Confused, he turned away from that thought.

"Is that why you have recommended those particular readings in the library?" he asked. "To sway me in my beliefs?"

Her face now mirrored his in intensity. "Of course it is, Samuel," she said, a note of annoyance in her voice. "Do you think you are the only one with passionate convictions? Do you think you are the only one who has read and debated?"

"I used to," he said, trying to make her smile.

"But you believe that women should not be allowed to

discuss and to read and to write about our faith...to preach the Gospel as they know it."

She stopped walking and turned to face him. He looked away. They were in a hollowed portion of the hills, open to the sea but protected from the wind. A heavy silence surrounded them.

"This is a debate I will have with the church elders," he finally said.

"Why not with me? Because I am a woman? Because I do menial tasks like cooking and cleaning the dishes?"

"No," he said, returning her steady gaze. "Because I don't want to argue with you."

"What if I want to argue with you?"

"I'm tired Maria. My life is full of arguments here. All I want is to walk and to be with you."

"You're right..."

He longed to take her in his arms but hesitated. "Let's walk up to the top of the hill."

She turned on her heel and they began to walk again. Relieved, his eyes watched the stony ground of the hill as it passed beneath his feet, but he could not shake the way she had looked, standing in the quiet dell behind them, her face flushed and indignant. "Tell me about you," he said.

"What do you want to know?" she asked.

"Did you grow up here?"

"No...my family lives in a village to the east."

"What brought you here then?"

"Lucia did," she said. "I heard her preach in my village five years ago. Every word she spoke—it felt like it was perfect. Not just true, but beyond that...as if she had access to some vast wisdom that others could only glimpse but not touch. I approached her afterward, and she told me that it was simply the power of the Lord speaking through her to me, and that the Spirit was available to any believer." She folded her arms and shook her head. "Two weeks later I left my home and journeyed here. I made the trek by myself, and asked to be taken into her congregation. I have been here ever since."

Samuel walked along beside her, unsure how to respond. For all the weakness he been brought up to believe women held, it was stories like this—stories of women like Alexandra and Michella—that jarred his sense of a woman's place in the universe. What could he, someone who had spent almost his entire life safely behind the four walls of a cloister and between the two ends of a book, possibly say to someone who had acted so passionately and with such resolution in the name of her beliefs.

"When Lucia died, it was as if a limb had been taken from each and every one of us," Maria continued. "But she is with the Lord now, and Anna has been a wonderful gift to our congregation—perhaps even more eloquent than Lucia in some ways."

"Did you ever see them again?"

"My family?"

"Yes."

She laughed. "Of course, Samuel. I visit them all the time…and we have very spirited debates about our religion. You see, my father is still stuck on the old ways. What about your family?"

"I have none. Only the Church."

"Oh," she replied, "I'm sorry to hear that."

"Don't be—all has happened as God has seen fit. The aspirations of the Church are my aspirations, and my hope is that I will dedicate the rest of my life to its causes," he said unconvincingly. "And what is it that you are searching for in life?"

"Are you sure you want to know?"

"Of course."

"I don't want to scare you—a woman actually wanting things."

"Maria, be serious."

"All right," she said. "I want a lover whom I can give myself to without reservation...a man I can give my heart to and accept his in return...a family to raise and nurture...and I also want to spread the Word of the Lord!"

He said nothing, a little intimidated by her boldness.

"I told you I would scare you."

"I've never heard a woman talk like that before."

She laughed. "Don't be so surprised. Love, children, marriage and all that it brings are among the joys the Lord has bestowed on us. I haven't realized those aspirations yet, but I know that I want them in my life. I also know that I can serve the Lord, but that in itself will not be enough for me. I want to be happy in every way, and I am not afraid to say it."

"That is remarkable...and you will not be swayed from your course?"

"I will not be swayed..."

She spun away from him and started back up the path. "Let's get to the top of this next hill!" she shouted back to him. "It has the best view on the whole walk."

Samuel jogged alongside the steep slope. *He was not prepared for this*, he told himself.

"See!" she said at the top, pointing. "From here you can see all the way back to the town and the church and all the way down the coast to the harbor village."

As he reached the top beside her, puffing harder than she was to catch his breath, the world lay before him as he had never seen it before. In the afternoon light, the sea shone like a blue jewel holding up the shimmering golden bands of the sun, and the land spread before in vast stretches of dry browns and whites. Samuel felt as if all the earth were visible from this point—as if this were how God must see the world. They embraced and stood for a long time with the breeze wrapping around them, both silent neither wanting to disturb the tranquility of the moment.

Moving apart, their eyes lingered for a moment and finally she spoke: "So is this how you see your life unfolding...in service of the Pope and the Church, walking where they bid you?"

"It is not as though I have no say in the matter," Samuel replied. "I have chosen this life, and I do as the Church bids me, because I believe in its teachings."

"And what happens when their demands run counter to your beliefs?"

"That will not happen."

"I have seen you in the library, Samuel. You are a lover of knowledge and the truth. What will you do when you are ordered to destroy all of those documents?"

A cloud passed in front of the sun, leaving them in the cool wake of its shadow.

"What makes you say that?" he asked.

"We aren't fools. We understand that the preferred method of the Roman Church for stamping out heresy is to destroy the writings that support the heresy, in order to eradicate the ideas that threaten their power. So much of early Christianity has been suppressed or destroyed that we fear if our writings are destroyed, they will be lost forever to history, and the diversity of our faith will not be known to Christians in the future." She paused. "You know you have been watched closely in your time here."

"I have?"

"Tell me the truth, Samuel. Do you have orders to destroy our writings if you find them to be in conflict with Rome?"

"Listen," he said. "I think..."

She interrupted him. "You need not speak if you are going to lie!"

They stared at each other and he felt embarrassed, his hands tingling with numbness.

"I was told that might be a possibility," he finally said. "But I am no fool either. It is clear that Anna and Joshua are aware of their position. They know that the Pope is dismayed by their practices. I do not believe that he will order the destruction of your documents—not if you renounce your ways and accept the orthodoxy of Rome. Gelasius is a powerful and ardent man, but he understands the importance of knowledge."

"Are you certain of this?"

"Yes," he said, but he knew that his voice betrayed him.

She shook her head sadly. "I am not sure our church will survive then. Always such differences between us," she said. "And our conversation always turns to them. Is there nothing else we can talk of?"

"The weather?" he suggested, similarly tired of such seriousness. "It certainly is dry again today."

"Ha," she said. "Not funny. There's a drought on, you know."

"I know," he said.

Before he knew exactly what he was doing, he stepped forward and kissed her on the lips. He closed his eyes. Her mouth lingered on his for just a moment. Then she drew back.

He looked at her and saw again how lovely she was. His passions burned beneath the surface, and he felt himself losing control. He turned away to look out at the shimmering sea.

"You can not conceal your distress, Samuel."

"I didn't expect this."

She looked at him reassuringly. "That's one of the joys of life…the unexpected."

"No," he said petulantly. "Predictable and understandable

has been the way I like my life."

But he did not resist when she took his hand in hers.

"Samuel," she said, "I can not tell you what to do with your life. No one but you can determine your path in life. But that is a matter between you and the Lord...not the Church, nor the Pope, nor anyone else in Rome."

"I couldn't have known...I could not have known the difficulties I'd face here."

"Difficulties!" she said. "You make it sound as if I am a torturer."

"You're not," he said quickly.

She stepped back. "You certainly are an odd choice for a messenger. It seems that an old and bitter man would do much better."

"I was given this task by my mentor, and I'm starting to understand the depths of this problem and his concerns. But do not underestimate me. My mission is to save the souls of those in this church, not the beliefs you hold, and if the word comes from Rome to deliver a message of excommunication, I will do that."

"But why?" she exclaimed, dropping his hand. "I know in my heart that you have doubts."

"Your views are not compatible with those of the Church."

"And what are your views, Samuel?" she implored.

He shook his head and put his hands up to press his temples for a moment. "Please, Maria," he said, "I'm only a messenger."

She sighed in frustration and moved away from him. He looked at her silhouette against the blue of the sea and felt again the ache in his chest.

"Maria," he said quietly, "will you tell me what you know of love?"

"Why?"

"Because I know very little of it."

She looked at him and touched his face. "It is something you feel. It's putting dreams together, it's struggling together, it's making love often. It lasts forever, and it is not always easy. From what I have seen of the world, the love of another person can be as trying as the love of the Lord. But it is wonderful and worthwhile and is the greatest gift that has ever been given to us."

"Does that leave enough room for God?"

"By truly loving each other, you love God. There is plenty of room for both!"

He moved close to her again and took both her hands in his, amazed at his own daring.

This time when he kissed her, he drew her in closely, holding her tightly in his arms. All the frustration that he felt, all the confusion, the anger, and the pain—all were transfigured as his lips met hers. They kissed for a long time, and he felt her tears warm upon his cheek. She pulled away from him, and they stood with their foreheads pressed together.

"What does this all mean, Samuel?" she asked him.

"I don't know—I just...all I care for right now is this moment."

Together, they walked home quietly, holding hands until they reached the outer limits of the church grounds. Samuel wished he could delay the setting of the sun—that they could keep walking together over the endless hills until they both grew weary. But as they approached the church, he despaired about what was to come. At the doorway to the kitchen, she paused to give him the chance to speak.

"Maybe tomorrow," he said, suddenly shy again, "or the next day..."

"I would love to," she replied. "You know where to find me."

"And you me," he said, and with a wave, she was gone.

Back in his room, he lay on the bed for a long time, looking up at the ceiling. Thoughts of Maria clashed with thoughts of his mission, while the voices of those in the stories he had just read raged against the scholars he had built his life around.

He prayed for guidance. Perhaps, he thought, it was time to write another letter to Flavius. The old man had been like a father to him, and had guided him through all the trials of his youth. Samuel had never been this confused, and his thoughts and emotions never in such an uproar as they were now. He no longer knew what to believe about himself, about women, about love, and about his Church. Flavius was the only person he felt he could trust.

After all, Samuel thought, *it seems that Flavius does know something of love.*

Chapter 23

⌒

T hat night Samuel left the candle burning in his room and kept the door closed and barred. He waited until he could hear that everyone else was eating the evening meal and crept quickly out the window, covering it behind him. He paused for a moment, looking out from behind the bushes below the window, fairly sure he had not been observed. When his eyes had adjusted to the darkness, he rose and made his way stealthily through the night to the library. Even though his intentions were benign, he did not like the idea of being watched while he read, or of having his choice of readings dictated to him. As he passed the kitchen and the room where Maria slept, he paused, contemplating her words and their walk along the hill. But he knew what he must do.

In the library, he searched the shelves carefully for the oldest documents he could find, finally settling on a set of scrolls titled "The History of Patricia and of the House-Church Which She Founded."

This is exactly what I need, he thought. The more recent history of Christianity was well known to him. The monastics and their strange practices, the waves of persecution, the famous martyrs like Saint Perpetua and Saint Felicity who gave their lives—all of these were well chronicled. Even the participation of women had been documented in Rome, although he had never encountered stories the likes of which he had found here. But the house-churches were much older. This is what he needed: a look at the historical roots of the issue. Standing in the library with

174

the ancient scrolls in his hands, he admitted that he needed it as much for his own peace of mind as he did to satisfy the demands of Gelasius. His time with Maria, the peace of this church, the stories he had read—as much as he wanted to deny it, all were beginning to take their toll on his beliefs.

He felt his hands begin to tremble and turned his mind away from that thought. He put the scrolls on the table, nervous that he might damage them. The thought occurred to him that he only had until morning to uncover the truths of this library. As soon as they knocked on his door and he did not answer, they would come here to look for him. He could take the scrolls off the church grounds somewhere, or bring them back to his room to read and conceal them—but they would certainly come here and discover which documents he had taken. They had not disturbed him yet, despite Maria's claims that he had been watched, so what was the point of going anywhere else?

Sighing, he suddenly felt very foolish for having climbed out his window. He would have to climb back through it when he wanted to go to bed, and was more likely to get caught in the process. *No turning back now*, he thought. He sat down at the table, and the first scroll unrolled stiffly in his hands. Holding it delicately, he began to read.

. . .

"Patricia! Patricia!"

It was her mother calling to her. The seven-year-old had grown accustomed to wandering from her parents' view, but she had also come to recognize the tone in her mother's voice that meant it was time to come home.

"I'm here, Mother!"

She came running from around the corner, laughing at the worried look on her mother's face.

"Where were you, child? You know how it worries me when you run off!"

Her girlish look of innocence and penitence was irresistible. "Mother, I was only off a short distance in the woods. I like it out there. He speaks to me in the wind."

Her mother scooped her up and gave her daughter a bewildered smile. "Does he? And who is that?"

"Our Father in Heaven. I see Him sometimes as He walks among the trees. He glows, mother, and He is always smiling at me."

"Really, now? And how do you know it's Him?" her mother pressed on, concerned for her daughter's well-being.

"He has told me. He tells me that one day I shall be a great leader for His Church."

Her mother looked up to the sky and sighed heavily. "My Lord, I know not what to make of this child." She turned to look at her daughter, whose eyes sparkled in the bright sunlight. "Inside with you, now! Supper's on the table, and you don't want to keep your father waiting!"

. . .

Patricia was the daughter of Timothy and Cecelia, Romans who had converted to the new religion of Christianity. They lived in a town north of Joppa on the eastern edge of the Mediterranean Sea and were members of a small community of Christian believers. This community met frequently on a ship owned by a merchant and trader named Bartholomew, for it was only in such a place that they could meet to escape the notice of the Roman authorities. Those presiding in Rome had begun to fear this new religion, believing that it attracts troublemakers and insurrectionists who want to overthrow the empire.

As soon as Patricia was old enough, her parents decided

it was time to take her to these meetings. They believed that their daughter was blessed with divine gifts, and felt that only in the company of fellow believers could she grow in the ways and love of Christ. To keep their meetings secret, though, the congregation had to move quietly down the wharves and onto the ship, travelling alone or in pairs, never in large groups.

Thus, that night Patricia set off with her father while her mother waited behind. They went forward with no light, finding their way in the darkness across the wooden pier and up onto the deck of the ship as it rocked with the tide. The tense walk was filled with the sound of ropes creaking in the darkness. At the entrance to the boat, a door opened in a flash of orange light. Her father then muttered a phrase she could not hear, and a man's dark eyes stared down at Patricia. Though she could not see the man's face, there was something in his eyes that told her he was smiling. With a loud creak of the wooden door, they were ushered into the belly of the great boat.

Here, the atmosphere was very different. The large hold was dimly lit, and the assembled people intermingled lightheartedly. Her mother arrived shortly after, and sat with her family, exchanging news with their neighbors, waiting for everyone to assemble.

"Good people of the church-of-the-sea!" a booming voice sounded.

Patricia looked around, her heart racing, and saw a large man standing before the group. His collared shirt was unbuttoned beneath a ragged blue vest, and many curly hairs poked out from his exposed chest. His beard was thick and wild, and many around her tittered as the man raised his hands for silence.

"Let us give thanks and pray."

She looked over to her father, who smiled reassuringly.

He gestured that she mimic him, as he bowed his head and clasped his hands together. Patricia prayed most nights before she went to bed, but here among these adults and strangers, gathered in this strange and wonderful place, she felt a new sensation wash over her as she closed her eyes.

A minute passed, and no one spoke. Patricia found it hard to keep her focus on her prayers, as she waited anxiously for someone to break the silence. She felt as if each movement of the boat, each breath of her parents and those next to her, made a ripple in the air washing over her skin.

"Amen," the large man's voice sounded again. He walked to the center of the hold and gazed out upon the forty or so who had gathered in a circle around him, and smiled broadly.

"Well, most of you know me, but for those who don't, my name's Bartholomew, and this here is my boat. If you're here, it's likely that you've heard the good news, and have come to worship in the name of our Lord and Savior come to earth, Jesus Christ."

He continued speaking, as he walked over to a table that had been set up towards the back of the boat, grabbing one of the loose scrolls that rested there.

"Now, we don't have much here by way of money or food, but what we do have is the Word as it's fallen from His lips, and been caught by His closest disciples. I'll do what I can to do justice to these holy texts, as they have been gathered from some of the house-churches throughout the land. Yet, as many of you know, these churches are forced, as are we, to hide from the watchful eye of the emperor."

He looked with great seriousness at those who sat before him, before settling his gaze finally upon Patricia. She shivered, and he winked at her.

"We will begin today with the Gospel of Christ's disciple Luke. Luke tells us of the holy birth of our Lord, and thus, we begin our tale in a manger, far off in Jerusalem."

As Bartholomew spoke, Patricia found herself filled with the fire of his reading. Though he seemed to read the story as it was written, he swung his arms and hands, as if drawing the story in the air before them. The congregation, circled around the large man, all sat on the edge of their seats, hanging onto each gesture, each word. There were long stretches where he hardly glanced down at the scroll before him, spinning in slow circles to face each man and woman who sat before him.

Patricia looked at her parents, whose faces were filled with hope as they followed Bartholomew's movements and words. As she took in all that was going on around her, she found it difficult to follow the words as they were spoken aloud—but even so, Patricia felt she understood the meaning of the tale Bartholomew wove. As his voice swung in grand arcs, filling the hold of the boat, she felt herself being lifted, moving in concert with the boat and with the beat of her own heart.

With a final raise of his hands, Bartholomew dipped his head back, almost whispering the final words of Luke's Gospel.

"King of kings, host of hosts—our Lord was born on earth, that we might never die again, and be with Him always in his Kingdom of Heaven."

He closed his eyes, and his words hung in the air as beads of sweat dripped down his face. Those around Patricia bowed their heads and reached out to hold hands with those around them.

"Brothers and sisters," he whispered. "Let us join in the strength of our prayer, and let Him know of our love."

Patricia felt chills and got goose bumps as those around her began humming softly. She peeked up at her father, and though he did not open his eyes, he squeezed her hand and smiled. Some in the great circle began to sway, while others began to shake their heads or twitch their shoulders. The hums grew louder, and the hold began to reverberate with the variegated tone of their joined voices. Patricia squeezed her parents' hands tightly, determined not to be afraid. As the humming grew ever louder, she was not sure if she herself was adding to the din with her own voice, or if the sound was simply passing through her and filling her.

Nearby, a woman launched into a fit, clutching at the air as she rolled on the floor. Patricia's eyes snapped open, and she felt her mother rise up. She clung to her father's arm as the woman began to mutter strange words, uttering sounds and syllables that Patricia had never heard before. Her mother, though, extended her hands out above the woman and turned her head, scrunching her eyes tightly as she listened intently to the woman.

"Our Holy Spirit Sophia speaks through this woman!" her mother shouted above the din. "She says...." Cecelia leaned in closer, as the hums grew ever louder. "She says that with new birth comes new death. And...and in the light, a new darkness emerges. To reach the light, we must love the dark...the dark edges."

The woman was now pulling at her own hair, a look of exhaustion on her face. Patricia shrieked and buried her head in her father's shoulder.

"He will return to us again. His disciples still walk among us. New converts are born to us each day from the darkness! I am with you! I am with you!"

As suddenly as it had begun, the hums ceased and only the sound of heavy breathing remained. The woman lay still upon the floor, and Cecilia kneeled beside her, one hand upon her forehead and the other pressing delicately into her palm. Patricia peeked out at the people around her, and saw each with their eyes still closed, their chests rising and falling with long breaths.

"The time has arrived for us to share the meal as our sign of peace, love, and community. Let us break bread and share the bread," Bartholomew said and passed the bread to the congregation. "Let us pour wine and share the wine," he said and passed the wine to the congregation. "Just as the bread was broken, so was his body broken for us. And just as the wine was poured, so was his blood poured for us." Patricia did not fully understand what was happening but felt she was a part of the community as she ate bread and sipped a little wine. "By eating the bread and drinking the wine, Christ makes good His promise to be present among those who are gathered in His name." Bartholomew paused to give all a chance to share in the bread and wine.

"Brothers and sisters," Bartholomew said once more, "we are blessed to hear from the Holy Spirit, and to give thanks to our Lord Jesus. As we open our eyes, let us embrace another as He has embraced us. Let us go forth, and bring His love to a world in need of good news."

With that, her father stood up, and all those around her began to exchange hugs and handshakes, blessing one another and nodding sincerely with their thanks.

"Patricia," her mother called. The woman she had tended to was now sitting up, drinking the water that Cecilia held before her. "Come here, my darling."

She walked anxiously forward, afraid that the woman on the floor might again lose control.

Her mother handed the bowl of water to the woman, and took Patricia lovingly into her arms, speaking softly in her ear. "My sweet girl—I am proud of you. Tonight was a very big night for you."

"What happened, mother? Is she okay?"

Her mother laughed softly, leaning back to face her daughter. "Yes, my dear. She is very well—though a little tired."

"What was that? Everyone...everyone was making noise, and she started screaming on the floor. I...I was scared and couldn't watch," Patricia said, hanging her head.

"What happened we call *glossalalia*," her mother replied. "It's a long word, and well...you need not worry about that. All you need to know is that the Holy Spirit sometimes speaks directly through those who embrace our heavenly Father."

Cecilia saw that her daughter was confused, and she kissed her on the cheek. "All will become clear in time, Patricia. You are very special, and I am very proud of you."

Patricia hugged her mother tightly, and as she looked up over her mother's shoulder, she saw Bartholomew looking towards her once again. The burly man winked once more before turning back to converse with his congregation.

. . .

As Patricia grew older, she soon became accustomed to the readings delivered in secret out upon the water and the wild prayers within the hold of the boat. Bartholomew had collected a number of documents from around the empire, and each of them told the story of Jesus a bit differently. The Gospel of Luke was always Patricia's favorite as a child, but as she grew and matured, she began to take to many of the others, like the Sayings Gospel, the Gospel of Mark, and the Gospel of Mary Magdalene.

The Sayings Gospel focused primarily on the parables of Jesus rather than the story of his life, and Patricia soon knew many of them by heart. In the woods, when her parents weren't watching, she recited these tales to her own private congregation of rocks and trees, answering their questions as Bartholomew did, and waving her hands in the air to mimic his grand telling.

The Gospel of Mark, which began with Jesus as an adult, said almost nothing about His family or childhood, and ended with Mary of Magdala returning to the cave where Jesus was buried to be told by an angel that He was not there. Because the story wasn't as straightforward as Luke's Gospel, Patricia grew up preferring the simplicity with which Luke expressed the life of Jesus. But as she grew into young adulthood, and the words of Mark became clearer to her, she began to feel the power of his story, and of the life that he led. Mark's life as a disciple was one of total service to others, and he seemed to preach that suffering in Christ's service was to glorify His life. Such devotion filled her with a desire to go out into the world that she might become a suffering servant of the Lord. She felt sometimes, after reading from Mark, that she would burst with the love of God she felt inside, and with her wish to tell everyone she could about Jesus.

She was also enthralled with the writings of Mary Magdalene who had shared a special relationship with both Jesus in his lifetime and with the Christ spirit after the death of Jesus. Mary, as the first witness to the Resurrection, was considered by the apostle John to be the founder of Christianity.

Often, when Bartholomew had concluded reading from one of the Gospels, someone from the congregation would rise and read from other writings of important Christians. Paul's letters to the congregations he had founded were read frequently, as were selections from a group of texts called the Didache—the collections of teachings from all twelve of Jesus' apostles.

Patricia's family had copies of the Gospel of Matthew, the Signs Gospel, the Gospel of Thomas, the Gospel of Mary, the Apocalypse of John, and the teachings of Barnabas —but many of these texts their congregation chose not to read. To many, they seemed to be speaking to groups very different from their own. Some, like the Apocalypse of John and several other apocalypses, spoke in metaphors of grand battles between the children of light and children of darkness. Patricia knew from her parents that these apocalyptic accounts of good and evil and the eventual triumph of Christ were very comforting to the terribly persecuted congregations in Rome—groups who were forced to meet in catacombs under city streets, and who risked their lives every time they stepped outside. Patricia's church was one of the lucky ones.

Despite the narrowed focus of her own church, Patricia read voraciously, taking in the teachings of all who spoke of Christ. When Patricia was thirteen, a preacher named Julia came and stayed with her family.

Julia was ancient, wizened, and a gentle soul, and Patricia took to her immediately, desperate for knowledge of the outside world. They often spent long hours together as Patricia did her chores, cleaned the house, or fetched vegetables from her family's garden. The old woman never seemed to tire of her questions, and walked slowly with her hands held behind her back as Patricia busied herself about the house.

"How did you decide to become a preacher?" Patricia asked her shyly, as she hung the last of the laundry outside the house.

The old woman's voice creaked with age, but she spoke slowly and clearly. "Child, no one decides to become a preacher, just as no one decides to become a Christian. The Holy Spirit commands it of you, and you can not say 'No.' Sophia, as you call her, commands that I preach far and wide until I take my last breath. Who am I to refuse her?"

"But when did you first know? When did you first hear that voice?"

Julia hummed, as if she were reaching far back into the long stretches of her memory. She coughed harshly, and Patricia leapt to her side.

"Are you all right?"

"Yes, my child," she said, dropping her hand back to her side. "It seems my body shall only be a vessel for His light for so much longer."

She chuckled and went on.

"To answer your question—I am one of the lucky few that was touched directly by our Lord. Just days prior to his crucifixion on the hill, I met Jesus and heard him preach." The old woman's eyes began to fill with tears as she spoke. "He reached out and placed His hand upon my head," she said, reaching out her own hand as she recollected the moment. "He was so...so kind...so pure in every way. It felt as if He would lift me from where I stood and bring me directly with Him to Heaven. What lasted mere moments felt to me a lifetime in His presence."

Her shoulders relaxed, and she came back to the present. "I knew then that my life was for Him alone. Our God is limitless and unknowable, my child—we can only act knowing what He places in our hearts. That is where God speaks to me."

Patricia looked lovingly at the older woman. She, like Mark, had seen and been with the Lord, and had given her life to His service.

That night, Patricia began to pray aloud that she too might be called to preach.

· · ·

For many years the little church went on this way, until the spring of 89 A.D. That year Bartholomew journeyed to Alexandria on a spiritual mission. He was gone for five months, and upon his return he announced he had been closeted with several church leaders there, receiving new Christian teachings that women would no longer be permitted to preach or have authority over men. These teachings were like a tidal wave that swept over their little church. Bartholomew, now clean shaven and buttoned up, declared that it was the duty and the requirement of women to be silent during worship meetings. The teachings had originated in Rome where the bishop claimed to be the heir to the apostle Peter. Bartholomew now stood at the front of his congregation rather than at its center.

As he spoke of these new teachings, murmurs and complaints began to break out among the crowd, which had grown to near a hundred since Patricia's first service.

"Are you actually saying that I am not to translate the gift of tongues?" Cecelia asked, aghast.

"Yes," Bartholomew replied.

"So I am to ignore the Holy Spirit?"

"No. I am just saying that you..." He faltered. "I think that we should now understand that the Holy Spirit will no longer call on women to speak in public."

A gasp went through the assembly. An elderly man stood and cleared his throat. "I don't want to misunderstand you, brother, but it sounds like you have taken it upon yourself to decide who and where and how the Holy Spirit will call us. I think that's a dangerous presumption. The Spirit moves where She wills."

A murmur of agreement went through the people gathered there.

A young woman with a toddler on her hip stood next. "We do not choose what gifts of the Spirit we are given. God chooses. If God chooses a woman to preach or speak in tongues, are you really saying we should ignore God?"

"No. I am saying that we must assume that it is not truly

God's work."

What had been a restrained din now erupted into uproar.

"Please," Bartholomew pleaded, "brothers and sisters, be reasonable. The leaders in Rome and Alexandria are just trying to strengthen our infant church—to bring us together. We are weak and vulnerable, outlaws in the Roman Empire. We must band together and listen to their leadership. They just want us to be safe, to not draw so much attention to ourselves. Women going around and preaching in public— it's a scandal to the Romans."

"Since when has the message of our Lord been about safety?"

"We must," Bartholomew replied, "try to blend in with Roman society."

"And we women are your bartering chip?" someone shouted.

"I don't think we should look at it like that."

"Then how should we look at it?" cried a voice from the back of the boat.

"Please calm down. Our Christian faith is growing and spreading. We must come together as a faith, unified instead of disparate little churches. We must band together and follow the churches in the big cities like Rome, Alexandria, and Jerusalem, for our own good and for our safety. It will help us to spread the Gospel. We must trust the leaders in Rome. They are wise, well read, and inspired."

"If these men are close to God as you claim they are," Cecelia said, "then they are not close to the God that I know. The God I know would not ask me to be quiet when proclaiming my love for Him. The God I know would not ask that I alter my ways to suit the whims of men. This God you speak of—this God who would ask that we submit to our captors—He is not the God we have worshipped at this church."

Bartholomew persisted. "It has long been understood by learned people that men's rational nature equips them to be leaders, while women's docility constitutes them to be followers, submissive, and obedient. All they are asking is that we recognize that this is a tenet of our religion as well. Can't you understand that?"

There was silence in the hull of the boat.

"I will trust you, brother," said the agitated man at the back.

"We'll try to understand," the mother with the toddler added.

But neither of Patricia's parents could understand, and neither could Patricia, although she was still quite young then. They were aghast at this turn of events and were even more perturbed at how many men and women just accepted it.

. . .

Patricia's parents had opened their house for those of their congregation who still believed in the old ways. Only a handful sided with them, while the rest were drawn by Bartholomew and the influence his beliefs seemed to be gaining in the outside world. Those who ascribed to his new philosophy vowed to continue meeting on his ship, their women listening and praying but not speaking. Many of them broke their friendships with Patricia's family, and as the months went on, they even refused to acknowledge them in public. Patricia's family and a few others persevered with their own meetings, praying and teaching what they believed to be the truth.

Chapter 24

T he house of her parents was a large and pleasant structure at the edge of the town. It was set back behind their flax fields and screened from view by a small grove of olive trees they tended. A large arbor stood behind the house, which they had built intentionally to conceal the religious gatherings from the road, and those who attended their services entered by way of this arbor. Patricia's parents shared the leadership duties in the congregation, and under their guidance the house-church began to grow rapidly, attracting new members little by little every week.

Patricia, for her part, did everything she could to learn about the evolving legs and arms of Christianity. She began to travel and attend meetings of the other house-churches in the region, and was amazed at the diversity of beliefs she encountered. There were churches that were run by women and churches in which women were not allowed to sit in the same area as the men. There were churches that claimed to have special secret knowledge, or *gnosis*, available only to the initiated, and others where claims to "special" knowledge were deemed prideful and contrary to the Lord. Some Christians taught that the material world around them was not in fact real and that Jesus had not actually taken the flesh and blood form of a man but only appeared to have done so, while still other Christians taught that all people had the ability to become divine, as Jesus was. Some Christians taught that the world was essentially good, others that it was bad and incapable of salvation without Jesus. Some taught that God was unknowable and distant from humans, while still others taught that God dwelled in each person's soul. Some taught that salvation came from within, while others taught that Jesus alone could bring salvation. The diversity of Christianity confused her.

Every church she visited claimed to have its roots in the earliest days of the religion, and many claimed to be in contact with larger churches in other places whose beliefs they shared. There were dozens of different documents and letters that the churches placed reliance on. Most relied on the Gospels of Mark, Luke, Matthew, and John and the letters of Paul, but others relied on the Gospels of Thomas, James, and Mary of Magdalene. At first, Patricia was mystified, but she soon grew to understand what was causing so much dissension in the Church.

She began to feel a stirring within herself to preach, remembering well the passion and commitment of which Julia had spoken to her once. Amid this growing milieu of Christian thought, she believed that there must be a middle ground that lay closest to the truth—as if each church were chipping away at different parts of the same sculpture. She often asked her parents if she could deliver a short sermon during their weekly ritual and celebration, and when they consented, she spoke passionately. Soon she became revered by the congregation. Many found it hard to believe that one so young could display such wisdom and insight into the words of Jesus and the works of the disciples.

As her sermon came to a close one day, she caught out of the corner of her eye a shock of dark hair of a male standing towards the back of the arbor by one of its most robust fig trees. It was not the first time she had seen this man standing by the back of the congregation. He appeared to listen very closely to everything that was said, but she often saw him scowling or shaking his head in disagreement. He was also, she could not help but notice, very handsome. Several times she told herself she would speak to him at the conclusion of the service, but he always disappeared immediately.

Today, she kept an eye on him, and when he darted out among the fig trees back to town, she followed him stealthily, always just out of sight. He wound his way through the brown buildings and the ramshackle huts of the town until, with a sharp right-hand turn, he arrived at the edge of the market. Patricia had passed by here before, and she knew this was a place where many came to proselytize their religions.

There were many men here, and even a few women scattered among them, talking loudly about everything from the worship of Ra to the benefits of sacrifices to Mercury. She stopped for a moment to listen with an amused smile on her face, when a silence fell upon the crowd. As she looked to find the cause, she spotted the dark haired young man, now standing above the gathered townspeople on a gnarled old tree stump.

"All you people—all who seek a life everlasting, and all the true riches of this world—hear me!" he shouted, raising his fist emphatically.

Those in the crowd responded: "Tell us, brother! Tell us!"

"Much have I seen, and much do I know," he went on. "Believe what you will, but there is one God, and He has come down to us to save us all."

"Tell us more!" came shouts from the crowd.

"I tell you—I have felt Him deep within my soul. Jesus Christ, Lord of all on earth, and His Father, creator of all in the heavens above—He asks only that you give yourself to Him. Do so, and you will walk with your heavenly Father in His eternal kingdom. But do not, then hear me when I say such souls will burn forever in the torments of hell!"

The cheers of the crowds continued as he preached

movingly of the teachings of Jesus. As he spoke, he placed
special emphasis on the teachings as they had been handed
down by Paul, the greatest of all Jesus' disciples. Patricia
walked in closer, drawn in by the passion with which he
spoke. Though in recent years the Roman garrison near the
town had been greatly reduced in numbers, she knew it was
still hazardous to proclaim one's faith in Christianity this
blatantly. As she neared the stump, he caught her eye and
smiled down at her with a wink, never losing his momentum
or train of thought. She flashed back to her first service in
Bartholomew's boat as a little girl, when the large man had
picked her out of the crowd. A chill ran down her spine.

The young man's voice was mesmerizing, and she
quickly realized that he knew more about the disciple Paul
and his writings and letters than anyone she had ever met.
When he finished his impassioned sermon and descended
from his makeshift pulpit, he shook hands and embraced
those who lingered to speak with him. Slowly the crowd
disseminated and drifted off to other parts of the town.
Patricia waited until all had left, and stepped forward to
introduce herself.

"My name's Patricia," she said.

"I know," he replied, taking a long drink of water. She
was surprised at the shyness in his voice.

"And yours?"

"Antonio," he said, nodding to her.

"You preach fervently," Patricia continued. "I've seen
you at our services."

"If I were half as eloquent as you, I would be happy," he
said while dumping the rest of the water on his head,
whipping his hair from side to side.

She stepped back to avoid getting wet.

"How do you know so much about Paul?" she asked after
a moment. "You talk as if you were intimately acquainted

with him."

"I am from Tarsus, as he was," Antonio replied. "For the last several years I have travelled widely, in his footsteps, learning as much about him as possible. There are still many places where stories of him abound that are not known elsewhere. I believe he was the greatest of the apostles and that his words need to be shared with the world."

"Don't you worry about the Romans stumbling upon you?"

"Why would I?"

Patricia eyed him skeptically. "Surely you must be aware of the dangers of being a Christian!"

He shrugged. "The soldiers in the garrison here don't care what I do. But if the Romans feel that they need to take me, then they will do so."

Despite the nonchalance of his words, Patricia saw sadness in his eyes as he spoke. She felt drawn to him, as if she might be his answer to a long sought-after yearning.

From that day on, Patricia and Antonio began to meet frequently. They walked together through the town, and spoke at length after the meetings in her parents' house-church. She often went to listen to him preach, and implored him to soften his rhetoric so as not to attract the attention of the authorities. He refused and continued to deliver his orations in a very open and blatant manner.

During their time together, he had informed her of his intentions to remain celibate, following the words of Paul. She also found that he was of a split mind about the participation of women in the church.

"Our religion is going to explode across the face of the world," he told her. "It will be a beacon to the downtrodden everywhere, for women as well as men. But it will continue to incur the wrath of the Romans as it does, and when this happens, we'll need the martial spirit of men and their rationality to lead us. Don't you see? Women are fine congregation members, but as the apostle Paul said: 'For it is shameful for a woman to speak in church.'"

"And if it ever does come to pass that we become a movement of more than a few people," she retorted, "where will we be without the patience and gentleness of women? Might we not become another empire of our own, run by men who embrace only the harsher side of our religion?"

This discussion soon became the focus of an extended debate between them. Patricia argued that Jesus' message was one of inclusion, pointing out that Jesus welcomed people whom others shunned, like lepers, prostitutes, and women, while Antonio stubbornly clung to the reasoning of Paul.

"Jesus treated everyone equally," Patricia argued as they ate bread and cheese and olives together one afternoon.

"But he chose only men to be among the twelve apostles," he countered.

"Yes, but Mary of Magdala was the apostle to the apostles! Jesus chose to appear to her first after He rose from the dead. Jesus chose a woman to be the first to preach the good news of His resurrection. How can you say women should not preach when Christ Himself chose Mary as the one to tell all the others?" As she spoke, she threw an olive at him, hitting him squarely on the nose.

"Patricia, it isn't just me who says this!" he said, scooping up the olive and popping it into his mouth. "Your aim is awful by the way."

He threw an olive at her, and she caught it in her mouth. The two were doing more than debating; they were falling in love. Discussion about religion had but become an excuse for them to meet.

Patricia rolled her eyes and pretended to throw another olive in his direction before dropping it in her own mouth. "I have two responses to your adherence to Paul's teachings—three, actually. First, it isn't at all clear that Paul wrote that particular letter. It's likely that one of his assistants wrote it and simply signed his name. Second, the statements in that letter completely contradict what Paul says in other letters. How can a man go from telling all women to be silent in church to saying that 'in Jesus Christ, there is no Jew or Gentile, male or female'?"

Antonio raised an eyebrow, and let out a long sigh. "I'm not sure, but I gather you're going to tell me."

"That's right," she replied, this time throwing an olive at his knee, "but I haven't even finished my point. Paul often acknowledged the leaders of the Christian communities at the end of his letters. Among the leadership that he acknowledged were many women. Of the twenty-eight prominent people that Paul saw fit to greet, many were women. Prominent women greeted by Paul were Prisca, Junia, Mary, Tryphaena, Tryphosa, Persis, Julia, Olympas, and Nereus!"

Antonio shook his head. "You're an excellent preacher, you know..."

"Thank you," she said, her nose held jokingly in the air.

"...for a woman," he said with a twinkle in his eye. He jumped out of her grasp, and she leapt up to punch him in the arm.

"No, really!" he said, holding his arms up as she pelted him with olives. "You bring up some interesting and important points, but I am still not convinced. Men and women have different natures. And..." he trailed off.

"And what?" she said, her hands resting on her waist.

"And women's nature is gentler, softer...weaker."

"I pray, Antonio, that you will see how wrong you are," Patricia replied. Their conversation had suddenly grown very serious, and she worried that he might never be convinced of the truths she felt so clearly in her own heart. *If my own Antonio can't be brought to see the light, what hope do we have?* she thought to herself.

As Patricia and Antonio continued to preach, the upsurge of Christian churches in the area began to attract the attention of the Romans. A soldier named Maxius was put in charge of the garrison in Joppa, and with him, the number of troops stationed there grew. Maxius had made it clear that he had a great hatred of Christians, and that the only religion he ascribed to was the paganism of the Roman state, where the emperor sat as the supreme deity throughout the land. Anyone caught practicing Christianity or preaching the faith was to be publicly scourged. If the action amounted to sedition, the violator would be executed.

When Patricia caught word of Maxius's growing power, she grew fearful for Antonio, who still frequented the market to preach to the following he had garnered. She hurried to see him, and found him waiting for her by the old stump, where once he had stood so boldly.

"Antonio—" she began.

"I've heard," he said, his face dark with anger. "This place is closed to me. I have no choice but to continue my wanderings."

"Antonio, you can stay. My parents—they can protect you."

At this, his face seemed to contort, split between anger and sadness.

"I'm not so sure that's true," he said.

She looked at him with concern. "What do you mean?"

He did not respond.

"Antonio, what do you mean that's not true?!" she shouted. "What do you mean that's..."

"They are not safe, Patricia!" he shouted back. She started to tremble as he spoke. "There are some churches in the area that are in league with the congregation of Jerusalem, and political bargains have been struck with the Roman governor. As long as they keep their services out of the public eye, they will be spared. Sadly, your parents' congregation is not one of them. Their church has been marked for destruction by Maxius."

Chapter 25

⌒

Maxius had acted more quickly than anybody could have expected. By the time Patricia and Antonio reached the arbor, soldiers had surrounded the house. At the sight of them, Patricia and Antonio left the road and plunged into the olive groves, sneaking among the trees until they reached the rows of trellised grapes behind the house. Unseen, they approached close enough to observe Maxius standing before a frightened congregation.

They stood in a line, surrounded by a cordon of Roman soldiers. As Maxius spoke, his voice was quiet and dismissive, as if he were speaking with children who deserved to be chastised.

"...sedition is a crime punishable by death," they heard him say as they approached. "The power to judge sedition has been granted to me as an officer of the empire, and my judgment is that your so-called teachings are explicit in their treason. To deny the divinity of our emperor is to ask for your own death."

He smiled and clasped his hands behind his back. "However," he said, "I am nothing if not a reasonable man. If you can convince me that your worship does not defy your emperor, I may see to it that your house is converted to a storehouse for the emperor's gold rather than burned." The sentinels around him snickered as members of the congregation gasped. "Tell me—I hear strange things about the rituals you Christians observe. Can you explain them to me?"

He looked at Patricia's father as he spoke, but it was Cecelia who stepped forward. She was short in stature, especially among the many tall soldiers, but her voice rang out forcefully.

"There are two essential rituals, which were given to us by our Savior, Jesus Christ," she said calmly. "We call them sacraments. They are baptism, which brings us into the faith, and the common meal of bread and wine, which strengthens this faith. We believe our faith is open to any who wish to accept it."

Maxius spat on the ground and turned again to face Patricia's father. "You allow a woman to speak for you?"

"She is equal to me in our religion," Timothy said.

Maxius chuckled derisively. "I can feel the flames beneath you already," he said. Turning to Cecelia, he spoke with a thick condescension. "Tell me, woman, what sacrifices do you make in this cult?"

"We honor the sacrifice of the Mass. We break bread together and share wine in memory of our Lord Jesus Christ."

Maxius' eyebrows slanted viciously. "Do not mock me, woman. That is no sacrifice."

"God hears all prayers that the faithful speak," said Timothy, stepping forward.

"I thought your women spoke for you in this religion, swine!" As he spoke, he slapped Timothy with the back of his hand, sending him reeling to the floor. Patricia cried out, but Antonio stifled her shouts with his hand, looking at her desperately as he told her to quiet herself.

Her father slowly picked himself up, brushing the dirt from his robes. "Any may speak, just as any may know the Lord."

"And where does this Lord of yours appear?" Maxius scoffed. "I see no idols among you."

"We worship no idols," said Cecelia. "The cross is our only symbol."

At this, Maxius broke into a long and terrible laugh. He bent over, and the members of the congregation began to look around, frightened and confused. As he rose, he made a great show of wiping the tears from his eyes, before turning to look at his soldiers. "These Christians truly are mad!" he shouted.

He turned back to Timothy, and an evil grin spread across his face. "The cross is your symbol? We only use your pathetic cross for executing the basest, most vile of petty criminals. Do you know how humiliating it is? How painful a death? And this is what you choose to worship?"

Timothy stood firmly before Maxius, waiting until all around him were silent. Maxius' grin slowly faded, and in its place came a wild look of fury.

"Speak, you swine—or die!" he cried, flailing his arms.

Timothy turned to look at his wife, who nodded sadly.

"Jesus, through His death and His miraculous resurrection, has changed the meaning of the cross," Timothy began. "Jesus has taken the symbol of Rome's power and might—a symbol meant to strike fear into all who see it—and has turned it into a symbol of life and love. We have the symbol of the cross to remind us that Jesus defeated death—the same way he defeated the mighty legions of Rome with his love."

For a moment, there was silence. Timothy stood before Maxius, and felt his heart beating violently in his chest. Maxius turned from him, and looked out at the members of the congregation.

"No! Father!"

Patricia's scream was too late. By the time the words had left her mouth, Maxius had reached for his knife, spun, and slit her father's throat. As the blood from his neck poured out onto the earth below, she fought wildly against Antonio, who had pinned her to the ground with his strong arms, cupping her mouth with his hand. Amid the shouts and screams of the congregation, no one heard them struggling in the trellises.

Cecelia fell to the floor, holding her husband's lifeless body in her arms. "You say your God performs miracles with the dead?" Maxius taunted her, looking around him. "Where is he now?"

The look in Cecelia's eyes was that of a flame choking on the end of a wick, burning wildly and brightly. "You bastard!" she screamed. "You godless bastard!"

She sobbed furiously as she held her husband tightly, rocking him back and forth in her arms. "The Lord does work miracles," she said, choking on her tears. "He does..."

"Your god is pathetic," Maxius said, spitting once more upon Timothy's limp body. Cecelia leapt up, but Maxius was too swift. He stepped to her side, and brought his hands down in a mighty blow upon her back. She dropped to the ground where she lay helpless. Members of the congregation shouted in fear, as he leaned over her, speaking maliciously into her ear.

"You see, my religion is the Roman Empire and its deity is the emperor. He is a real deity, in contact with real gods, who give him real power. And through him, I partake in that power. He makes laws; he commands armies and levies taxes; this is true power. And he trusts me to wield this power in his name." In a swift motion, he grabbed her by her hair, pulling her up to face him. "So here is the miracle I will perform on his behalf: If you do not renounce this pathetic God of yours before me and swear an oath of fealty to the emperor, I will have everyone here killed."

In her mind's eye, Patricia imagined she could see her father's sheepish smile. He stood before her, and she watched as he mouthed the words with a final breath, "Live to fight another day."

Maxius threw her back to the ground, and began to walk ominously among the congregation, spinning his knife in his hand. Many of the men and women were crying as Cecelia dragged herself back to her husband's side. Maxius approached her slowly and crouched down beside her, dragging his knife along her cheek.

"What will it be, swine? Shall you live, or shall I kill everyone here as a sacrifice to the gods of Rome?"

Cecelia looked helplessly up at the quaking masses before her. Around them, the soldiers gripped their spears, waiting anxiously for the word from their master.

Cecelia spoke so softly that Maxius could not hear her.

"Speak up, woman, or I kill you now."

With one last sob, she turned to look up at him. "Let them live...I will not have any more death in this house. Let my people live."

With that, she hunched over her husband's body. Maxius stood up, gesturing grandly to the people before him. "It appears as though she is ready to prostrate herself before the might of Rome!" he declared triumphantly. "Any of you who believe in miracles from this invisible God of yours, stay where you are, and you may join Him," he said, pointing his knife to Timothy. "All who wish to live, step forward and take joy in your emperor's endless mercy."

One by one the people in the line, all people Patricia had known since childhood, stepped forward.

Her mind was racing. She had spent all her strength struggling against Antonio, and she lay exhausted in his arms, feebly trying to break free. *This can not be happening. This is not happening.*

She watched as Maxius forced each of them to their knees, and as they groveled and chanted the emperor's name. All the while, her mother lay in a heap above her father, shaking occasionally with fresh tears. The world began to spin around her, and as Patricia looked to see her father's pale face, there was nothing more.

. . .

Patricia snapped awake. *Where am I? Where is my father?*

She looked around her, and saw nothing but forest all around her. As she made to stand up, a hand fell gently upon her shoulder.

"You should rest, Patricia."

"Antonio!" she exclaimed. "What happened?"

He hung his head. "Maxius, he...your father..."

Patricia looked off into the trees. No glowing figure wandered there now, and no voice came to comfort her. She closed her eyes and saw her father's face, looking down at her as they sat together on Bartholomew's boat. How could that all be gone now? How could so much have changed?

"But how did I...?"

"You passed out," Antonio replied. "I brought you here...for your own safety."

Patricia was furious. "I don't need to be safe!" she cried. "I need my father! I need answers!"

For many days, Patricia was distraught and inconsolable. Maxius had taken everything she believed in and cast it underfoot. Where had God been? Why hadn't He responded? Even though she understood what had happened, and why her mother relented, she realized that amidst her anger, she felt ashamed. Ashamed that her mother submitted to Maxius, and ashamed that she had not broken free from Antonio's grasp and killed him herself.

She sat amid the trees in silence, refusing to eat or drink. A week had passed in this fashion, and Antonio began to grow concerned until one morning she approached him as he lit a fire to make breakfast.

"I'm leaving," she told him.

He nodded. "When?"

"This afternoon."

"I'm going with you," he said.

"Antonio..."

"Lest you forget Patricia, I was the one who had that idea first. There is nothing left for me here either. Especially...if you go," he said, turning towards the fire.

"Do what you will, but I can't stay here any longer."

She turned away, and went off into their shelter among the trees. There, she spent the rest of that day writing a letter to her mother. It had taken her a week to sort through the calamity of emotions that stirred within her chest. With each word, she felt she was pushing her fingers a little deeper beyond the lip of a closed door. All she had wanted to say and to ask poured forth until, finally, she could no longer bear the weight of the pen in her own hand. Her body was wracked with sobs as she folded up the thick parchment, ready to leave her home forever.

As they prepared to leave, she found a small boy from the village and paid him to carry her note to Cecelia. He looked up at her, smiling innocently, and she wondered if he too had not run away from home as she once did, just a little beyond the earshot of his parents. With only a brief glance back at the town she had grown up in, she and Antonio rolled their few belongings in blankets and tied the ends around their shoulders. They left the town without saying good-bye to anyone.

．　．　．

Their first night out of the city, they camped on a rocky ledge above the road and built a small fire. Patricia was very quiet, and she could feel Antonio watching her from across the fire. At last, he spoke.

"I've never told you what it was that convinced me to leave Tarsus, have I?" he said.

She shook her head, and he waited until she looked up to speak again. "My parents were also devoted Christians. They were arrested for their beliefs and given the chance to renounce them, much the same way that yours were, except that their trial was held publicly. I was in the crowd, along with my younger brother, and I was not so old myself. They declared boldly that God would save them—that they would never relinquish the faith that was like water and food to their soul."

He paused, throwing another log onto the fire. "I watched as they were trampled by wild animals. My brother could not contain himself...he ran to their side. He was killed as well. I watched them all die."

Patricia gazed at him over the fire. His face was very still as he spoke.

"Patricia—I couldn't let that happen to you," he said. No longer able to hide his emotions, he looked at her, and she saw the pain etched deeply into his face. "Don't judge them too harshly, Patricia. This world is a dangerous place for those who believe."

She nodded, feeling a great surge of affection for him.

"I'm sorry," she said.

He shrugged, looking away. "I'm sorry, too. For me, it feels like a long time ago, but I know the pain and confusion you must be feeling now."

She watched as the light from the fire wavered on his face. "Is this," she asked slowly, "why you feel the way you do about a life of celibacy?"

He gazed at her a long time before answering. "In part, I told myself that I would never have children, that they might never be exposed to such pain. But...it goes beyond that..."

He sat up straight as he went on. "Patricia, I also came to believe that chastity is simply another way of disciplining oneself, hardening oneself to prepare for the trials of being a Christian. This is the discipline that will see me through my torments when my moment with the Romans comes."

"The same thing might not happen to you. Our religion might triumph."

"It will. I know it will," he said, a serious look in his eyes. "There will come a time when the savagery of Rome is tempered by our faith, when the laws protect ordinary people instead of oppressing them, and when the emperor makes peace instead of war. It is bound to happen, because it is right—but I know it won't happen in my lifetime. Nevertheless, I fight, and I preach, because I know I must be an instrument of His will on earth."

She moved around the fire to sit next to him and took his hand in hers.

"Is there not strength in love also? Jesus taught that there was."

She squeezed his hand, and he looked desperately at her.

"I have not known enough of it to be able to tell."

. . .

They travelled together from that moment on, preaching wherever they had the opportunity. It was a time of great difficulty, but they found that their message carried renewed strength, especially as they preached among the poor and dispossessed. In some places, they were chased out of town, while in others, they gained followers like streams flowing into a mighty river. A single conversion would lead to the conversion of a household, of a guild, of a neighborhood, and ultimately of an entire section of the city. Their faith spread quickly, and Patricia and Antonio could hardly believe their own role in the events. Theirs was not simply a rogue religion anymore. Christianity had begun to put down lasting roots, and congregations bonded through an understanding of common traditions and beliefs, recording them in songs and writings. Patricia and Antonio would stay long enough for this process to begin and to ensure that the congregations had leaders strong enough in their faith to carry forward what had been begun. As they travelled, they stayed connected with their various congregations, and engaged them in a dialogue with larger Christian congregations all across the Mediterranean. Letters flew in all directions, in an attempt to bring conformity to the teachings of Jesus and the beliefs of the men and women who had followed Him.

Patricia and Antonio played an active role in this maelstrom, reading and responding to the letters that reached them daily. But there were always more towns on the road before them where people were in need of the Word. Slowly, as the months passed, Antonio's unbending belief in the strictures of their new faith and Patricia's commitment to love and equality for everyone, regardless of gender, merged into a single message of Christ's love for all.

They moved like this for nearly two years, and the letters they received told of Christianity spreading like wildfire. Patricia threw herself into her work, telling herself that Antonio was right, that salvation lay in self-discipline and love of the Lord. They allowed themselves that perhaps the day would come when they could walk freely as Christians through the streets of Rome.

Then a letter came to them one day from Joppa. It had been sent nearly four months prior, and was written by

Bartholomew. Patricia, having not heard from anyone in her hometown since their departure, opened the letter with great curiosity.

Dear Patricia,

I know it has been some time since we've spoken. I've heard from many who pass through Joppa that you are accomplishing great things, and spreading the glories of our Lord with fervor across the land. I always knew you had been given a gift from God, and feel truly blessed to have watched you grow for a time.

It is with great sadness then, that I must tell you of your mother's passing. Though it pained me deeply when your family parted ways with my church, I never forgot all that they gave to our small congregation, and the love they shared. Thus, it was with great happiness that I welcomed your mother as she returned to our church several months ago. She told me that she could no longer bear the weight of the guilt she felt, living in denial of her faith. She spoke often of how she wished to see you, that she might tell you of her love for you and of the forgiveness she found in Christ.

Know that, whatever your reasons for leaving, she loved you deeply, and forgave you. She walks in Heaven with her Lord now, and here on earth, we hold her memory close.

Be well, Patricia, and may your mother's strength guide you on your journey.

Yours,

Bartholomew

Her hands shook, as she fell to her knees, sobbing.

.   .   .

"I should have gone back to see her," said Patricia quietly after a long period of silence.

She and Antonio had left the town they were staying in that night and travelled to the countryside to be alone with one another. They built a small fire and ate little, the way they had once, before they had become well known.

Antonio took her hand in his. "I'm sorry," he said. "You could not know this would happen."

"I wronged them."

"The Lord will forgive you. And there is no doubt your mother heard of you and your successes and was proud."

"I wish I could see them again," she said. "I wish I could see the house again. They were my only family."

"We could travel there if you want to."

"No," she said. "It's too late for me now."

He moved closer to her, and held her, not knowing what to say. She laid her head upon his chest and wrapped her arm around his waist.

"We've gone so far, Patricia, and done so much. Perhaps it's time we settle down. We could find a large town, somewhere where our work is particularly needed. We could stay there and build a congregation ourselves instead of leaving that up to others." He paused for a moment, staring into the fire. "We could get married and start our own family."

She looked up at him, poring over the expression on his face. Without saying anything more, he took her head in his hands and kissed her. It was only a moment before he felt her kiss him back, her lips pressing firmly against his, as they fell slowly together towards the rough earth. "I love you," she said.

"I have always loved you," he whispered.

He smiled. "I am asking you to marry me." She took his hand and nodded her assent. They sat on a blanket next to the fire. Above them the stars seemed to shine brighter, each as bright and hot as the campfire next to them.

. . .

The next day they returned to one of the congregations they had founded and asked a priest, Martha, to marry them.

After a week of discussion, Patricia, Martha, and Antonio decided on their next location for spreading the Word, a small town called Areppio which was notoriously poor and dangerous. They also planned a different strategy than any they had used before. Upon arriving at the outskirts of the town, they did not immediately begin to preach, but instead went into the fields to help the peasants with their harvest. They asked for only food and lodging. This was a time for building trust, respect, and friendship—while toiling from dawn to dusk. Eventually, they built a small house, which became the house-church for the community. Within months they had converted many in the community to Christianity, not only because of the tenets of the religion but also their good works.

They repeated their plan many times in the southern area

of Italia and gathered many converts to the faith. They also gained the support of Linus, the bishop who supervised the loose conglomerate of churches throughout the area. Linus answered many questions they had about disciples and presbyters."The disciples were those that followed Jesus. For Jesus, discipleship demanded a break from the past. Mark, Luke, and John wrote that to become a disciple was to enter into a lifelong relationship with Jesus, even to share in his suffering and death. The disciples had common meals with Jesus and one another, and followed prescribed forms of prayer. Such discipleship drew one into Jesus' own mission, where the disciple was to act as Jesus himself: with compassion, humility, generosity, and suffering in the service of others. The characteristic mark of disciples was love, in particular, love for one another," Linus told his three guests.

"And after the Resurrection of Jesus, what role did the disciples assume in spreading the faith?" Patricia asked.

"Since Jesus was no longer physically present, Matthew wrote, 'He becomes present when two or three are gathered in His name.' The Church itself became known as the 'community of the disciples,'" Linus replied.

"Our concern," Antonio raised, "is that once we have established a local congregation, we can leave behind those who can lead the congregation."

"Heretofore, we have appointed elders, both men and women, to supervise the congregations and to preside over the Eucharistic ceremony," added Patricia.

"You have done well. As the Apostles began to pass away, there was a growing recognition of the need for order in the Church. The disciples provided this order for a period of time, and as you know, the disciples consisted of both men and women.

"The Apostles and the disciples appointed elders to provide order, preside over the Eucharistic service, and

211

preach. As Christianity spread to different cultural areas, different models of the ministry evolved. The bishops are now trying to establish a clear line of authority from God to Jesus to the Apostles to the bishops and to the presbyters."

"And what are the requirements to be a presbyter?" Martha asked.

"The people holding this office should be of good judgment, prudent, and temperate; able to manage their own household; married no more than once; neither greedy nor given to violence."

"And who should appoint the presbyters?" Antonio asked.

Linus hesitated to answer, seemingly perplexed by the question. After a few moments of deliberation, he responded:

"The most that can be said at this time is that the presbyter should serve at the consent of the local congregation."

"Why did you hesitate to respond, Linus?" Martha asked.

"The bishops are considering whether the appointment of presbyters is to become the exclusive privilege of bishops. But for now we will leave that responsibility to the local congregation."

In this manner the three established both the strategy for the development of local churches and the procedure to designate its leadership. They continued their work for many years in search of converts and a place for their final destination to establish a church and a school.

. . .

Over the course of the next few years, the three managed to build a small church overlooking the sea. Two years later, it was destroyed by the Romans. Martha died shortly thereafter, but Antonio and Patricia persevered and lived to see a new church built on the same spot. Their congregation was not large, but the members were very devout, and they handed down this devotion year to year in the church by the sea.

Chapter 26

⌒

S amuel walked slowly back across the grounds of the church by way of one of the small gardens. It was very late at night, and the church was quiet and mysterious, shrouded in the silver silence of the moonlight. Patricia, Martha, Alexandra, Michella, Antonio, and Joseph —Samuel felt as if they were all a part of a Christian tradition he had never heard of before. He paused for a moment and gazed at the twisted limbs of the dark trees, reaching up towards the stars and sky. The peace of this place seemed to course in its grasses and branches, in the sound of the distant ocean, and yet all of it felt inaccessible to him as his mind grappled with what he had been sent here to do. *How many of these traditions are there? How many churches like this one with their own deeply held traditions and histories?*

He moved on through the garden, breathing deeply the sea air, in hopes that its gentle breeze might clear his mind. Like a splinter beneath his skin, the thought of different Christian traditions had begun to pierce the strong armor of his faith, and he struggled to ignore this fact as he made his way back to his room. *Don't be a fool*, he thought to himself. *Gelasius, the Pope, has personally given you this mission. You must do what you came here to do.* He knew that the time was drawing near. He only had to wait for Anna to convene the church elders. At that point, he would have to either reason them into submission or deliver the order of excommunication and destroy all evidence of heresy in this place.

But even as he had this thought, a deep sadness took hold of him. He could not just ignore all that he had seen and learned. He could not go forward in his faith, forever setting aside the questions that now burned within him. Back and forth, growing doubts raged within him until he was exhausted. All he wanted to do was to fall from the world and sleep.

He grasped the handle of the door to his room, and as he struggled with it, his forehead fell against the hard wood. His earlier attempts at stealth came back to him in a flash, and without thinking, he slammed the door with the bottom of his clenched fist. Frustrated by his doubt and at his lack of control, he looked around to see if anyone heard his tantrum before trudging to the window and attempting to climb in, banging both his knees and the toes of his left foot. He cursed under his breath. He threw off his clothes, and fell into his bed, hopeful that sleep would help subside the troubling torrents of his mind.

A loud knocking sounded on the door. A glance at the window, and Samuel knew that he had slept long past dawn, and that everyone else in the church had already begun doing the tasks of the day. Joshua would be working tirelessly on the meeting hall, and Maria would be cleaning the breakfast crockery. Samuel buried his face in his pillow, the anger and frustration from last night still rife within him.

The knock came again, accompanied by a muffled voice, and he dressed himself quickly. He threw open the door to find Maria, hand raised, almost falling forward, a little shocked at the violence with which he had opened the door.

"Oh!" she said, with a look of surprise on her face. At the sight of her face, his anger softened, replaced by a new rush of thought and confusion.

"Are you feeling all right?" she asked with a smile. "We're not used to missing you at the breakfast table."

215

"I'm fine," Samuel replied. "I was up late. That's all."

There was a moment of awkward silence as they both recalled what had taken place on the walk the day before.

"Doing what?" she finally asked.

He felt himself blush. "Ah, about yesterday," he said, trying to change the subject. "I wanted to say..."

"You don't have to..."

"I wanted to say that I had a nice time," he finished over her objection.

At this, she blushed a little. "I did too."

She smiled, and despite all his frustration, he felt the urge to lean forward and kiss her as he had yesterday.

"I hate to change the subject,...and I think we should talk more about this..." she said suddenly, "but I came to tell you that Anna wishes to discuss with you when to convene the church elders."

"She does?"

"Yes. She was up very late last night. She said she thought she saw you in the garden when she was in the garden, but no one was sure what you would be doing there in the middle of the night."

How much does she know? Samuel thought to himself. He knew that if he had been spotted, he couldn't just lie about being out of his room. "I was just thinking," he said, reaching up innocently to scratch the back of his head.

"Thinking about what?"

"About the discussion I'm going to have with Anna and the elders."

"Oh," she said, averting her eyes from his. Samuel couldn't help but feel that he had disappointed her somehow with his response. "Well, if you want to talk to her, she's probably in the garden with Joshua."

"I do," replied Samuel. "And I'd like to talk to you also. Will you have time before you have to start preparing the noon meal?"

"You've slept a bit too late for that," she said, cocking her head slightly to her left. "I have to start dinner now. But later this afternoon?"

"I'll be there..." he paused, thinking again that they might kiss, but they simply looked at each other for a moment before she turned and went off towards the kitchen.

As he made his way out to the garden, he found Anna and Joshua sitting on a bench, holding hands and talking intently. Anna spotted him and waved him over, and he approached cautiously, with both of them watching him.

"We haven't spoken much since your return, but how was your trip to the south?" he asked.

"Very difficult, but we were able to help," Anna responded. "We gathered enough food from the people of the countryside between here and there to hold them over if their drought continues, and several fishermen from our congregation have agreed to take on some men from the village as temporary help, to aid them in feeding their families. Perhaps the greatest blessing is the number of people who were inspired by our good works, and who have taken Christ into their hearts. There is a church in that village, but it is a small and poor church, and it has been that way for years. We worshipped with them, and I left one of my ablest aides down there to help them organize and grow."

"You have done a wonderful thing," said Samuel, meaningfully.

"It sounds as if I am not the only one—Joshua tells me you've been helping on the meeting hall."

Samuel fidgeted, still unable to accept a compliment with self-assurance. "Yes, or at least I tried. I've only had so much time between visits to your library, which I've also found to be quite..." Samuel paused, realizing he had been about to say "enlightening." Changing his mind quickly, he finished by saying, "which I've found to be very extensive."

Anna eyed him curiously. "That's good to hear. We're very proud of our collection of texts, as you've probably guessed."

"Yes, well," Samuel said, not wanting to dwell on the topic, "what I really wanted to speak to you about is when you could convene the elders of the church. I've been here long enough to find out what I needed to, I believe, and I think it's time that we all had a frank discussion."

Anna smiled brightly. "Joshua said he believed as much. I've already called a meeting for later in the week. Since there doesn't seem to be much chance of rain, we'll hold it in the meeting hall, if that's all right."

"That's fine," Samuel said stiffly. Though he had known the moment was fast approaching, the realization that he would have to argue with these people and present the Pope's ultimatum ran like a cold wave over his body.

He had been with the congregation for nearly twenty days, and yet it had seemed a lot longer. Despite all his years of formal education under the greatest minds of the Church, and months upon months of tireless training in Rome— training in rhetoric, grammar, philosophy, theology, natural sciences, arithmetic—his mind had never been stretched and challenged the way it had reading the books housed in this little church's library. He had been taught, and absolutely believed to be true, that Christianity had developed in an inevitable line of right thought and right action, and that the prohibition of women in the priesthood was an intrinsic part of that development.

But now he had come to realize how very many threads of tradition there were in the early church. He had started to doubt that the concentration of power with the Pope, the Bishop of Rome, was so divinely ordered and necessary. As he stood on the brink of delivering his ultimatum to this church, his unquestionable faith in Gelasius and the papacy was shaken. His will to do Gelasius's bidding—excommunicating these fellow Christians and destroying their precious library—was faltering. He no longer knew what was right and wrong.

How, he wondered, *could Gelasius suppress women's leadership when women had been priests, prophets, healers, preachers, and martyrs from the very beginning?* It was all part of a deep-rooted prejudice against women held not only by Gelasius but many of his predecessors, he concluded.

And knowing this, how could he stand in front of Anna's congregation, in front of people who personified Christianity in a way he had never seen in the halls of Saint Peter's in Rome, and tell them that they were wrong, that they were heretics?

Samuel shuddered. He was suddenly overwhelmed with how little he truly knew about his faith and about Jesus' will for His church.

"Are you all right, brother?" Joshua asked as he extended a hand to him.

"Yes, I'm okay." Samuel took two steps back. "I, I…"

Joshua stood and looked concerned. Anna, it seemed to Samuel, had looked right through his eyes and into his mind. She knew of the turmoil that he felt, and of the truths he was wrestling with. But she did not look at him with anger or frustration—only with unending love and compassion.

"If you'll excuse me," Samuel said, regaining his composure, "I have several things to take care of. I'm glad your trip went well."

"So am I," said Anna. "We'll see you at the noon meal?"

"Of course."

He could not help but notice as he was leaving that Anna and Joshua were still holding hands, nor could he keep himself from thinking how happy they looked.

Chapter 27

From where he sat in the shadowed corner of the library, Flavius could see between two shelves to the door of the small room that was his study. He had been here for most of the day, unnoticed, and he had spent the previous day in the same way. He needed to think and to pray, but he did not want to lose sight of that door.

Several days earlier, he had decided to leave his study only a few moments after he had entered and had nearly run over a young papal aide crouching outside. The aide apologized and made a show of picking up the several papers he had dropped, but it was clear to Flavius that the young man had been trying to peer through the keyhole. It was also clear he had no reason to undertake such actions on his own. Flavius was being watched, and he stood, waiting to catch another of Gelasius's spies in the act, although he didn't know how much good it would do.

Besides the cover they provided, the tall shelves holding row after row of books and manuscripts brought Flavius a sense of calm and comfort at a moment in his life when he sorely needed that. They held all the knowledge and debate and argument sanctioned by the Church of Rome, and it was for the sake of these things, he knew, that he had strayed from the path of the Church. In lying to the Pope and about the nature of Samuel's mission, he had put these two great passions of his life at odds. Sooner or later, he would have to find a way to ask repentance for his actions, but now was not the time.

First, he had to decide what to do with the history he had

been writing. If he was indeed being watched, it meant that the history he had been writing was likely in danger. He could not abide the thought of having it destroyed, which is surely what Gelasius would do if he found out about it. Yet a part of him was dismayed knowing how far he had strayed outside the bounds of orthodoxy to compile this book. Had he gone too far and tried to keep his secret for too long? *What secrets can be kept from God?* he thought to himself. Helpless, he sat in the library among the things that comforted him and watched the unmoving door, waiting for the Lord to reveal what he should do next.

Flavius heard footsteps on the stone floor and stiffened. They were not the steps of the portly head librarian, who rarely came to this part of the library, but were light and quick, purposeful. He stood up and peered around the bookshelves to get a better look at the door. If he could catch someone in the act, he could beat Gelasius at his own game. *Invite them in,* he thought, *and show them that there's nothing to hide.* The false bottom of the drawer that held his manuscript was nearly impossible to detect, and whoever it was would have to report back to Gelasius that his suspicions were unfounded. He had been sitting here for nearly two days clinging to this vain hope, and listening to the approaching footsteps, he began to question if his plan would work. Would such a ruse, even if it worked, buy him enough time to finish his manuscript? He suddenly felt like a fool for sitting alone in this darkened nook in the library, an old man paralyzed by the circumstances of his life. *Circumstances of your own making,* he reminded himself.

The footsteps drew closer and another young papal aide appeared. He did not move tentatively or crouch before the door as Flavius had expected. Instead, he walked boldly up to the door and rapped it officially with his knuckles.

Flavius rose and hurried down one of the long rows of

shelves to appear to have been at the opposite end from which he had been hiding. He adjusted his cassock as he went and tried to look preoccupied, as if he were simply returning to his office after a contemplative walk. The aide, not hearing him, raised his hand to knock again.

"Hello," said Flavius. "Can I help you?"

"Father Flavius—I've been looking all over for you."

"Have you?"

Taking the large key from where it hung around his neck, Flavius unlocked the door. "Would you like to come in for a moment?" he asked. "I would invite you to sit, but as you can see my study is nearly unfurnished. I've only my chair and the desk, which is mostly empty." He moved towards the desk, but the young aide frowned.

"I'm sorry, sir," he said, "but we've no time for that. The Pope requests that you join him immediately in the courtyard."

"He does?" asked Flavius, turning back to the aide. He walked back to the door and smiled nervously, pulling the door shut and locking it, suddenly glad to have the bolt back in place. "Well, we mustn't keep him waiting then. Did he say what this was in regards to?"

"No, Father, not exactly. Something about a squad of soldiers we're sending to the south."

Flavius felt his heart sink. The aide turned, and they went rapidly through the dim halls beyond the library towards a small courtyard that stood next to the stables. In it, a group of armed men was saddling horses and preparing to travel. Gelasius stood to one side talking to the captain of the horsemen. At their approach, he turned, his look of concern shifting slowly into a contented smile.

"Flavius," he called loudly, "thank you for coming to see Jason and his men off. I thought you should know that I'm sending them down to that church of yours to finish this business in a proper manner. There is, as you know, only one way to deal with heretics."

Flavius steadied himself, refusing to give in to the Pope's baiting.

"Your Holiness will do as he sees fit," he said agreeably walking towards the Pope.

"I've just been giving Jason here his final instructions and thought, since you're more familiar with this particular issue than I am, you might have something to add."

Jason was a large man with a nose that had been broken several times and shoulders like a bull. Flavius could well imagine what his instructions were regarding any documents he found, and he thought immediately of his own book. Samuel could not stop what was going to happen there, but with every piece of history that was destroyed, those that remained would become all the more precious.

"Be certain to remember," Flavius told Jason, "that these are fellow Christians you are dealing with. Despite their wayward beliefs, they believe in our Lord and Savior and do not need to be harmed or bullied."

"Yes," said Gelasius, "we've just been talking about that, haven't we, Jason?"

The big man nodded, smiling as his nostrils flared.

"Very well, Flavius, if that's all you have to say," Gelasius looked momentarily at Flavius before continuing, "Jason, you and your men can embark on your godly journey. God blesses you!"

The Pope offered his hand, and the big man knelt to kiss his ring before mounting his warhorse and rallying his armed men. Flavius and the Pope watched the men ride out of the courtyard, the hooves of the huge horses drumming loudly on the stone beneath them. The white banner emblazoned with a gold cross, the banner of the Christian Church since the time of Constantine, fluttered in the breeze atop the staff held by the lead soldier.

"I'm glad to see that that matter is dealt with," said Gelasius when it was quiet again. "Don't you see how easily these things can be solved, Flavius, with an order from the Pope and a few well-armed men to back it up? None of this cajoling and convincing you're so fond of."

Flavius nodded dejectedly.

"I'm only sorry I didn't resort to this course of action sooner—before things got out of hand the way they have," Gelasius asserted as he turned and began to walk back towards the hallway with Flavius at his side.

He felt as if he were back in the library, waiting, powerless and hopeless. Did he really think he could alter the divine will of this Pope? Despair washed over him, and he wondered if this was his punishment from God for disobeying Gelasius, His voice on earth.

"Tell me, Flavius," Gelasius continued. "I was made aware last night that you've been writing a Christian history, and I must admit—I'm a little concerned that you hadn't come forward to tell me."

Flavius stopped in his tracks, unable to hide the fear in his eyes. Gelasius paused, a look of feigned concern upon his face. "You know how I respect you as a scholar, Flavius. It saddens me that you didn't think I would be interested in your work." His lips turned up at the edges as he glowered at Flavius.

Flavius felt everything slowing down around him, as if he had been thrust into a stupor. His vision began to cloud, darkening around the edges, and his hands and feet went numb. He stifled a gasp.

"The history...it is not finished yet. I thought it should be complete before presenting it to you, Your Holiness." His lips were trembling as he spoke, and Gelasius stared at him woodenly.

"That won't be necessary, Flavius. You wish to finish your book—I wish to finish my business with the heretics in the south. It seems that only one of us can get what he wants." His voice dropped low as he leaned in close to Flavius.

"Your manuscript is on my desk, Flavius, and I plan on reading it immediately. Tell me, Flavius—is there anything you wish to tell me before I begin?"

Is this your will, God, that such things should come to pass? Does it have to be this way...with armed soldiers riding off to destroy the church and homes of fellow Christians in the name of Jesus, a peaceful carpenter who professed love to be the foremost virtue? he asked himself. The implausibility of this strange destiny struck him like a boulder falling on his head from Heaven.

Flavius thought of his treasured history. He had struggled for many years to develop a unifying theme for his manuscript, but was never able to settle on the right idea or structure to truly bind the work together. It remained a piecemeal story of scattered heresies and Christians who were banished from the Church. But now, watching these men—papal men-at-arms—ride off bearing the symbol of the cross along with weapons of war to destroy the tradition of equality between men and women, the message that Jesus himself had preached, was all he needed to realize the overarching theme of his history: the corruption of truth through political power.

The early church, before Constantine declared it the official state religion, had been scattered, believers clinging together, searching for a way to live the message of Jesus in a hostile world. They had made mistakes, and had lost their way a few times, but it was all in the search for truth, not gold or power. These churches, found in people's homes or in the catacombs running beneath the streets of Rome, gave little thought to how Christians might appear to outsiders. They were led by the Holy Spirit, who chose women as often as men to lead the people gathered, to break the bread and say the blessings, to speak in tongues, and to prophesy about the future.

When Constantine declared Christianity a legal religion, no Christians could have foreseen the sea of change that was about to inundate their infant faith. They were too joyful, relieved that they no longer had to fear for their lives every moment. Their little congregations no longer had to hide, so their meetings and worship services moved from houses, the realm of women, to public churches, the realm of men in the Roman Empire.

Just a generation later, basilicas and cathedrals as great as any monument of ancient Rome sprouted up in cities and towns across the empire. Bishops changed almost overnight from the pastors and protectors of endangered people to princes living in houses rivaling palaces, with temporal power to match the size of their newfound wealth. Christ would rule not just in the transcendent world but in the temporal one as well. Female leaders were excluded from this new vision of Jesus and Christianity.

Christianity had forever shifted, from the faith of the poor and the downtrodden to an institution led by the rich and powerful. Once the churches moved from the homes of its followers to cathedrals, chapels, and basilicas, the leadership of women as it had been known for three hundred years began to vanish. Texts that told the story of women priests were declared heretical and burned. Now there were only a few dozen churches remaining that were pastored by women priests. Once Gelasius's edict was enforced, there would be none. All that would remain of this strong tradition would be the history—Flavius's history.

Flavius looked squarely into the eyes of the skeletal man

standing at his side. "There is nothing to tell you," he said, hearing his words die along the stone walls of the hallway. "Like any history, it is no more than a true record of things that have happened. I hope that that alone will make it valuable to the Church."

"I wish that were the case, Flavius, but you know it's not that simple," Gelasius replied firmly. "If this document is what I believe it to be, then you have done a great disservice to yourself, to the Church, and to God."

He looked sternly at Flavius. "You can not serve two masters, Flavius. There is the truth, as it is decided by God and imparted to me, and there is everything else, which is heresy. I hope dearly that you have remained on the proper side of that bright line."

Chapter 28

❧

"I t is always difficult to see so many in great need, but to have been able to help so many was a great blessing." Anna looked around the table of people who had gathered to welcome her back. Loaves of bread sat before men and women who had broken from their work to greet her. Among them, children giggled in their small seats, caught up in their own precious worlds.

"Rebecca," she said to one of the blond girls who had been sitting quietly before her plate. The young girl looked up nervously, sitting on her hands and swinging her legs back and forth. "Would you be willing to say the prayers over our meal?"

The young girl looked questioningly over at her mother, who nodded and gestured towards Anna. Her legs came to a stop, and she hopped off her chair, walking briskly over to Anna's side. Anna took the girl under her arm and whispered gently in her ear.

Samuel could not hear what passed between them, but he watched as the girl stood up in Anna's chair and began the grace. When she finished, there was a resounding "Amen," and many began to clap their hands as the little girl dashed back to her seat.

Anna looked over at her beaming. "My friends—I believe we have a future priestess in our midst!"

A month ago, this would have sent Samuel into an uproar. But as he saw the look of pride on the young girl's face, mirrored in Anna and the others around the table, he stayed quiet. There was an undeniable purity to what had just taken place. The blessing had been said, and a young child had been brought closer to a love of Jesus and His teachings. *How could this be so wrong in the eyes of the Church?* he thought. There were those out there who did not bless their food, and who had never heard the word of God. Those were the people who needed saving, he realized. How could he possibly denounce the wonderful and simple exchange that had just taken place?

As he sat in his chair, others laughing and enjoying themselves around him, he came to realize that his initial reaction had been based not on history or theology, or even on the principles Jesus himself had espoused, but on his own fear and pride.

He glanced over at Maria and saw her laughing and talking with friends. She had an energy that seemed to draw in and welcome everyone around her, and seeing the way the people of the town embraced her, he knew one day she was bound to follow in Anna's footsteps. There were a number of men who watched her with affectionate eyes, and he could not restrain the jealousy he felt welling up inside him. He wondered if they too waited to see her pass by a window, or thought about her in the midst of their work. Samuel wondered if anyone could feel the way he felt at that moment.

Gelasius had taught him once that celibacy was the surest route to salvation for one who wanted to dedicate his life to Christ. Samuel had always assumed that he would finish his studies and become a priest, that the only family he would ever want or need would be the Holy Father and all of the brethren in the priesthood. He was content to remain a celibate all his life because he had been taught and believed that this was most pleasing to God. But being in this parish, working on the hall with married men, seeing families and children playing together, and thinking of Maria—all this made him doubt that such restraint could somehow be more holy or righteous.

Samuel shook his head. *What is happening to me? How is it that I never saw these things before?*

His thoughts were interrupted by a timid knocking at the entrance to the dining room. Conversation stilled and heads turned. A small boy from the town stood with his hands clasped in front of him, standing on his toes as he looked out over the room. Seeing that he had their attention, he took a deep breath.

"I'm looking for a man named Samuel. Is he here?" he said in a high, reedy voice. His chin pointed upward as he spoke, as if raising his head might allow him more volume.

Samuel couldn't hear what he had said, but as the people at several long tables turned to look at him, he realized that he was being summoned. He met Maria's eyes and tried to smile as he walked towards the door. The boy stepped outside and waited for him.

"You're Samuel?" the boy asked as he approached Samuel.

"I am."

The boy's eyes lit up. "Come with me—quickly!" He took Samuel by the hand and began to run forward.

Samuel pulled back, slowing the boy to a stop. "Wait! Wait! Who are you, and where are we going?"

The boy looked ahead anxiously. "My name is Jonas, and we're going to where I can earn a copper piece just arrived from Rome." He squeezed Samuel's hands, pulling him forward.

"Come with me, please," he said again.

Just arrived from Rome? What could this mean? Samuel wasn't sure, but he could sense the boy meant him no harm. "Very well," he said. "But I would appreciate it if I didn't have to be dragged there," he said with a smile.

The boy dropped his hand, looking embarrassed, and began to move quickly forward again. Samuel followed the boy's determined strides around the side of the church and through one of the gardens towards the village. As they approached the rows of houses, standing at the edge of the road, Samuel saw the outlines of a dark man, his clothes ragged and a cutlass hanging from his right hip. *Of course,* he thought. It was the old rapscallion whom Samuel had contracted to deliver his message north to Flavius. He grinned when he saw Samuel and raised his hand in greeting, but did not step forward.

"This is the man," reported the boy when they neared. He stuck out his hand towards the old smuggler. "For another copper, sir, I'll find anyone you want back there. This was easy."

"You've did well, boy," said the old man, dropping a coin in the boy's palm. "Run along now. If I need other errands, I will find you."

The boy trotted off, holding the copper lovingly in both hands and examining it as he ran.

"It's good to see you again," said Samuel. "I've been expecting you for several days."

The old man coughed violently into his hand and spat on the ground. "Dat I am sorry for. Dere's bin trouble to the north involvin' a devilish man, collectin' what he calls 'taxes.' He had a few large friends, but..." he said looking down at the three fingers on his right hand. "...as you can see, everything came out in one piece," he said as he chuckled. He reached inside the loose, ragged vest that he wore. Samuel instinctively braced himself, and the man gave him a curious look as he pulled out a thin document. It was embossed with the personal seal of Flavius.

"I'm a man of my word," he said.

"Thank you," said Samuel, looking around them. "I was

not expecting to see you now, and so I don't have your payment with me."

The man's grin turned quickly to a sinister frown.

"But," Samuel said quickly, "though I feel it may be a strange thing to ask, would you accompany me back to the church? I can pay you there."

The old man shifted in his boots and looked nervously towards where Samuel had come from. "I'm no Christian, and dis seems to be the ground of your temple dere." He pointed to the line of turf that began at the edge of the road. "I was not sure what would happen to me if I set foot on it."

"The boy you sent is not a Christian either, to my knowledge," said Samuel.

The old man grinned again. "Yes—but he's too young to have done anything to offend your God. Myself, on de udda hand—I've spent most of my years doing such things."

Samuel could not help but chuckle. "I said when we met previously that when you returned, I would show you that you had nothing to fear." He reached up and put his hand on the man's shoulder. "I know you're a busy man, with many places to be. But I can promise you that no harm will come to you. I have another letter I hope you will be able to deliver, and I'll be able to pay you for both when we get there."

The man looked unsure for a moment and then shrugged his shoulders. "I'm old, boy," he said. "There's not much I have to fear in this life."

"But perhaps there is still some peace you can find?"

Samuel looked at the man earnestly, unsure exactly of what he was doing. He felt as if he were caught in the flow of a will greater than his own.

"I never caught your name," he said, offering his hand.

The old man took it slowly. His grip was calloused and as hard as an old piece of ship's rope. "Abbas," he said.

232

"Abbas, then. It is up to you. If you come with me now, I promise no harm will come to you, and by the time we are done, you will have a new letter and money to take with you."

The old man seemed to warm to this idea, and at his nod, they both walked out across the dry earth and into one of the gardens that ringed the church. As they walked, Samuel pointed out the buildings that housed the personal quarters, the kitchen, and the dining room. He then led the way towards the large roofless main hall. He was surprised, stepping back from it now, how much work had been accomplished in the past several days. The walls had been completed, and the bell tower had been rebuilt, topped with a large stone cross that looked proudly out over the sea. All that remained was to rebuild the roof. Samuel realized with a stab of sadness that he would not be here to see this, nor to see the building whole once more.

He brought Abbas through the main door into a space that was empty except for a large heavy table in the center and a few chairs pushed up against the far wall.

"Dis is de building dat was knocked down several months ago, isn't it?" asked Abbas.

"Yes. This is the building where we worship," said Samuel. Like his new and surprising affection for the building, he was taken aback at the pride in his voice. *What's happening to me?* he thought. He was not a member of this church, but he was certainly acting like one. "This is where the sacrifice of the Eucharist is held," he corrected himself.

The old man chuckled. "You're talking to a man who's never bin to church, boy. I don' know what you're saying."

"Oh, of course," Samuel offered. "Well, it means that all the members of the church gather here on the Sabbath and worship our Lord, and a part of that worship includes breaking bread and drinking wine together."

"Dat's all?" The old man looked very skeptical.

"Well," Samuel hesitated. The temptation to give a detailed theological explanation of the meaning of the Eucharist, the importance of scripture, and the meaning of sacrament was bursting within him. But following the strange sense that had taken hold of him, he decided a simpler path would be wiser in this case. "Yes, as simple as that. We believe that Jesus Christ is with us in something as simple and necessary as eating a meal together."

Doubt still hung heavy in the old man's eyes, and he sighed heavily. "I'm not sure if you Christians are as strange as I thought."

Samuel laughed, and the smuggler joined in with even heartier laughter.

"You've done a fine job with the rebuilding," the old man said as he ran a hand along the new wall. There was something strange and beautiful about the sound of his rough skin along the stones. Samuel knew that those hands had more stories to tell than he might care to hear.

"It is a wonder to step back and view now. Admittedly though, I only helped a little bit."

"Mmm..." the old man murmured. He turned again to Samuel. "I must ask you somet'ing."

Samuel nodded.

"What has happened to all of de idols and ornaments here? Have dey bin stolen?"

Samuel laughed again. "No, my friend." He raised his arm, pointing to the large wooden cross standing at the back of the platform. "The only ornament you'll find here is the cross." He responded, pointing to the large wooden cross.

"I've seen you Christians in many places during my travels. The ornate temples in Rome and elsewhere are filled with statues and fancy tapestries. In de deserts of Africa, I've seen you starving yourselves and beating yourselves with sticks and ropes. It's all very strange to me. And everywhere I go, you have dis symbol of a sword stuck into de ground. I've never understood it."

Samuel held back his smile, and began to explain the history of the cross. He told Abbas about Jesus and what He had taught about peace and love; he told him how Jesus had died on the cross and risen again. Since then, different people had been trying to understand for themselves what the Savior's life had meant, which explained the differences Abbas had seen in his journeys. Across these developing sects of Christianity, though, the cross was the symbol of Jesus' death and resurrection that unified them all.

As he concluded his story, there was something in the old man's face that seemed to soften. "Love your enemy as you love yourself, you say?"

Samuel nodded.

"Wouldn't last long in my line of work," the smuggler said with hearty laughter. Curious, he continued to look at the cross, as if seeing it truly for the first time.

"You know, Abbas, we all have an eternal soul inside of us, and for the Lord, anything is possible. He has offered all of us an eternal life after this one. You and me both."

The old man reached up to scratch his chin and spoke with a twinkle in his eye. "Doesn't sound dat bad after all. Nuttin' like killing chickens and praying to little idols and all dat! These things I have known all my life." The old man paused, looking down at his feet. "Say I was interested doh —how would I buy my way into dis eternal life of yours?"

Samuel laughed again. A feeling of pride and joy surged through him. Here he was, finally able to talk to a stranger, a non-Christian, about his faith. All these years he had been walling himself off from others with thick treatises and philosophy and doctrine—he felt for the first time as though he were actually spreading the good news of Jesus. *What would Flavius think if he were here to see and hear me talking with this old pirate?* Samuel asked himself.

"If you'd like to, you can stop in anytime to hear someone talk about the ways of the Lord." Samuel moved towards the man and saw out of the corner of his eye Anna standing just outside the church, watching them.

"The person you'd do best to speak with is actually just over there," Samuel said, beckoning Anna over. "Her name is Anna. She leads the services here, and can tell you a time when you could stop by."

Abbas watched the woman approaching, an odd look of delight on his face. "She is a priest?"

Anna stepped forward. "We've both priestesses and priests in our church," she said. She smiled at Samuel, as if to let him know she wasn't trying to start an argument. "And you're welcome to come by anytime to hear us preach. There will be a short service the day after tomorrow during the afternoon, and we always worship on the Sabbath."

"You have a beautiful temple," said Abbas.

"Thank you," she said. "It is always open to you. We'd be delighted if you came to hear us speak sometime."

"I just may at dat," he said. "Try anyting once is what my brudda always says." He winked broadly at them and then turned to Samuel. "If you need anything, I'll be down at the docks for de next few days."

Samuel looked at the man in surprise. "But what about your...?"

"I will be dere for some time," he said, cutting Samuel off. "I trust you will find me."

The grin on his face was the same Samuel had seen when they first met, but it was as if years of salt and pain had been subtly washed away. "Thank you," Samuel said.

The old man bowed, and with a last look at the cross,

headed off through the gardens. After he had gone, Anna turned to Samuel. "I imagine there's a good story there?"

Samuel felt the letter from Flavius buried in the folds of his robe. "Indeed—a story for another time perhaps."

"You did quite well with him," she said, changing the subject. "Have you ever considered missionary work?"

"The written Word has always been the most comfortable for me."

"Well," she said, stepping towards the doorway, "one never knows how things will turn out. If you ever feel the urge, we'd be glad to have you work with us."

He opened his mouth, but she stopped him with a motion of her hand. "I know," she said, "heresy and orthodoxy and all of that. We can only do what we feel we're compelled to."

She stepped out the door then, leaving him alone in the big empty hall clutching the letter from Flavius.

Chapter 29

ᔕ

S amuel looked up from the letter, his mind racing. As the minutes and hours of the day waned, he knew the moment was approaching when he would have to stand before the congregation. He looked to the sky, hoping that a sign would come to him.

What had come over him? He was sitting back idly as women were teaching their daughters to lead in the church; he was proselytizing to scoundrels he had never met; he was allowing himself to feel things he had never felt before—things that he had once been so sure were fallacious. Gelasius and Flavius had sent him forth with the authority of God, and yet he did not know if he knew anymore what that authority represented. Was it the true God—the God who had come down to earth as a man that all men might be saved? Or was it another idol, elaborately built to draw believers away from the truth?

All he knew was that he couldn't stay where he was, wallowing in these thoughts. Folding up the letter and placing it in his pocket, he set off. He headed into the hills that rimmed the town, thinking and praying as his steps kicked small clouds of dust up into the air. The sun hung over him, its rays playing softly along his cheek and hands, and the land around him, though dry and brown, seemed vibrant, filled with the glow of the late afternoon sun. He remembered how the town had first appeared to him when he arrived, how much younger he had felt then. He had difficulty imagining what his life would be like back in Rome, with its crowded dirty streets and the deep solemnity of the papal palace. Things were bright and fresh here, and he felt in touch with the Lord here more than any place he had been in life—certainly more so than in Rome, where the Spirit often seemed to be conjured up by empty words, thrown out among gilded enamel and ornate trappings. With a long sigh, he looked out to the landscape once more before turning to walk back down the slope to the church. Unexpectedly, he heard his name being called, and glanced up.

Maria was climbing the slope towards him. She waved at him happily, and he returned the gesture, meeting her halfway down the slope. Her dark hair was pulled back from her forehead, and she was dressed in simple white clothes. *Nothing more in the world could add to her beauty*, he fancied.

"I thought it might be time for a walk," she said when she reached him, "and I saw you up here. I hope I'm not intruding."

"Of course not," he said, shielding his eyes from the sun. "I was just on my way to try to roust you out of your chores."

They smiled at each other, and he put his hands out. She took them in her own.

"I've been thinking of you," he said.

"And what have you been thinking?"

He looked back up the hill. "Do you think we could talk about this somewhere else? I need someone to speak with, and you're the only one I feel will know how to listen."

"Let's talk then," she replied. "Up there? Where we can look out over the sea?"

Samuel nodded.

They hiked off in the direction of the sea along the line of bluffs until they were well out of sight of the church. Next to the path stood a large flat boulder that Samuel had passed several times, each time daunted by its smooth, tall sides, standing like a guardian before the gates of the cliffs. He told Maria that he had often wished to see the view from the top of this rock, and she laughed, taking his hand. As they approached the edge of the bluff, he grew nervous, but the look she cast back at him calmed his rushing heart. She led him on a narrow path around to the seaward side of the rock, where to his surprise there was a crack running upward. This crack was wide enough, and its surface rough enough, that it appeared to be a natural stairwell. They climbed easily up to the flat top of the stone and settled themselves side by side looking out at the sea. Below them, the churning waters were starting to turn a burnished gold as the sun fell towards the thin lines of clouds on the horizon. The hills stretched dryly in either direction, with a small dusty grove of trees in the distance offering the only color. They sat facing the sea, and for a long time, neither of them spoke. Samuel understood that she was waiting for him to begin.

"I'm going to be meeting with Anna and the church elders soon," he finally said. He shifted his weight off of his palms and sat forward, feeling Maria do the same beside him.

"Which means that my time here is coming to an end."

She looked at him stoically, the golden light of the fading sun illuminating her simple dress as its fringes rustled in the passing breeze.

"I've read most of the important documents in your library, which was an important part of my task. All that is left to do is to deliver the official proclamation of the Pope and learn the response. I...," he paused looking in her direction.

She was smiling suddenly. When she noticed him watching her, she lowered her head slightly. "Why are you smiling?" he asked.

"It's about the library," she said, "the thought of you sitting there, studying and reading. I couldn't help but smile."

"Why?"

"Does it matter?" she asked frankly.

"Were you thinking that I'd be converted to your way of thinking by the documents there?"

She hesitated for a moment. "Something like that."

"Well," he said softly, "that's one of the things I wanted to talk about."

He began to wring his hands, as he looked off to the side.

"There's so much to say. My mentor, Flavius, believes that one of the best things we can do when we are confronted with challenges to our faith is to discuss it. 'Give it some air, Samuel,' is what he always said to me."

He felt like he was rambling, but her expression did not change. She nodded that he might continue.

"I could not have imagined this, but you've become someone, in the short time I've known you, whom I trust. Two months ago I never would have believed I could talk to a woman about serious matters of any nature, much less have her understand me and even argue with me. This is one of the things you've done for me here—one of the many things. You've opened my mind to things."

Samuel paused to take a breath, and then pressed on. "And soon I have to do what I have been tasked to do, and it is something I am no longer certain is right."

Maria raised an eyebrow. "I was chosen to come here because I was young, I think," Samuel continued, "and because neither Flavius, who picked me, nor the Pope, who approved my designation, could imagine that I would have an agenda of my own. They both, in their own way, believed that because of my youth, I would do exactly what they asked of me. And now I'm adrift."

As the breeze picked up, he felt again the letter in the pocket of his tunic. He instinctively reached up to touch it.

"Soon I am to go before the church elders, and if they do not renounce their practice of ordaining women into the priesthood, they will be branded as heretics and excommunicated from the faith. I will only argue enough to make the Pope's position clear, but I no longer feel I can endeavor to convince anyone otherwise. I have seen enough to understand that I will not be able to convince anyone to turn back on their beliefs."

Samuel inhaled slowly and deeply once more. "As for my mentor, Flavius, his priority was that I report on the state of your library. I did so, informing him that you have many works of important historical value, and today I finally received his response."

He took out the letter, and after a moment's hesitation, handed it to Maria. Rather than read it though, she simply kept it in her hand, waiting for him to continue.

"Maybe all of this is in vain. I know that whatever I say to the elders, I will do so with misgivings. I have based my life and founded my faith on the things I learned in Rome, and they are becoming undone here in this place. The Pope believes that his own understanding of the Word of God is the only truth possible. But how many histories has he not read? How many voices were ignored by his predecessors? And what writings were discarded because they were written by women or referred to women in positions of power? Who have the Popes been but simply the heads of the largest Church, the one with the most money, in a religion that is supposed to value neither of these things?"

Maria took his hand, and Samuel shook his head, feeling the frustration and anger of years of false devotion welling up inside of him. "And Flavius—he believes that all knowledge is valuable, but only as an end unto itself—of what we may learn from it to embolden the beliefs we already hold. He has turned his back on the search for truth. He has forgotten that ours is a religion that strives for righteousness and against repression. He has forgotten the passion that filled Jesus for equality among all people. Sadly, his interest in your library is only for the sole purpose of history."

She squeezed his hand tightly, as his lip began to quiver.

"His letter is simply an order to copy whatever documents I feel are of importance or to secure the originals —to steal them—and bring them back to Rome. He would have me delay the Pope's declaration for however long it takes, as long as the documents are preserved and returned safely to him. But the ideas contained in the documents are not foremost in his mind."

His eyes were red, and he bit his lip to keep himself from crying. Maria was now sitting directly beside him, and he rested his head on her shoulder, as she ran her fingers through his hair. They sat like that for awhile, a respite from the obligations of the moment.

"Maria, he has misjudged me," he said, wiping his nose on the back of his sleeve. "Flavius believed that I would remain as insulated from the world as he is. Instead, I have become a man with no realm of my own, no place to call home. My duty impels me to follow the Pope's instructions and excommunicate the members of your church, but at the same time, I know what I've seen, and I feel in my heart that what I've read is true."

He looked at her with so much doubt on his face, and said, "How can I answer either of these callings with a clear heart and mind?"

"Samuel," Maria began, "that's not all is it?"

"I can not find it in myself to agree completely with the things you teach here. Your beliefs are based on fragments of history, but they have no firm foundation that I can find. The truth is the most important thing to me, and the fact that people have believed such things in the past is not enough. I have given too much of my life to the study of the New Testament to be wholly convinced by the few writings that I have read in your library."

She said nothing.

"Where is the truth? In your library or in Rome?"

Samuel looked at the horizon where the sun had fallen between two layers of clouds, filling the sky with a fantastic explosion of yellow and pink. Its beauty, however, seemed to exist separately from him, and could not touch the deep sadness within. For a long time, neither he nor Maria spoke.

"You sound like a man at the beginning of a spiritual journey," she said, their hands still clasped. "When you arrived here, you sounded like a man who believed he had already completed most of his journey."

He nodded.

"I don't think this is a bad place to be, Samuel."

"Maybe, but...I feel as if I've lost my way. My trust remains in the Lord, but He seems to have shrouded himself from me."

He had begun to grow tired of his own weakness. He had just poured out his soul to Maria, and wanted nothing more than to be strong enough for her. What was this fascination he had for her? He was bewitched by her charm, her daring, the effortless way she coped with life.

"Samuel," she said very quietly.

He turned to look at her, hopeful that she would sense his longing and show him the way.

"What if there are more documents than those you've seen?"

At first he did not know if she was serious, but the look in her eyes gave him the answer. "Are there other writings?"

She was silent.

"Does your church have documents that are not in the library?"

"I can't say just now," she said. She moved suddenly away from him and began to stand up.

"That means you do," he said, grabbing one of the loose folds of her dress. "Tell me if you do!"

"I can not say, Samuel!"

He let go of her dress, and looked up at her inquisitively. "Of course you can't," he responded.

She looked at him for a long time, a strange and troubled look on her face. Before he could say another word, she began to climb back down from the rock. She turned back to him momentarily.

"I will talk to Anna."

Chapter 30

W hen they reached the church, Maria asked Samuel to wait for her in the meeting hall. Before she walked off, she leaned forward and kissed him on the lips. He closed his eyes and put his hands up to her face. Then she pulled free and was gone.

He sat in one of the back pews for a long time, glancing at the cross before him and watching as the sky overhead turned from pale blue to deep blue, and the stars began to appear. If there were more documents in the church's possession, especially those that made Maria so eager, it could change everything. He had possibly earned their trust, and if he did, he did not wish to violate it. He had assumed from the start that as the representative of the Pope, he would be granted open access to everything these people had, even though they knew that he was a threat to their deepest beliefs and most cherished traditions. He kneaded his hands in frustration and anticipation. The roofless building was silent around him.

Eventually, he heard footsteps approaching the entrance. Anna entered, followed by Joshua and Maria. He stood to greet them as they arrayed themselves in front of him. It was Anna who was first to speak.

"Maria has asked us to do something...something unprecedented," she said solemnly. "And yet it is not only on her behalf that we are considering it. Joshua has also told me that he believes you are a man of character."

Samuel glanced at the big man, whose face remained impassive in the gloom of dusk.

246

"But even this would not have been enough for me to consent to such a request," Anna continued.

Samuel began to speak, but she silenced him with a patient motion. Her small frame commanded amazing authority when she wished it to. "The only reason I can see for granting her request is believing in my heart that it will help to ensure the continuation of our traditions, heritage, and beliefs. We all know that unless our traditions are shared with the generations that will come after us, they will die, and that would be a loss for all Christianity and for Jesus' message."

He realized that the feeling that he had sensed all along—the feeling that he was being judged at all times—all of it had led to this moment. There was nothing he could hide from them, and so he met Anna's gaze, as if opening himself to her wholly.

"It is not lightly that I am making this decision, Samuel. Tomorrow, the world may change, and this may be our last chance to save our way of life."

Samuel realized what she meant. A blast of fear like a cold wind chilled his soul.

She stared at Joshua intently, who, in turn, nodded his consent. "We've decided to show you documents we had no intention of showing you upon your arrival."

Samuel remained stoic, not able to respond to the trust they were about to place in him.

"But we must ask you to do something for us in exchange," she went on. "We must ask you to swear that you will never reveal the existence, without our permission, of what we will show you."

"By simply revealing the existence of these documents, you know you are placing them at risk," Samuel replied honestly.

"Of course," she smiled.

"I don't know if I can swear such an oath."

"That decision is yours alone. But if you can not swear to us, then I can not go forward. Should this secret be revealed to the Bishop in Rome, our library, our church, and, yes, even our parishioners could be destroyed."

When rationality returned to him, he asked himself whether he could swear such an oath. He looked first to Maria, hoping she would help him to make a decision. But she remained impassive.

"Why do I feel," he asked, "as if I was converted from the moment I set foot on the grounds of this church?"

Anna smiled again. "Maybe it's the will of God that you play a greater role in the Church than what was envisioned by Gelasius. Christian women have been struggling against people like Gelasius for hundreds of years, Samuel. We have had to struggle to make our voices heard, and to make sure that our rightful place in Jesus' ministry is not erased from memory." Anna's voice grew stronger. "Sometimes I think that if your Bishop and others like him had their say, there would be no record at all of Mary, Martha, Veronica, Phoebe, Priscilla, or Mary of Magdala."

She held her hands out, leaning in closely to Samuel. "Look at the writings that are in the canon of Scripture now —those women are barely mentioned at all, their work as disciples barely mentioned. There's no record of the hundreds of women who have served our Lord as presbyters over the last five hundred years, and that record will be forever lost unless our history is preserved. Slowly but surely your theologians and bishops in Rome have been painting over the truth—spreading the slander that Mary of Magdala was a whore, wiping out the ministry of the sisters Martha and Mary, denying that many of the earliest house-churches were led by women, and now promoting Augustine's bizarre theory that original sin was caused by the inferior nature of women tempting man to sin."

She stepped back, a look of sadness and desperation finally creeping into her eyes. "So, yes, Samuel, we have been trying to convert you and help you to understand the history of our little church ever since you first stepped foot here. We tell the story of Christian women to everyone we meet. Why would we do any less for you?"

Samuel turned away from the three of them, looking back at the simple wooden cross that hung on the wall. Night had gathered around them, filling the roofless meeting hall with patches of heavy darkness. The stars had come out strongly overhead, and he could tell from the glow in the east that the moon was about to rise.

His heart was thumping loudly in his chest. He prayed and searched for the right words. The cross before him seemed to be cut out of space and time, hanging before him like an eternal truth. All else around him was darkness, and the faces before him faded. It was only him, and the spirit that had taken hold of his heart.

"If the search for truth is pursued with a clear heart," he said, "no harm can come of it. The Lord is the Way and all truth leads to Him." He turned back to face them. "I swear to Jesus never to reveal your secrets without your consent."

The world came back into focus as Anna nodded, and the three of them turned and filed silently out of the meeting hall. Samuel followed them without question. They waited in silence at the edge of the courtyard while Maria went to the kitchen for candles, and then together they proceeded towards the library. None of them spoke until they were inside, among the rows of old books and manuscripts. Maria placed the candles on the desk where Samuel had spent so many hours and lit them.

"If what you have to show me is here, I believe I've already looked through everything of importance," Samuel said, showing some disappointment that no new revelation had been made.

"You are right, Samuel. You *have* seen everything here," said Anna.

"Then what…"

"This is not our only library, Samuel."

"But I've been everywhere on the grounds of the church…"

Samuel hushed up as he saw Joshua grasp the bottom of the heavy desk. They stepped back to give him room as he pulled it aside, and from the back of a dusty shelf near the door, he took a thin metal bar and inserted it into a gap between the two big flagstones that made up the floor. He strained mightily, throwing his weight against the lever, the muscles of his forearms and biceps bulging under the strain. With a crackling of stones, one of the flagstones budged far enough for him to lift it with his other hand. Slowly and carefully he removed it, leaning it against the wall. The dust settled to reveal a narrow dark hole.

"There is a ladder in place," Anna said. "It's steep, so we must be careful."

She set her candle on the ground next to the hole and then eased herself down into it, descending slowly. In the wavering light of her candle, Samuel could see that she was climbing down a wooden ladder with broad steps, moving the candle down step by step as she went.

"After you," said Maria, smiling as if she couldn't contain herself any longer.

"Just below where I sat every night," said Samuel, shaking his head.

"The truth is always close at hand," she said. "Sometimes you just need to know where to look."

Joshua chuckled to himself as he handed Samuel a candle from the table.

"Is it safe?" Samuel called looking down the shaft at the now distant candlelight.

"If a woman can do it, surely..."

"I get it," Samuel said, cutting Maria off.

He turned and climbed into the hole as Anna had, making his way carefully down the ladder and moving his candle as he went. Above him, the square of light where he could see the faces of Joshua and Maria grew smaller and smaller. He did not look down. Around him, he noticed that the walls were braced by heavy beams and slats of wood. He went slowly, moving his feet and hands one at a time, very conscious of the sound of his own breath hissing through the darkness.

After a long time, his foot reached the rough stone of the floor. He staggered for a moment, surprised, and caught himself. Taking up his candle, he turned carefully. He was in a small chamber, reinforced by a number of wooden beams. He had been so consumed by his descent that he hadn't noticed the light of Anna's candle, and she now stood next to him. She gestured to a low tunnel that slanted away from them.

"We still have to go down," she said, "but the grade is more gentle."

Samuel looked all around him. It was difficult to tell if these caves were natural or sculpted by human hands. The effort required to dig so deeply into the earth would have been immense, but it was clear that the fingerprints of generations of men and women had left their mark here.

"Where did this all come from? Did you create these tunnels, or were they here before you?" he asked.

"They've been around much longer than we can remember. The tunnels are quite old and have served as the parish's trove of rare documents."

Samuel's attention had been diverted to the crumbling

timbers he spotted.

"After the tremors that shook the earth and collapsed the roof of our church, much of this upper part shifted and became unstable. Joshua took it on himself to brace the walls with salvaged timbers from the collapsed roof to prevent a cave-in. As you can see, the work is not done yet."

"Is it safe to be down here?" Samuel asked with some trepidation.

"They have been safe for over two hundred years, which is when they were discovered. When church members built the library, they discovered the caves. With a little work the caves became a natural hiding place for a number of precious books and artifacts that needed to be hidden from the Roman emperor. How ironic that today they are being hidden from the Roman bishop! The ladder was constructed and secured to the foundation of the library, and then the building was added to conceal the entrance."

Just then Maria reached the bottom of the ladder. She had climbed down quickly and gracefully, the light of her candle growing steadily brighter as she neared, and Samuel sensed because of her dexterity in the tunnel that this wasn't the first time she had ventured to these caverns. Joshua had waited at the top, guarding the entrance.

With Maria by their side, Anna turned and led the way into the reinforced tunnel. It slanted down for a ways and then began to slope gently upward again. At this point the wooden bracing stopped, and Samuel could see in the light of the candles that the walls were made of solid rock, hollowed out to form a gently undulating passage.

"Are we moving in the direction of the sea?" he asked Maria, behind him.

"I don't think so," she said, "but it turns subtly, so it's difficult to say where it ends up."

The air here was dry and cool, and he knew there had to

be an opening to the sea, maybe in one of the steep cliffs. The roof of the tunnel rose and fell, and at points Samuel had to stoop as he walked. He moved slowly, and Anna's candle grew smaller in front of him. Just as he thought he was going to lose her, the light suddenly grew much brighter.

He rounded a final corner, and stepped out of the tunnel into a large cave. Its walls were formed of the same hard rock as the tunnel through which they had passed, and the rough surface seemed to soak in the light of their candles, magnifying it and casting it about the room. In the center of the cave, three long tables had been arranged at right angles, and each held a line of neatly ordered books and scrolls.

"These," said Anna, "are our most precious documents."

Samuel barely heard what she said. He moved forward in a dream-like state, looking from one carefully ordered stack to the next. Some of the titles were vaguely familiar to him, others he had heard of from Flavius, and still others, he had never heard of before, their existence resting tenuously on the secrecy of the tunnels.

"There are writings here from the earliest times in Christianity," Anna said. "Everything we've been able to collect rests in this place. There is one in particular that I would like you to see."

She led him to the middle of the center table where a stack of papyrus seemed to occupy a special position. Delicately, she lifted the sheets and held them out for Samuel.

Neither of them spoke a word, and Samuel could only imagine its content. It was wrapped in cloth and bound with twine. Despite its plain appearance, a shiver of anxiety shot up his spine. He stood motionless as if possessed by the document.

"Do you know Aramaic?" Anna asked softly.

"The language that Jesus spoke? Is this text that old?" His

hands began to tremble at the thought.

"A small part of it is. Maria will help you translate if need be."

Samuel still stood, his feet rooted to the floor. He felt as though his fate had just been handed to him, and if he wasn't careful, it would flee like water slipping through his hands.

Maria brought him a chair and several extra candles. He sat and slowly peeled back the outer layer of cloth that held the bundle together. It had been some time since he had read Aramaic, and he sounded out the title slowly.

"The Gos...pel... the Gospel of... of..."

He stood back from the text and looked back at Maria. The light from the candle cast deep shadows in the lines of her face as she beamed at him.

"The Gospel of Mary?"

Samuel had never heard of this Gospel. "Is this...who... how did you?" He didn't know where to start. He could see that the fragile, brittle parchment was very old and the ink faded. He took a deep breath. "How old is this book?"

"It was first written down in the late first century, about sixty years after our Lord's resurrection. But as you will read, it had been passed down orally since Jesus' ascension."

"Where did it come from?"

"This copy is from Egypt, where it was first recorded. This is the only copy we know of. Maria is transcribing and translating it, but it is slow work, and there are many documents she is trying to preserve."

Anna paused, moving closer to the young man before her. "Samuel, when the Roman Church decreed that there would be one set of ecclesiastical canons, it also decreed that many other writings were heretical. They ordered them burned, that the truth they chose for themselves might never be questioned. At first, those groups that refused were excommunicated. But once Emperor Constantine converted to Christianity, the Roman Church had the political and military might of the Roman Empire behind it. The Popes no longer settled for excommunication—they ordered that many writings be destroyed and its followers persecuted. We had no choice but to hide these documents from all who seek to destroy them."

Samuel blanched. Anna and Joshua, and even Maria, must have known that he was sent here to destroy the very documents he held in his hands. Did they also think that he had been sent to burn their homes to the ground? Yet even if they had, they still brought him down here to read these precious writings. At this thought, tears filled his eyes.

He looked at Anna and Maria. "Mea culpa," he said ominously.

"Stay for however long you wish. We will check on you periodically," Anna said.

Maria stayed next to him for a while after Anna had started back towards the tunnel. He took her hand in his and pressed it gently. "Thank you for your trust in me."

She nodded and squeezed his hand in return. When she was gone, Samuel was left alone with the ancient texts.

He began reading.

Chapter 31

〜

Mary of Magdala leaned against a tree, her body shaking as she cried uncontrollably. It was a clear, cool day, and the sky above was patched loosely with clouds. The land had blossomed around her and turned green from the recent storms. Wildflowers were once again beginning to dot the countryside. But she noticed none of this. To her, the landscape looked gray and dead. The people around her seemed hardly to exist. The past days had been like a dream, a nightmare from which Mary could not awaken. She felt like she was moving through a fog. It hurt even to breathe.

The day before had been the Sabbath, and she had spent it mourning with Jesus' mother, his sisters, Martha and Mary, and another of His most devout followers, Joanna. Though they found strength in one another, they felt lonely and deserted. All the disciples, the men He had chosen to be His first students and His best friends, had fled into hiding after His crucifixion and were still nowhere to be found. When Jesus' mother had collapsed with grief, none had emerged to comfort her.

And so it was that Mary of Magdala went alone to His tomb that morning to pray and observe His memory.

Mary Magdala was not a young woman; at thirty-seven, she was well into middle age. She had already buried her husband, Aaron, but nothing could have prepared her for the crucifixion of her beloved rabbi, Jesus. She was not simply heartbroken—she felt that the world beneath her feet had been rent to pieces. Whatever good was left seemed to flee from the towns and cities. All who had followed in His footsteps appeared lost and confused. Mary had truly believed that Jesus was the Messiah, the Chosen One. She had sold off her entire fortune and used the money to fund Jesus' and His disciples' travel, preaching, and ministry. She had given up her power and considerable status in Jewish society, and become the closest confidante of a poor, itinerant, and radical peasant teacher whom she thought would change the world.

Had she been a fool? How could this have happened? She berated herself as she walked through the outskirts of town to the cave Joseph of Arimathea had provided to lay Jesus in. How could Jesus have died, and died as a petty criminal? How could He have suffered so much...when He sought only to bring love into the hearts of men and women?

When the tomb came into sight a few hundred yards ahead, she broke down into sobs that convulsed her body. She could not help feeling betrayed. The disciples were in hiding and she was alone. The thought only increased her grief. She had loved Him so much, like a brother, like a son, like a husband. To ease her own grief, she had tried to imagine the pain He had gone through, imagined her own body nailed to the rough wooden timbers, the tip of a spear thrust in her side, the fires of hell beneath her feet. Could it be greater than her pain now, the emptiness she was left to face? Who among us, she wondered, could ever understand His humiliation and His agony? Her tears blinded her; she wanted to tear her hair out at the injustice.

She stumbled the final few paces with her hands in front of her, blind with despair and lost in her grief. She felt the cool touch of solid rock and rested her forehead against it. The tears flowed through her, as if from a deep well, washing her spirit clean. It was some time before she caught her breath and dried her eyes. Before her, the mighty stone that had concealed His body had been rolled back.

Oh God, couldn't they have left His body alone! Couldn't they have done that at least! she wondered.

"MARY!"

She spun around, looking frantically about her. The voice seemed to have come from all around her. She stepped backward slowly, and froze, looking up. Two immense figures clothed in blinding white light stood atop the cave.

"WHY DO YOU SEEK THE LIVING IN THE PLACE OF THE DEAD?"

Their voices came at her like the crack of thunder, like a river in flood, like the thousand trumpets of an approaching army.

She gazed up at the ghost-like figures, and fear gripped her throat. She tried to answer but could not. Her words hung like icicles in her chest. Their light seemed to grow, weighing down upon her with crushing force. As she stood on the verge of collapsing, a familiar voice called her name from behind her.

"Mary."

The light of the ghosts retreated, and the world again settled into its normal state before her.

"Mary, turn around," the voice called.

She turned to see a young man walking towards her. His face was clean and pure, and His smile was full of joy. He seemed to know her. She took several steps back, afraid that another apparition had come to steal her away.

"Leave me alone!" she shouted. The grief of the last days had transformed into a sudden explosion of rage. "Why can't you just leave me alone!"

The man, still smiling, stretched His hand out to her. Very gently, He said, "Don't you recognize me, Mary?"

She gazed at Him, poring over His face, His robe, His hands. Her eyes went wide as she looked deeply into his eyes.

"No...no! It can't be! I don't believe... You... You..." She fell to her knees convinced that her grief had made her mad. The man could not be Jesus. His face was so much younger than she had known, so perfect and unsullied by time or age. Yet despite what her eyes beheld, she knew in her heart that it was He, raised from the dead. She began to shake and could not bear to look upon the figure before her. "My Lord. Rabbi...."

She felt His hand on her cheek. The touch of those fingers filled her with light and comfort.

"Do you know me now?" He asked.

The trembling was so violent that she could barely speak. "Rabbi?" she whispered.

"Yes."

"But how? I was there. I laid your body in this tomb. I was there when your mother drew the cloth across your face. You died. How can this be? How can this be?" Her voice cracked. Her grief felt like a liquid that was slowly falling away, back into the earth.

He took her by the hand and helped her to her feet. Together, they walked into the shade of the tomb and sat on a low boulder. As He sat next to her, He took her hand softly in His. She remembered all the conversations sitting next to each other this way, but she still could not stop trembling.

"I know you were there, Mary. I did die. And now through the power of God, I have been raised from the dead, to live again."

"But you're...different. I didn't recognize you. Are you real? Why did you come back? Are you here forever?"

He interrupted her and held up His hand. "Peace, Mary."

At that instant she understood that it was really He. That gesture, that phrase—she had seen and heard it a thousand times. She closed her eyes and took a deep breath. When she opened them, she leaned into Him and threw her arms around Him. He was real, tangible, and solid.

After a moment, she broke the embrace, and He smiled at her and stood. For a long time He was silent, looking back towards the town. She could not guess what He was thinking. Everything around Him seemed to glow with new life—the rocks, the dirt, the grass, and the flowers. He turned and squatted before her, with His heels flat on the ground. She had seen Him do this many times when conferring with the disciples, a habit from His upbringing. Peasants and working men squatted like this, gossiping or trading or seeking a bit of shade while they waited for the day to pass. It had always been considered below those in polite society, where people were more fond of lounging on couches to conduct their business or join in idle conversation.

Seeing Him like this once more, she recalled the time He had argued gently with a rabbi in front of his provincial audience. The farmers and laborers who had gathered all squatted as He did now, and they watched closely as He dropped down before them, illustrating His point by drawing a figure in the dust. The peasants watched in amusement as the rabbi bent over uncomfortably to examine the figure. As Jesus continued to speak, the rabbi knelt awkwardly in front of Him, staining his embroidered robes with dry earth. This simple mannerism had shown the people of the village more clearly than anything else that this man Jesus spoke for them —as a common person, born from among them to raise them up.

"I know this is hard for you to understand," He said, looking her steadily in the eye, "but I need you to listen to me carefully, Mary. I have much to teach you, and little time."

"Little time?"

"Yes. I need you to listen closely."

She nodded. "Whatever you ask, I shall do."

"In the months and years to come, it will be up to you and those around you to continue to spread the message. My words are simple, but many will use them for their own means if you are not there to guide them."

"Tell me what I must do, Rabbi."

He stood then, and gesturing with His hands as He had when delivering His sermons, He began to talk. He explained again all that He had spoken of during His life, and more. His words were etched like lines of fire in her memory. He spoke of the eternal nature of the human soul, of the nature of God, and of the way to find peace from within. He told her that the salvation of humanity is rooted in the good and the true, and how His resurrection negated the power of death. He told her to beware of those who would usurp power in His name or decree laws beyond the simple rules He said: to love God, to love one another, and to turn the other cheek. He told her that, above all, she and the rest of humanity must live in love and protect the truth.

Mary listened carefully and asked many questions. As the sun began to set, Jesus looked to the sky, and she sensed that it would soon be time for Him to leave.

"Mary—there is much I have told you, and much I have asked. Before proceeding though, it is essential that you call together my disciples and tell them what has passed between us."

"But they are hiding in fear, my Lord. They have been hiding since the day of your crucifixion." Her voice dropped to a whisper. "They truly do love you, Rabbi, but they are confused and afraid."

"I know," He said. He had turned again to look at the city. His face did not show it, but Mary knew that it had broken

261

His heart to see that some of those closest to Him had abandoned Him and His message.

"You don't have to protect them," He said, turning back to her. "I knew this would happen. That is why I have chosen you, Mary, to bring to the world the message of my resurrection, which will serve as a strong symbol of my love for women and their leadership in the faith."

There was nothing she could do to express the gratitude she felt. She bowed deeply, and held His hand, returning His look of joy and hope.

"I shall carry forth your message," she spoke firmly, her earlier fear completely gone.

He turned to her and smiled. "It is no easy thing I am bestowing upon you. You must find them and proclaim my resurrection. You are the first to preach the good news of salvation, Mary. You are the first and will always be the most important of my disciples. You have an understanding as deep as the ocean. You are the apostle to the apostles, and all those who will preach the good news until the end of time will stand on you."

He took her hands and pulled her gently to her feet. "Find the eleven and tell them not to be afraid." He then shook His head and laughed light-heartedly.

"What are you laughing about, Rabbi?" she asked.

He looked for a moment as if He were contemplating His answer before speaking, and He shook His head once more. "It seems that I am always telling those men not to be afraid. Only you and the other women who have believed in me have conquered your fear. The men never seem to listen, Peter especially. He is so headstrong..."

His look became grave. "I'll warn you now, Mary. They will not want to listen to you and will willfully misunderstand my message. You must make sure that my teachings are not lost or changed by those who fear its meaning. The light of truth and equality must never be allowed to go out. The truth will scare people, and they will turn away. It will not be easy for you, Mary, nor, I fear, for the women who come after you."

"I don't understand why it has to be that way," she said, shaking her head. "I don't understand why the world is so unjust."

"We do not get to make the world, Mary; we can only try to affect it. I have always treated women as equals of men, but my teachings challenge people. This teaching challenges them as much as any. I know many call my teaching radical, but there is no love more righteous than love for each other. You must be strong."

"I will be," she said firmly.

"Find the eleven tonight and tell them all to gather tomorrow afternoon at the house of Levi. I will meet you there." He took her hands one more time. His smile was like a vast, joyful ocean, and He seemed larger now, with the stature of a king. He walked into the mist and was gone.

.   .   .

Mary ran as fast as she could back into town. She spent the whole night in search of the eleven apostles. She found them hidden in stables, in olive orchards, behind barricaded doors, and under false floors. Some had shaved their heads and beards to change their appearance. Andrew even pretended not to know her when she found him.

To each of them, she proclaimed the truth: Jesus had been resurrected. He had triumphed over death so that every person could do the same. She repeated it over and over again until they listened to her.

Some were angry, some were incredulous and amazed, some did not believe her at all, and some even took pity on

263

her, thinking she had gone mad. But one by one she found them and gave them the message, and one by one they agreed to meet at the house of Levi.

The last one to find was Peter. None of the others knew where he was, and she had already looked everywhere she could think of. In desperation, she began asking around at the local market, trying to determine who might have seen him last. As it was only as she had given up all hope that she saw a man, hanging his head, spinning a half-full cup of wine between his fingers.

He stood up as he recognized her, and his eyes opened wide in fear.

"Peace, Peter—you have nothing to fear from me."

He slowly settled back down into his seat, watching her closely as she began to tell him what she had seen. By the time she finished, his face was pale, and his eyes shot around the market wildly. Without a word, he shot up from his seat and shoved past her, upsetting the table and spilling the bottle of wine. He took off running through the night, and as she followed after him, she realized he was headed towards the tomb. She arrived to find him frozen in front of the massive boulder, rolled aside from the entrance. Without looking back at her, he entered the cave. Mary expected him to shout with happiness or cry with amazement, that he might fall to his knees in exultant joy and join her as she brought the eleven back together. But when he emerged from the dark cave, his face held only anger.

"Are you lying?" he asked.

"I am not."

"Are you mad?"

"I have spoken the truth, Peter."

He ran his hands through his hair and looked up at the sky.

"It can't be," he muttered to himself. "This can't be true."

"It is, Peter, and we must go. He has asked that we meet him and the others within the hour. You must believe me!"

Peter laughed at this, and Mary looked at him, scared and confused. "What is the meaning of this, Peter?"

"Believe you?" he shook his head. As she moved close to him, the anger flared in his eyes once more.

"I can't believe He appeared first to you!" he yelled. "You! A woman!"

Chapter 32

⌒

Samuel, oblivious to time, continued his reading of the ancient documents.

. . .

Jesus spent forty days with them, eating, talking, laughing. But He also taught them, and He preached to them, and tried to help them understand His message fully and completely so they would be prepared to spread the good news. They reveled in His presence and in His infinite wisdom and kindness, their faith and strength restored by His presence.

Mary of Magdala, His closest confidante and most trusted advisor in life, became His most trusted helper. The other disciples came to her with questions when Jesus was busy, and she was a pillar of strength when they were afraid or confused.

Then one day, Jesus said: "I will be leaving you again, my disciples."

A grave silence fell over the room. "You must not be afraid. Be strong in your faith, and go out to preach to all you see. Tell them that peace is found within, and that the love of God is for all humanity without distinction. Be on your guard, and let no one deceive you by saying 'Look over here!' or 'Look over there!' for the seed of true humanity exists within you. Follow it! Those who search for it will find it." All listened intently.

"Go then, and preach the good news of the Kingdom of God. Learn, live, and love and be guided by my words and deeds. Do not lay down any rules beyond what I ordained for you, nor promulgate laws like a lawgiver, or else they will dominate you."

Some of the men began to weep, some cursed loudly, and others shouted, begging Jesus to come back. Only Levi and Mary of Magdala remained calm.

"Brothers, listen to me," Levi said, raising his hands for calm. "You must hear what our Lord has told us. We must go forth and spread Jesus' message; we must remain focused on helping others. We must find the peace of Jesus Christ within our hearts."

"How are we going to go out to the rest of the world and preach the good news of love and the new humanity of Christ?" Thomas shouted out. "As they crucified Him, they will crucify us!"

Mary stood up, and her voice rang loudly above the din of doubt and fear. "My brothers and sisters—do not weep nor let your hearts be irresolute. His grace will be with you and will shelter you. We must trust in Him, for as He has joined us together He will give us the strength to persevere." As she spoke, a calm descended upon all in the room.

Peter turned to her and said, "Sister, we know that the Savior loved you more than any other woman. He confided in you, and trusted that you would uphold His will on earth. What has He told you that we do not know?"

Mary paused, looking out over the anxious men and women before her. They all seemed so lost without Him. Could they not see that He lived on in them, in their hearts and souls? Did they not hear the message that He had given to them, or feel the love that He had given so freely to them?

Slowly, and with great strength in her voice, she told them everything that Jesus had passed on to her. She told them about their conversations, her questions and His answers, the parables and stories, and her attempts to understand a sometimes subtle message. She told them about her visions of God and Christ in Heaven. With her arms raised high, she told them to be brave and strong and to find peace in their hearts, as Jesus taught her. She said they must conquer their fear and go out to tell the world about Jesus— about His death and victory over death; about His healing of the sick; about His acceptance of all, even tax collectors and prostitutes and lepers; and about His parables and sayings regarding the Kingdom of God and the true nature of humanity.

When she finished, dusk was gathering outside the windows. The disciples were silent for a long time, until finally Peter stood up among them. Peter was a tall, powerfully built man, a fisherman by trade, and fiery in all aspects of his life: quick to anger and quick to regret, and passionate in love and hatred. He loved Jesus enormously— everyone gathered there knew that—but he often misunderstood Jesus' message, and distanced himself from his fellow disciples when he felt threatened or confused. He had also been quick to belittle Mary whenever the opportunity arose, yet was careful to do so when Jesus was out of earshot, for every one of the disciples knew that Jesus considered Mary to be His most trusted advisor.

Peter and his brother had once asked Jesus if He would pick them as the official leaders of His movement once He was gone. At the time, Jesus had just brushed them off and told them gently that they need not worry.

Peter had tried to argue with Jesus, but Jesus was quick to cut him off. There were certain things that must be, and must be for a reason He told Peter then. But the fact remained that Peter very much desired to play an important role in Jesus' ministry, and his jealousy of Mary had not decreased with

Jesus' death and resurrection.

His face and neck were flushed, and his body was shaking lightly as he turned to face her. "Did Jesus speak then? Speak to a woman in private without our knowing about it? Did He choose her over us, the twelve apostles?" Peter exclaimed, his eyes bulging and spittle spewing from his mouth. He seemed like a man possessed.

He realized he was hurting her, and Mary felt the pain like a blow to the stomach. *After all we have been through,* she thought, *after all Jesus had preached, and in light of the great danger they still faced from the Romans, how could he demean her this way?* "Peter, my brother, what are you saying? Do you think I've made all this up to anger you? That I am telling lies about our Savior?" She strained to hold back her emotions and to remain calm. The very thought of what Peter was accusing her of was overwhelming.

It was Levi who came to her defense. "You are treating Mary like she is an adversary. We all know that Jesus loved her, that He chose her to be a leader to the disciples. Why are you challenging her now? If the Savior considered her to be worthy, who are you to disregard her?"

"Who am I?" Peter raged. "I am the 'Rock' upon which Jesus said he would build his Church...and you all heard Him say it!"

"Peter," James spoke up. "We did hear Him say it. And you are the chief apostle of Jesus, and Jesus did give you the name *Kepa*, which conveys that you are His rock. You were also the first amongst us from our little fishing village to be called by Jesus. And you will be the *Kepa* to the disciples going forward. But Jesus did not intend for you to be the *Kepa* that crushes Mary Magdala, or other women for that matter."

"You're wrong," Peter responded, glaring venomously at

James. "How do we know she's telling the truth about what Jesus said? She might have just made it up—He never once told us that she was to lead this movement. He may have favored her, but He never put her in charge of me or the rest of us!

"I have had a revelation that many of us will be executed and become martyrs for our faith, but I have had no such revelation for Mary of Magdala. I have also had a revelation that I was handed the keys to the Kingdom of Heaven, which is a sign of my authority over others, certainly including the women disciples. I will consult with the other apostles on matters of importance, but that will not include Mary of Magdala! I will be the guardian of the true faith and the rock on which our Church is to be built."

"Peter, we will all accept you as our leader, but not at the expense of others who were so close to Jesus. Remember, you denied Him three times as he predicted you would and Mary Magdala has never denied Him," Levi responded.

"No, Levi—what Peter says is true!" Andrew had now jumped into the fray. "Jesus said to Peter at our last supper, 'I have prayed that your own faith may not fail; and once you have turned back, you must strengthen your brothers', which seems to me to give a special position to Peter."

"And the risen Christ appeared to Mary Magdala for He must have recognized she was capable of understanding the great mystery of the Resurrection and to pass on to others the good news of His rising from the dead, which seems to me to give a special position to Mary," replied Levi.

Mary responded with tears in her eyes. "My brother, Peter, what can you be thinking? Do you believe that this is just my own imagination, that I invented this vision? Or do you believe that I would lie about our Teacher?"

. . .

Samuel rubbed his eyes. He had been reading for hours, but he had to know more about the feud between Mary Magdala and Peter. The reaction of Peter was a reflection of the times they lived in. There was a refusal to accept the truth especially if it came from a woman. As Mark had so eloquently captured the moment in his Gospel: *Now as he arose from the tomb early on the first day of the week, he appeared first to Mary Magdalene, from whom he had cast out seven demons. She went and told those who had been with him, as they mourned and wept. But when they heard he was alive and had been seen by her, they would not believe it.*

And similar words in the Gospel of Luke: *Now it was Mary Magdalene and Joanna and Mary the mother of James and the other women with them who told this to the apostles; but these words seemed to be idle rambling, and they did not believe them.*

And Peter in his writings adds: *How is it possible that the Teacher talked in this manner to a woman, about secrets of which we ourselves are ignorant? Must we change our customs, and listen to this woman? Did he really choose her, and prefer her to us?*

Many of the writings in the secret cavern revealed Peter's mistrust of women, such as his morning prayer: *God, I thank you for not making me an invalid, poor, or a woman.*

This is so unlike the writings of Mary of Magdala, Samuel thought as he read her works: *Therefore let us atone, and become fully human so that the Teacher can take root in us. Let us grow as he demanded of us, and walk forth to spread the Gospel, without trying to lay down any rules and laws other than those he witnessed.*

It was apparent to Samuel as to which of these thoughts

more fully embraced those of Jesus, but still two schools of thought went forth to spread the Gospel, with only one transcending gender.

Chapter 33

⌒

There was nothing left to say or do. He had gone through and read or skimmed through every document contained in this secret library. The secrets that had unfolded before him, the knowledge that had come to light—he could never look at his Church in the same way.

The foundation that he sought—that he had claimed to Maria did not exist—he found here in the Gospel of Mary. The laws that Mary had outlined, and the words she had caught from Jesus' mouth were undeniably comprehensive, and ran like a thread through many of the disparate works he had discovered in the texts that lay above him. Her Gospel fit with much of what Samuel had grown up knowing all his life, and to some extent, it was even simpler and purer. The message of love that she put forth, a message of unfettered, radical love for all creatures and all beings—it made sense. It just seemed right. After a lifetime of ascribing to the dogmas of the Catholic Church, arguing his way around the loopholes and the confusion, Samuel finally felt as though he had heard the Word of his God, ringing truly and clearly from within himself.

He unconsciously picked up many of the ancient documents and wound his way through the tunnel to the ladder. Gingerly, he climbed the ladder with the documents underarm and the candle in the same hand. As quietly as he could, he returned the heavy rock floor to its place over the opening. Clandestinely, he went to his room and placed a few items and the documents in a satchel and took flight from the church on its fastest steed.

He knew the journey to Rome would take a few days and decided to spend the first night at the house of his newly found friend. Rachel was surprised to see him but welcomed him warmly. He gave a brief account of what had happened and awaited her response.

"Christianity swept across the empire like a firestorm but also caused a firestorm of controversy. Jesus provided hope of salvation, a loving way of life, and equality for women. All powerful forces...and if I were to change from my pagan ways and adopt Christianity, I would need all three: hope, love, and equality. But the men of the Church promulgated along the way that humankind is weak and insisted that the path to God could only be found through the Church, the bishops, and its priests."

"Which meant that Christians could no longer find God for themselves and had to abide by the laws and rules laid down by the men of the Church," Samuel interjected.

"And now that you are filled with this information, what do you propose to do with it?"

"I am taking the documents to Rome to show them to the Pope. I believe that once he studies the documents, he will reverse his course to destroy the documents in the library and excommunicate the parishioners."

"You are so naïve, Samuel. Gelasius will destroy the documents, excommunicate the heretics, and persecute those that do not change their ways. Return to the village, Samuel, and I will carry your message to the Bishop of Rome!"

Just then they felt the thunder of hooves heading towards the house.

Samuel looked out the window. "Papal soldiers!" he exclaimed.

"Give me the signet ring and leave through the back of the house. There is a path through the woods that will get you back to the road. Go! Go quickly!"

He tossed her the ring and was out of the house and on the forest path with his horse when he heard the order of the commander: "Check the back and break through the front door." He heard the door collapse, following a blow by a soldier, and then loud voices clamoring in the house. He now feared for Rachel but knew it was urgent for him to bring a warning to the church by the sea. He continued on the path, leading the horse by its bridle until it led him to the road, and then spurred it to a full gallop heading to the south.

"Who was here with you before we arrived?" Jason growled.

"Nobody!"

"Then why is the table set for two?"

"Oh, a neighbor stopped by before dusk."

"And why is the porridge still warm?" he said while sticking his finger in the bowl. "Do what you want with this lying bitch!" he told his soldiers. "I am going to bed."

A centurion reached out and grabbed the front of Rachel's tunic. He pulled hard on the rough linen cloth, ripping the tunic. He kept pulling until it tore all the way down the front. She screamed and tried to cover herself with her arms. Another centurion grabbed her by the hair and pulled her outside while the others worked themselves into a frenzy. As the soldiers took turns raping her, she began to cry. They held her legs apart and when she cried too loudly, a soldier struck her in the face with his fist breaking her nose. She cried out and blood spurted onto the soldiers, making them more delirious. They ravished her most of the night until the soldiers were drained.

At daylight a centurion stumbled into the bedroom. "Captain, it is time to rise and continue our journey. The men are ready."

"What did you do with the lying bitch?"

"She is sleeping outdoors....Oh, by the way, we found this signet ring in her possession."

"Let me see that," he said as he examined the ring. "You stupid fool! This is the Pope's signet ring. That's who was here last night. Samuel! He will warn the outlaw church of our approach. Hopefully, he is on foot and we can overtake him. Let's ride!"

They walked by the naked body of Rachel, bloodied and in a fetal position. Jason spit on her and paid her no further heed.

When they had left, she dragged her bruised and beaten body to the well and drank of the cool water. She poured water over the dried blood and scrubbed forcefully to get the scum of the soldiers off her body. Slowly she got to her feet aching all over, her face swollen, and her groin throbbing with every step as she moved to the house. She gently placed a cloak over her naked body and slowly sat in a hard wooden chair staring blankly out the small kitchen window. At first she could think of nothing but the horrific scene she had been through. She prayed for strength to whatever god would listen, and gradually the pain eased a little and she was able to listen to the birds singing outside and feel the soft breeze flowing over her bruised skin. She picked up the mirror on the table next to her. She gasped. Her face was barely recognizable, it was so swollen. And her nose was out of shape, and her skin bruised a deep purple. Repulsed by the reflection, she let the mirror drop to her lap. She longed for someone to comfort her and help ease the pain.

Hours later, she awakened with fear in her heart. *I must have fallen asleep,* she thought. The cruelty of the night before came rushing back to her, and she saw it all in front of her, in all its horrors. *Nothing will ever be the same,* she lamented. However, she sensed that there was something left to be done; she did not know what, but she knew it had to do with the church by the sea. She packed a small bag, and before she left, she went to a drawer and pulled out a long dagger. The dagger was in a leather sheath that she could attach to her belt. Rachel looked at the dagger, realizing that she was taking the deadly weapon with her for a purpose other than her own protection.

A few miles from the village, Samuel's horse was spent. He left it at a nearby farm and continued his journey on foot. He wondered about Rachel and whether she was safe. He thought of Maria and what she now thought of him. He thought of Anna and Joshua and how he had deceived them. He reflected on Flavius and wondered what would become of his mentor. He called to mind the edict of Gelasius and how unjust it now seemed. *Were it not for the edict of Gelasius, none of this would have happened*, he thought.

But his first priority was to get to the church before the papal soldiers, so speed was paramount. It was a clear day, but the road was dusty from many days without rain. After a while he reached the top of a hill. Looking back, he could see along the road for a long distance. He feared seeing a cloud of dust along the road, but he saw none. He descended the other side of the hill feeling buoyed by his lead but did not slow down his pace. He ran for long distances and then walked, never stopping to rest. Whenever the road provided him with a long rearward view, he would stop momentarily and look back for the dreaded cloud of dust then quickly resume his pace of alternatively walking and running.

Jason and his squad of soldiers were travelling at a furious pace, doing their best to overtake Samuel before he arrived at the church. "We must rest our horses, Jason. They can not continue at this pace much longer," yelled one of the centurions.

"With God's help they will run right up to the church...ride as hard as you can. We are on God's mission," he responded, spurring his horse to go faster.

The centurion caught the irony of that statement: "We live as pagans but do God's work," he muttered.

Rachel moved agonizingly down the road, too weak to even turn upon hearing a wagon behind her. "Oh my God, what are you doing on this road in this condition?" the driver of the wagon said as he pulled up next to her. She turned gingerly to observe a rugged handsome man with a concerned look halting the wagon and coming to her assistance. "Please get into my wagon...I will take you to wherever you are going."

"I am going to the church by the sea," she responded weakly.

"Then that is my destination," he replied. "There is wine and cheese in the back. Please eat and then rest."

"As you wish."

The man smiled humbly and nodded.

.   .   .

"Anna! Maria! Samuel is gone!" Joshua said in a shocked tone of voice.

"Gone...gone where?" Maria asked.

"To Rome with our ancient documents and our fastest horse. You convinced us that he was trustworthy, and we opened our hearts and our most valued possessions to him!" he replied in an angry voice.

"Joshua, it was our decision to allow Samuel into our inner sanctum," Anna reminded him. "And I am saddened to say that our most prized tradition may now vanish from the face of the earth. The documents were our link to Christ, and they will certainly be destroyed. That is our sin to bear Joshua, not Maria's!"

"We must inform the elders of our grievous sin. Maria,

278

toll the bell to signal a meeting of the elders," Joshua ordered.

The three with heads bowed walked slowly to the meeting hall to face the elders of the congregation. As they reached the hall, they could see the elders coming out from the kitchen, the stable, and the fields. They arranged the chairs in a half circle and placed three chairs before them.

When the elders were seated, Anna rose to address them. Most of the elders seemed happy to have been called from their midday chores. They passed clay cups and a bucket of cold water around which an elder had drawn from a cistern outside the meeting hall. No one was prepared for what they were about to hear.

"Samuel has left us and in so doing has stolen one of our horses," Anna announced sadly.

There was a murmur of discontent from the elders.

"He rode off like a thief in the night with much more than a horse," Anna continued.

The elders looked at each other quizzically.

"He left with many of our documents..." she said as her voiced trailed off.

"But the documents in the library have been copied...and they were there mainly for show. We all know that they were there as a diversion to protect our ancient documents," one of the elders said.

"He left with more than the documents in the library."

The group gasped in horror. "How can that be?" an elder asked.

"Samuel took ancient documents from the secret cavern," she replied.

"How is that possible!" an elder exclaimed. "The elders never authorized his admission to the cavern."

"Joshua and I allowed him into the cavern to peruse the documents."

"But…but one of you must have stayed with him. He…he had been sent from Rome to destroy these documents."

"We trusted him…yes, we trusted him," she responded weakly.

Suddenly the doors to the meeting hall swung open with a loud crash. All heads turned to see Samuel standing on the threshold of the hall. His clothes were pressed with perspiration, and he was pale and haggard from miles of running. "Yes…yes, they entrusted me with your most historic documents. And I violated that trust by absconding with the ancient documents in the dead of night…" He paused to catch his breath. "But I was well intentioned. My purpose was to show the documents to the Pope and change his mind in regard to your traditions."

"Foolish, but sweet, man," Maria whispered under her breath loud enough for Anna to hear.

"And did you succeed in your mission?" an elder asked.

"I never made it to Rome. A woman of strong character convinced me otherwise…"

"Not so foolish after all," Anna whispered under her breath loud enough for Maria to hear.

"But there are papal soldiers not far behind me…who will arrive shortly!"

This sent a chill through the group of elders.

"Give the documents to Maria," Joshua commanded.

Maria grabbed the documents and instinctively followed Joshua to the library.

Samuel looked from one face to the next, meeting the eyes of each elder in turn.

Chapter 34

F lavius heard the crashing sounds as he raced through the halls, his old legs protesting under the strain, his heart and lungs laboring. He prayed desperately, knowing as he did so that it was in vain. He had been alarmed when interrupted in prayer in the chapel by a young messenger announcing that the Holy Father demanded his presence in his study near the library. Now the loud sounds as he approached his study could mean only one thing: His office was being ransacked.

Rounding the corner, he saw that several burly servants had busted the door to his office wide open and were now smashing his plain furniture with clubs. Little remained by the time he arrived, just wooden fragments scattered around the floor.

Gelasius stood to one side, staring at the wreckage, and holding Flavius's history casually in his arms. Flavius slowed to a walk as he entered the room, panting.

"My messenger finally found you?"

Flavius nodded at the Pope, catching his breath.

"I thought you should know that I've read your work in its entirety," Gelasius said, "and much to my surprise, it is repugnant." A look of utter fury crossed his face.

Flavius's eyes flitted between the servants, who had stopped their work, listening intently to Gelasius with an unsavory delight in their eyes.

"As such, I'm consigning it to the fate it deserves." Gelasius' voice seemed to lick forth like flames along Flavius's cheek.

"Gelasius, you can't do this!" cried Flavius. "The contents of that book are irreplaceable."

"Remember your place, Flavius!" roared Gelasius. The tight skin of his face had gone as pale as ivory. "Do not disgrace yourself more than you already have."

"Your Holiness," said Flavius, struggling to control his voice, "I beg you to reconsider. My work is not a promotion of heresy—it is simply a record of such thought. It can be used as a tool of our Church against future heretics—a peaceful way of demonstrating the error of their ways. Please...please reconsider..."

"Reconsider?" spewed Gelasius. "There can be no reconsideration of these damnable writings. The New Testament is our guide, and all writings that disagree with it are by definition heretical. My reaction is a result of my vigilance against the works of Satan. I will not be dissuaded by any man or any argument that defies this."

"Your Holiness, it is simply a record, a history," he said nervously, his earlier defiance completely gone.

"There is no history but the history recognized by the Church. All else is heretical and an aberration of His teachings."

"But, Your Holiness!"

"Enough, Flavius! The records contained in this book are not the work of any pious man, and I fear you have allowed yourself to be led astray by Satan. He cloaks himself in such arguments, in such lies and filth. You have disobeyed my direct wishes and spent your time undermining the Church you claim to love so much. Look within yourself and cast out the demons you find there. You should not be pleading to save this book of yours—but rather you should be pleading for forgiveness and salvation."

Flavius watched helplessly as the two servants held forth a stack of papers. "We found these in the desk, Your Holiness, and there's nothing else here."

"More of the same, Flavius?"

Flavius bowed his head. "Yes, they are, Your Holiness."

"Very well," said Gelasius, accepting the papers. "Clean this room out, and burn anything else you find."

He started down the hall, and Flavius followed him instinctively. Gelasius' words rang in his head. *Should I beg for forgiveness? Should I drop down on my knees, tearing at my hair, digging my nails into my own flesh that I might demonstrate my penitence? Or should I bludgeon the man before me, smash his head into the granite, grab his precious manuscripts, and flee?* He felt lost, as if he had blundered into a place where he did not know how to survive. He managed to keep up with Gelasius only by staring at the blurry white image of the papal robes dragging across the stones.

As they made their way through the opulent halls of the palace, all the things that might happen to his history and to him flashed before his eyes. He had seen Gelasius before with this kind of holy fire in his eyes, but it had never been directed at him. He felt both sinful and sinned against; shame and anger grappled in his turbulent mind. Their footsteps echoed in the unusually silent building, sounding to him like a succession of stone doors closing on him, dooming his soul to live forever in darkness.

They emerged into a grey, overcast courtyard. Past the corner of the building lay the grove of olive trees where Flavius had spent so many of his days walking, reflecting and thinking of one long gone from his life. But he could not see the trees because the courtyard was teeming with men; all the priests, monks, and servants who occupied the palace were present. When Gelasius and Flavius entered, the crowd hushed and parted, forming an aisle to the center of the courtyard.

"Your time is at hand, Flavius," Gelasius said in a harsh tone.

Flavius followed, feeling everyone's eyes upon him. In a circular space at the center of the crowd, a stack of firewood had been placed on a hearth. Gelasius walked to this open space and waited until Flavius stood next to him. With a grand gesture, Gelasius then turned in a complete circle, looking around the silent assemblage of men.

"I have called us together today," he said, "because I have learned that even here, in the bastion of our Church, in the heart of the kingdom of Christ on earth, in the very resting place of our beloved Saint Peter, we are not free from the terrible stain of heresy." His voice echoed loudly against the walls of the basilica. "One of our number, living and working amongst us, has succumbed to its stain. And this," he said, holding the bundle of papers high above his head, "is the result...heresy."

This is ecclesiastical justice, Flavius thought.

Gelasius nodded at one of the priests standing nearby, and the man stepped forward to strike a flame to the firewood. The fire immediately crackled to life and roared upward.

For a moment Flavius thought gloomily of Samuel. *What was he doing now? What would happen to him next?* Flavius had no doubt that the papal soldiers would arrest him. *What would his fate be with Gelasius? Would he escape, and if he failed how would he be punished?* Flavius realized he might never find out.

"In these pages," bellowed Gelasius, "the oldest and most central doctrines of our religion are defiled. In these pages, the teachings of our Savior Jesus Christ are desecrated. In these pages, the foundation of our Church is assaulted."

I am on trial for heresy. Gelasius is my judge and jury...and I have already been found guilty, Flavius surmised.

Gelasius glowered at Flavius. "This man who stands before you, once our trusted brother, claims that these writings contain only a benign history. He claims that these writings merely recount the beliefs of women. He claims that these writings will serve to combat the heresies of the future. Well, I say to all, that these are the claims of all heretics when they are caught, confronted, and convicted. For they know now that unless they repent and are absolved, they face an eternity in the fires of hell."

S*o that is my fate for recording a true history of women in the Church...an eternity in the fires of hell*, Flavius thought ruefully.

Gelasius took on a patristic air and said: "Recall the words of the poet Adam: 'This at last is bone of bones, and flesh of my flesh. She shall be called woman, because she was taken out of man.' Thus, let us always accept the domination of men over women as the proper God-given order, not only for the human race but also for the Christian Church."

Slowly, Gelasius pulled a single sheet from the stack of documents and began to tear it into thin strips, watching as they fluttered down before Flavius.

"When it comes to our beliefs, there are no benign attacks. These writings portray a misunderstanding of the order of the world that our Lord has decreed. They portray a deliberate perversion of that order. If this is not heresy, then the Word has no meaning."

Gelasius turned to the fire. "Lord!" he prayed, "Let us be cleansed of this heresy! Let it be purged from us and from this world like the righteous flame before us consumes this desecrated papyrus!"

With that, he hurled the manuscript and loose papers down onto the fire, and its flames leapt up hungrily as if to accept them.

285

The history of Christianity will never be told in the same way again, Flavius thought as tears rolled down his cheeks.

"Any writings or symbols of women's participation in the leadership of the Church shall henceforth be anathema and destroyed," Gelasius concluded.

All his years of work, the extensive research, the meticulous copying of documents, the difficult translations —all were gone in an instant. This was punishment from God for his hubris. Flavius felt his limbs turn cold as he collapsed, trembling visibly as the dying fire of his heart met the icy hands of grief and despair. Flavius now understood his punishment, and it would be worse than death.

As the flames burned down and only the ashes of the book remained, Gelasius turned to him. Flavius found the strength to draw himself up slowly, still trembling and terrified of the man before him.

"Flavius, I have known you for a long time. Until this moment, I have known you to be a good and faithful man." There were murmurs of agreement from the assembled priests.

"But we must be vigilant against sin and punish the wrongdoers, and set an example for our followers. Our faith must be defended at all costs."

I lost my sense of right and wrong along the way...could I not just be forgiven...must I also be punished for my transgressions, Flavius said to himself.

"We are under attack from all fronts. Our authority must be complete, and our beliefs must never be questioned."

Murmurs of consent floated across the courtyard.

"Heresy is evil. It corrupts the souls of men and women. It must be dealt with severely."

It was amazing, Flavius reflected, *how the truth could be just a little changed and sound so sinister*. "But our Lord also tells us that mercy is a great virtue."

I would prefer death to the mercy of Gelasius, Flavius thought.

Gelasius reached out and touched Flavius gently on the head. "If you confess your sin, ask for forgiveness, and say you are repentant, I will be merciful."

Flavius fought down a rising feeling of fear. He looked around desperately. He could have run, but he was surrounded by dozens of priests and monks, and would not have gotten very far. He bowed his head and did what had been asked by Gelasius. "I confess my sin of heresy, I ask for forgiveness, and I am repentant for my actions, Most Holy Father."

Gelasius removed his hand. "Very well," he said. "You have confessed your sin and I will give you absolution...but there must be a reconciliation between you and the Church and ultimately with God. If you are truly contrite and this is demonstrated in your actions, you will have reconciled with your Church and God. The glory of Rome has corrupted your mind, so for you to find reconciliation with the Church and God, I will take this temptation from you. You are condemned for the remainder of your earthly life to the hinterlands of Gaul where there are no books, no libraries, no heretical writings to entice you to sin again."

"I have faith in the mercy of God, I have contrition in my heart, and I will do penance in Gaul as imposed by the Holy Father."

"You will leave for Gaul immediately, Flavius, never to return to Rome!"

Chapter 35

⌒

The horses gave out on Jason and his band of soldiers. "Damn, we have driven them too hard!" Jason snorted.

"We are still miles from the church," a centurion said.

"We are soldiers, and we must reach our destination quickly. Fall into formation, and we will go into a forced march," Jason retorted.

Jason had to prevent Samuel from concealing the heretical documents. He didn't understand the philosophy of the Pope, but he understood that his mission was important and that Gelasius would not accept failure. He second-guessed whether he should have stopped to rest last night and why he did not immediately pursue the scoundrel leaving the house. *Am I losing my edge?* he wondered. Well, he would have his edge when he arrived at the church. He would be merciless, and if that meant executing the congregation, he would not give that a second thought. As they marched, he made his preparations carefully. If he succeeded, he would fall in the good graces of the Pope and would command his legion in Rome. If he moved fast enough, he would catch Samuel before he reached the village. He commanded the troops to go from a forced march to double-time.

"He will destroy us, like he destroyed the horses," murmured a soldier.

. . .

Far behind the soldiers, Rachel awakened in the back of the wagon. The food, wine, and rest had served her well, but the pain of her brutalization still wracked her body.

"You are awake," the driver said. "You have been sleeping for hours."

"The sleep did me some good. Are we close to the church by the sea?"

"We are still hours away, but I would love some company up front if you are up for it."

She struggled to get to the front seat. "What monster did this to you?"

"Papal soldiers...for no other reason than for their pleasure."

"When you are ready, I will straighten out your nose, but it will hurt. And then you will be as beautiful as ever."

"Why are you being so kind to me?" she asked.

"What is your name?"

"Rachel."

"Well, Rachel, I am a Christian...and part of being a good Christian is helping others. Those men who did this to you are not true Christians."

"And my nose . . . what makes you think you can fix it?"

"Rachel, I am a farmer and I am constantly caring for my animals. But before that, I was a centurion and I cared for many of my wounded soldiers."

"Then you will fight with me if I ever find that bastard Jason?"

"No...but I will let no harm come to you."

"So you are not my enemy, but you are not quite my ally either," she quipped.

. . .

289

Maria returned from the caverns to find Anna and Samuel in deep conversation. "The papal soldiers are coming and they will soon be here," Samuel said. "What can be done to save our congregation?"

"Pray...pray...and pray some more," Anna responded.

"They are coming for me. I could leave," Samuel suggested.

"Samuel, they are coming for our documents, to excommunicate us, and to execute us, if necessary. Your leaving will not help."

"They are only a handful of soldiers. Let's set a trap," Maria suggested.

"Then the Bishop will send a legion. We must conceal our documents for future generations and stand our ground. God help us!" Anna retorted.

"They will destroy our church and take the documents from the library," Joshua said as he entered the room. "When they leave, we will rebuild our church and library, practice our faith as we see it, and propagate the teachings of Jesus as expressed in our ancient documents. Toll the bell to gather the congregation, Maria."

. . .

The soldiers were nearing the village. None had dropped out, fearing Jason's wrath. The sun beat down mercilessly on them, and there was no breeze to cool them off. "We will be there soon," Jason said encouragingly.

. . .

"We should arrive in about an hour, Rachel." Rachel nodded grimly and settled down to wait. She could not help thinking about her encounter with the soldiers at her house in the woods. It was not her fault, but still she felt ashamed.

. . .

When the soldiers arrived, the entire congregation awaited their arrival outside the church. The soldiers fell at attention and withdrew their swords at Jason's command. He stood at the head of his squad and faced the congregation. Jason loved to fight. He had been a soldier in the Roman army. He had always been ready to lead a raiding party, set an ambush, or lead a charge in battle. His brutality was legendary, always willing to fight to the death. Even though vastly outnumbered, he stood ready to eliminate all opposition.

Anna approached the papal envoy. "We have prepared a response to Gelasius, the Bishop of Rome. I would ask you to deliver it to him."

"What does it contain?" Jason asked gruffly.

"Our theological arguments for the inclusion of women in the priesthood and all aspects of church life and leadership," she said, "along with a disputation of our status as ex-communicants, and a summation of the history of the early church, which we believe demonstrates the correctness of our views."

Jason looked at the papers, laughing heartily as the packet was handed to him. "Gelasius has no interest in your document. He will pay it no heed, let alone read it."

"No one can tell ahead of time what chain of events the Lord will set in motion," replied Anna.

His interest piqued. "And what would the Lord say to Gelasius?"

"This is about convincing Christians as well as non-Christians that the teachings of Jesus Christ apply to everyone equally, weak and strong, poor and rich, women and men. If we cut ourselves off from the Bishop of Rome, we will be cutting ourselves off from some of the people we need to reach the most. We need to make this a story that resonates around the Christian world."

"Your story will not resonate beyond this courtyard."

Just then a voice came from the crowd. "My name is Samuel," he said as he moved towards the soldiers. "I am the Pope's representative."

"Then where is your signet ring, Samuel, the representative of the Pope?" Jason asked sardonically.

"Well…well, I misplaced it."

"Here it is, Samuel," he said as he reached into the leather bag that hung from his belt and tossed the ring to Samuel. "I found it in the bed of the whore, Rachel, a day's walk from here."

He heard Maria gasp, but he knew now was not the time to explain. "The story will resonate, if not today, then tomorrow. Jesus came to liberate women, not to enslave them."

"Hold your tongue, Samuel," Jason interrupted. "I am here to do your work. Now, point me to the library."

Samuel looked at Joshua, and Joshua nodded his assent. "That is the library," Samuel said pointing at the nearby building.

"Burn it!" Jason ordered.

A gasp came from the congregation.

Within moments the conflagration spread rapidly through the old wooden building. "Ransack the other building…take anything of value and throw all the documents that you find in the fire," Jason ordered.

.   .   .

"Damn!" Rachel said seeing the billowing smoke in the distance. "Those bastards are destroying the church buildings! Whip this mule to go faster!"

. . .

"You, come here!" Jason said pointing to Joshua. "I will ask you but once. Where are the other documents?"

"There are no other documents." As the last word came out of Joshua's mouth, Jason ran his sword through Joshua's chest.

As he lay there gasping for air, Jason ordered, "You, come here!" pointing to Maria.

"No!" Samuel cried, rushing towards Jason, who easily shoved him aside striding towards Maria. He drew his dagger and asked her, "I will ask you but once. Where are the other documents?"

The wagon came into the courtyard unobserved by the soldiers. Rachel stepped off the wagon and limped towards Jason, taking the dagger from its sheath. Instinctively, Jason spun around to face her, and she thrust the sharp blade into his chest. He gurgled as she spit in his face...he made a gruesome choking noise as the dagger reached his heart. She let go of the knife and stepped back. The soldiers raced towards her, but with the alacrity of a cat, her escort jumped in front of them. They halted. One of them called out: "Dionysius!"

"Sheathe your swords, soldiers. There will be no more blood shed on this sacred soil!"

"We have followed you in many battles, Dionysius, and were it not for your bravery, we would not be standing here today. We will follow your command."

The fighting done, they all gathered by Joshua, who was barely breathing. "With the help of God, you must carry on!"

He said barely audible.

"I love you, Joshua. I will see you on the other side," Anna said, sobbing.

"I love you, Anna."

"Samuel, please get blankets to keep him warm," Maria asked.

Before Samuel could answer, there came a great rumbling like a groan from the earth beneath them. For a moment it drowned out the roaring of the flames. The ground shook beneath them so violently that Samuel was thrown off his feet. A roar went up from the burning library, and the entire building fell deep into the ground, as if the ground beneath it had given way.

"No!" Anna had thrown her body over Joshua to protect him, but she now leapt to her feet, running towards the library. "Oh, no!" The tears sprang from her eyes and flooded down her face. "The tunnel has collapsed!" she sobbed.

Samuel got to his feet and ran to her side. "What is this place?" cried a soldier. "There is something accursed here!" He had been thrown off his feet as well, and scrambled to organize his men. "The works of the devil make the ground shake and speak here," he said to them.

"It is time for you to return to Rome and tell the Pope that Jason and Joshua lost their lives in the name of Christianity; that all the ancient documents have been destroyed; that women priests will no longer be ordained; that the church will send tithes to Rome annually; and that you have prevailed and the church by the sea will live by the rule of Rome," Samuel ordered with Dionysius by his side. "And also inform him that Samuel will not be returning to Rome."

"Now march to Rome, soldiers, and deliver the message...before the devil takes his due," Dionysius ordered.

The soldiers scurried from the courtyard to the road to

Rome.

"Now let's see if we can put out the fire," Dionysius cried. They made their way as close as they could to the raging flames. Through the gap that had once been the doorway of the collapsed building, they could see a large sinkhole that had devoured the burning building. Where the opening to the tunnel had once been, there was now a deep indentation in the wreckage, burning hotly. Samuel shielded his face and turned away, realizing that the ancient documents now laid beneath tons of rubble.

Anna was sitting at one of the outdoor tables saddened to tears by the events of the day. As Samuel approached, she said, "We have lost Joshua, we have lost our library, and I fear that we have also lost our ancient documents, Samuel."

"It is as you fear, Anna," said Samuel, slumping to the ground. He felt numb and sat staring down at the earth. Maria sat next to him and took his hand.

"I don't understand," said Anna. "What happened?"

"The tunnel collapsed and is burning," said Samuel, not looking up.

"That can't be right," said Anna.

"It is plain to see," responded Samuel.

"So all of our work has come to this," said Anna. Her voice sounded as numb as Samuel felt.

"We will start again," Maria said. "The soldiers will return to Rome and deliver our message. Gelasius will leave us alone, feeling content that we have returned to the fold. We will continue to ordain women priests, teach to those that come to our shores for education, and rebuild our library."

Samuel took Maria by the hand, and they walked to the bluffs overlooking the sea. "Look out over the sea," said Joshua. "There are clouds building."

"Could it be rain? The end of the drought?" asked Maria anxiously.

"It may well be," replied Samuel. "It's difficult to tell in this light, but it has the look of a mighty storm."

The great bank of clouds drew nearer, and a gust of wind came up suddenly. Maria grabbed Samuel. He held her closely. They smelled the wind from the sea, which held the scent of rain. The wind softened, and a light rain fell upon their heads. They held their embrace, standing there on the top of the bluff for a long time—behind them despair, ahead of them hope.

Epilogue

~

Southern Italy, Yesterday

At the bottom of the excavation site, a large group of people stood around a complicated hydraulic winching system hanging from a structure of aluminum piping. Archaeologists, scientists, historians, a politician or two, and a smattering of graduate students, assistants, and workmen had gathered, and several film crews had set up their cameras and were conducting interviews.

The site had initially been dug up to lay the foundation of a new, ultra-modern condominium building, situated on a high bluff overlooking the Mediterranean. But the construction had been halted ten days ago, and the machinery stood motionless. Now a high fence around the edge of the deep pit held off a thin crowd of curious tourists.

Two weeks before, the workmen, digging with a large backhoe, had begun to unearth a trail of burned timbers leading straight down into the soil. They had called the local archaeological society, which had sent a representative; tests were done, experts were consulted, and work on the condominium building was canceled. Excitement had begun to build in the Italian archaeological community and quickly spread around the world. The timbers bore the markings of what appeared to be an early Christian church. Carbon dating set them at nearly fifteen hundred years old, and they appeared to have formed the walls of a tunnel leading into the ground. At some point the timbers had burned, sucking the oxygen out of the tunnel, extinguishing the flames, and causing a collapse. All of this in and of itself was fairly mundane, but advanced geological mapping tests, borrowed from the natural gas industry, had revealed something else: The collapsed timbers led to an intact tunnel and a sizable cavern.

When the news of this spread, archaeologists and historians started to arrive from around the world. Slowly and with infinite care, they began to extract the timbers and dig towards the cavern. They set up the aluminum frame and removed the timbers one by one, using the hydraulic system for the heavy beams that still remained. They labeled the timbers carefully and took every care to make sure they were preserved. More experts were contacted, who confirmed there *had* been a church on this spot, surviving until 1553 when it had been razed by the Inquisition. All other records of it had been lost. Excitement continued to grow.

Finally, they reached what they believed was the last tangle of timbers and old wood. These had been too deep to be touched by the fire and had simply collapsed. It was assumed that they had been preserved by the lack of moisture at this depth, but already a heated debate was raging on the topic. They stuck out from the rock wall like a clasped pair of hands. Behind them, it was believed, stood the tunnel and the cavern.

A hush fell over the assembled crowd as two men approached, wearing gloves and masks to protect them if the air beyond the timbers was poisonous. The cameras whirred. The men conferred for a moment and then stepped forward to take hold of the timber, which appeared to be light enough for them to lift unaided. They grasped it and pulled very gently. The timber came free as smoothly as if it had been oiled.

From the small dark hole came a flow of air. The crowd stepped back. The air smelled fresh as it flooded out around them. In the darkness, a set of shelves holding reams of documents could be seen...

Made in the USA
Charleston, SC
09 July 2010